5,000,000 people —

The bar graphs on the right hand side of the pages in this book show the development of the population numbers of China's megacities between 1950 and 2025, based on an analysis by the Population Division of the United Nations in 2009. The figures show the number of inhabitants of the urban core.

1,000,000 people —

500,000 people —

HOW THE CITY MOVED TO MR SUN

CHINA'S NEW MEGACITIES

HOW THE CITY MOVED TO MR SUN

CHINA'S NEW MEGACITIES

MICHIEL HULSHOF &
DAAN ROGGEVEEN

SUN

江景华宅
m² 起
热销
起
太

CONTENTS

Authors: **Michiel Hulshof, Daan Roggeveen**
Research: Song Xinlin

Photography: Daan Roggeveen, Michiel Hulshof
Translation: Martin Mevius
Graphic Design: Job, Joris & Marieke
Publisher: Martien de Vletter, SUN

PROLOGUE

The city centre is as large as that of Frankfurt. Gleaming skyscrapers surround an artificial lake. The brand new roads are six lanes wide. A circular, two kilometre long mall surrounds the water. Porsche recently opened a flagship store here, but the real eye-catcher is the new theatre: five golden egg-shaped globes designed by Uruguayan architect Carlos Ott. It all looks very cosmopolitan.
Apart from one thing.

The city has no inhabitants.

Yet.

1. ZHENGZHOU

(1950)

'THIS IS A BUSINESS TOWN'

ZHENGZHOU

HENAN - VIETNAM
With 94 million inhabitants, Henan province has roughly the same population as Vietnam

One word: pandemonium. Thousands of travellers move in a massive jumble. Women try to sell us maps while men offer us taxi rides. We walk past hundreds of people queuing in long lines next to peasants sitting on their luggage. Bored youths with bleached hair stand around smoking, while girls hand out leaflets advertising newly built properties, circumventing the begging vagrants on the ground. We see busses, taxis and scooters arriving from all directions. Everything is for sale. Kentucky Fried Chicken, McDonald's and Dong Fang Ji Bai compete for hungry voyagers. Customers in small supermarkets throng around instant noodles, green tea and sunflower seeds. There are call shops, souvenir stalls and liquor stores. Thousands of bags are stacked in piles in front of a row of shops. Above all, the deafening noise characterises the chaos, an indistinct blend of shouting, honking cars and the train station announcer. Almost all shopkeepers tout their wares from large loudspeakers on the street. 'Special offer. Don't miss it. Special offer. Don't miss it. Special offer. Don't miss it. Everything cheap. Doesn't matter what. Everything is two yuan. Doesn't matter what. Two yuan. Special offer. Don't miss it.'

It is February 2009, and the two of us, a journalist and an architect from Europe, are standing on Station Square in Zhengzhou. A fascination with the unknown megacities in the heart of China has driven us here. We live in Shanghai, and up to several weeks ago, the name 'Zhengzhou' meant little to us. Friends in Shanghai dismissively speak of 'that pokey provincial town' or even 'that village,' despite the fact that, according to the *Statistical Yearbook*, Zhengzhou has seven million inhabitants. The reason for this obscurity is obvious: Zhengzhou's precipitous growth started only very recently. Thirty years of Chinese reforms caused the boom of East Coast mega-metropolises like Beijing, Shanghai, Guangzhou and Shenzhen. Other coastal towns have similarly grown into flourishing cities of millions. This trend is now moving westward at a furious pace. In a few short years, economic growth and the pace of urbanisation have reached unprecedented rates. Far from the ocean and out of sight from the world, Zhengzhou, Chongqing, Shijiazhuang and Wuhan are growing into the (big) brothers and sisters of international metropolises such as Rio de Janeiro, Madrid, Dubai and Chicago.

We visit Zhengzhou as a prelude to a two-year investigation into the burgeoning metropolises in the heart of China. Over time, we will examine sixteen of them: fifteen provincial capitals and one future boom town. Their populations vary between two and thirty-two million. Their economic growth is gigantic: well over ten per cent annually over the last decade. Almost all of them have pristine new international airports, in anticipation of direct connections to Tokyo, Bangkok or Amsterdam.

In the next twenty years, an estimated 280 million Chinese villagers will become city dwellers, attracted by the profusion of jobs and opportunities in the city. The urbanisation rate will increase from about fifty per cent at present, to almost seventy per cent by 2030.[1] This means that, in the coming century, China will change from a rural into an urban society, a modernisation project influencing the lives of hundreds of millions. This transformation involves numbers that thrill the imagination. Consulting firm McKinsey, for instance, notes that in the coming years China will annually construct 'more than fifteen hundred buildings of thirty stories or higher,' boiling down to 'the equivalent of a new Chicago every year.'[2]

The effects of this colossal urbanisation are felt far outside China. The enormous increase in construction has provoked an explosive demand for steel, and causes price rises and budget overruns in construction projects in the rest of the world. Consumers

in Europe and the United States buy sunglasses and phones flowing from the new factories in the interior of China. The growing urban middle class has ever more money to spend, driving up demand for luxuries world wide, ranging from French wine to gold watches, designer bags and sports cars. Chinese students are conquering the lecture halls of Harvard and Yale. The new metropolises produce artists, movie directors, athletes and scientists whose paintings, movies, achievements and inventions are gaining growing recognition abroad. On the other hand, urbanisation has severe implications in terms of sustainability: it causes higher emissions of greenhouse gasses and puts further pressure on dwindling oil and gas reserves.
All the same, China's large-scale urban development is an example for other countries. The experience gained in the interior of China benefits other developing areas in the world. Chinese architects are already designing new cities in Africa and South America.

During our walk through the station district Zhenghzou at first sight leaves a dreary impression. The predominant colour is grey, thanks to the quality of the air, a suffocating mixture of fog and coal dust. Here and there between the buildings, factory chimneys jut into the sky. The traffic is congested in many places, and where it is not, pedestrians risk their lives crossing the road. Concrete apartment blocks with barred windows stand next to gleaming malls, half-completed hotels and undeveloped plots of land. The disarray continues inside the buildings. We enter a tower block at random and find shops, guest houses, an online gaming café, a bowling alley, a hairdresser and numerous restaurants under and beside each other. Despite February's wintery cold, life takes place largely on the street. Old people dance or play table tennis in the park, while young people play billiards in the open air. Street vendors sell telephones, mp3-players, phone cards, gloves and scarves. On the markets traders are hawking trousers, T-shirts, coats, toys, household appliances, meat, vegetables and fish. And everybody is eating: roast potatoes, fried tofu, chunks of pineapple, sausages and pancakes.
People shout at us every hundred metres or so, a sign that the locals are not used to seeing foreigners. The only Westerners in the street are the models on gigantic billboards plastered all over the sides of buildings. A few international fashion chains have discovered Zhengzhou as a promising consumer market: Adidas, Jack Jones and Miss Sixty. The architecture is an eclectic post-modern mix. Besides drab communist

apartment blocks and modern business buildings we see a restaurant shaped like a French chateau, a government office with Roman columns and a massage parlour in a Texan ranch. In the park a dilapidated Chinese temple stands next to a new Egyptian sphinx. This leads to absurd conversations. 'Is that a mosque?' – 'No, a mall.' As evening falls, the city changes from grey to multi-coloured. Neon lights cover literally everything – hotels, restaurants, offices, clubs, karaoke bars, the Ferris wheel and viaducts. Giant video screens everywhere display adverts, news and trailers for the latest movies.

Zhengzhou lies about 600 kilometres west of Beijing and is the capital of Henan province. To get a feel for the size of Chinese provinces it helps to compare them to American states or European countries. Henan is four times smaller than France, but has one and a half times the number of inhabitants: ninety-four million to be exact. This comparison also illustrates the regional importance of the capital. What Paris is to the French, Zhengzhou is to most inhabitants of Henan.

China has known large cities for thousands of years. Over 3600 years ago, Zhengzhou was one of the most important Shang Dynasty cities. Today, nothing but a few ruins remain. The development of the modern city started with the construction of the train station in 1903. Industrialisation commenced after the communist takeover in 1949, with Zhengzhou appointed as a centre for textiles and tobacco. Factories sprang up everywhere, along with residential communes for the workers. In the 1960s and 1970s urbanisation ground to a halt as Mao ruthlessly attempted to transform China into an agrarian society. After Mao's death China's new leader Deng Xiaoping opted for another economic model, putting cities centre stage. Urbanisation gathered pace, at first slowly, then faster from the beginning of the 1990s. The number of city dwellers rose from 18 per cent in 1978 to 23 per cent in 1992 and 44 per cent in 2005.[3]

Zhengzhou at first noticed little of the new policy. The economic miracle manifested itself primarily on the coast, in a number of specially selected cities permitted to experiment with market forces and foreign trade. Investors from abroad, from Taiwan and Hong Kong, and migrant workers from the depths of China moved to the coast, first to produce jeans and T-shirts, later also electric razors and walkmans. The southern province of Guangdong developed into the 'factory of the world'. Foreign trade and investment brought riches in the coastal provinces, where annual disposable

income now exceeds 1,650 dollars per capita. Party leader Deng Xiaoping believed that 'some must become rich first,' as an example to the rest of the country. His 'ladder-step doctrine' divided the country into three regions: the Coast, the Centre and the West. The plan proposed to 'speed up the development of the coastal region, to put the emphasis on energy and raw materials production in the central region, and to actively make preparations for the further development of the western region.' [4]

She points at the most important tourist attraction around: the new Central Business District.

We move into the Home Inn, a chain of cheap hotels identifiable by its bright yellow walls. A girl sleeps in the lobby, slouched on a red sofa. The pretty Chinese receptionist behind the counter introduces herself in English as Patsy. She takes out a city map. We ask her where the historical town centre is. She stares at us blankly and requests us to write our question down. We scribble 'old buildings' on a piece of paper. She picks up our pen and writes the answer underneath.

'NO'.

Then, in Chinese: 'This is a business town. If you want to see old buildings, you have to take the train to Luoyang.' She bends over the map and points at the most important tourist attraction around: the new Central Business District.

And so, one grey morning, we find ourselves at the edge of an enormous lake surrounded by a double ring of sixty residential and business tower blocks, each at least one hundred metres high. By the lakeshore lie a convention centre, a car park and a combined theatre and museum consisting of five golden globes, varying from fifteen to thirty metres in height. Construction workers are building a skyscraper that eventually will rise from out of the lake. Billboards advertise it as a luxury hotel-to-be.

The chaotic inner city of Zhengzhou seems very distant here. The opulent use of corporate architecture with plenty of glass and steel gives the district a futuristic look. This environment breathes structure and order. When you squint through your eyelashes, you see a business world filled with successful men and women in tailored business suits clinching one million dollar deal after another in boardrooms overlooking the new skyline. However, nothing of this furious future activity can be noticed just yet. The new business district is deadly quiet. We hardly see any pedestrians or cyclists. Cars drive past only once every now and again on the wide streets. There are no shops, apart from perhaps the newly opened Porsche showroom. In the empty car park next to the convention centre a few tradesmen have transformed their minivans into mobile supermarkets, targeting the rare visitor to an occasional conference.

Not far from here lies an exhibition centre completely dedicated to the new neighbourhood. Inside, an enormous model makes it clear that the area surrounding the lake forms only a small part of a new city district named Zhengdong. Its size is gargantuan: Zhengdong has a surface area of sixty square kilometres, which makes it as large as Paris within the Périphérique. Ultimately, the new city area is to become twice that size, even bigger still. A photo gallery in the exhibition area proves the new district is not merely a local project. President Hu Jintao, Prime Minister Wen Jiabao and various members of the Politburo have had their pictures taken wearing construction helmets, against a background of cranes.

Japanese architect Kisho Kurokawa designed the master plan for the district, consisting of several parts: a Central Business District, two logistical zones, a university quarter, an economic development zone and an ecological neighbourhood. When we drive through the area in a taxi, we see that the infrastructure for the whole area is complete. Even in sections where building has yet to commence straight roads run equipped with street lighting, fully grown trees and cultivated road dividers. In between there are still some fields with a few remaining farms. Closer to the central lake we pass residential areas, all with themes of their own. We drive past 'Vancouver Town' and a district with balconied apartment blocks and tiled roofs that from a distance vaguely reminds one of Spain. Next to it stands a nursery dubbed 'Little Harvard.' Most apartments are empty, but inquiries teach us that the majority have been sold to speculators. In the sales centre of Westlake Spring No.1 an employee tells us to come back next year. 'Only a few people live here now, but that will change swiftly.'

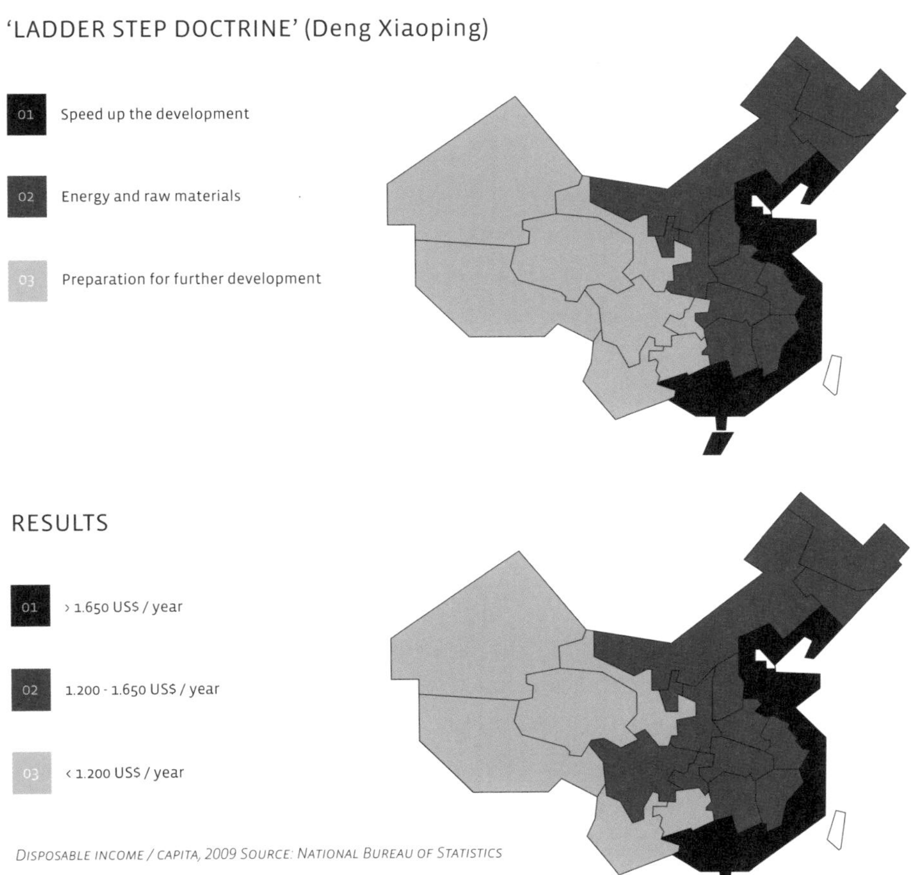

DISPOSABLE INCOME / CAPITA, 2009 SOURCE: NATIONAL BUREAU OF STATISTICS

Most inhabitants of Zhengzhou point to the year 2000 as turning point in the development of their city. In that year the government initiated the Go West policy, aimed at bridging the gap in the development of China's interior. The Gross National Product per capita then was only forty per cent of that on the East Coast.[5] The government financed the construction of railways, motorways and gas and oil pipelines, power plants and hydroelectric power plants, and paid for large environmental projects such as the planting of forests. As gas and coal are found namely in Central and Western China, critics believed the growing need for fossil fuels on the East Coast particularly inspired the policy.

In November 2008, Go West received a new impulse. To reduce the impact of the global financial crisis, Hu Jintao's government announced it would pump 586 billion dollars into the economy. Much of it ended up in infrastructure projects intended to unlock the Chinese hinterland. Besides building new airports, the network of high-speed trains was to be expanded. In 2020 almost all provincial capitals will be connected by trains running at speeds between 250 and 350 kilometres per hour.

A review of ten years of the Go West policy by the Chinese University of Hong Kong estimates that the economy of Central and Western China grew between 1999 and 2008 by an average twelve per cent per year.[6] In the same period, the GDP per capita in the area increased from 521 to 2303 dollars. Partly thanks to the stimulus package, economic growth remained strong in Western China during the financial crisis, even though it diminished on the East Coast, as it did in the rest of the world.

'Is that a mosque?' – 'No, a mall.'

As we walk through Zhengzhou, economic development is obviously still behind that of the major cities on the coast. To begin with, prices are lower. The starting rate for taxis is half that of Shanghai. We also see fewer luxury hotels or shopping centres. But hard work is being done to bridge this gap: construction sites with cranes stand in every street. The sounds of pile drivers, pneumatic drills and circle saws drift into the centre of town. In a country of tea drinkers one can link the size of the middle class to the popularity of *frappuccino* and *latte macchiato*. In Shanghai chains such as Starbucks, Coffee Company and 85°C together have hundreds of branches. In downtown Zhengzhou, Amy's Café still has a monopoly. Owner Tao Ying has her coffee shop on the twenty-first floor of an apartment complex in which various entrepreneurs have set up small businesses. Twenty-three year old Ying serves coffee to an audience of Chinese and foreigners, the latter mostly English teachers.

Just as the Zhengzhou of 2009 has rapidly become unrecognizable from that of 1979, changes will pile up in the next thirty years. While Ying prepares Brazilian coffee behind the counter of her café, she talks about her grandmother and mother. Her grandmother worked in a cigarette factory where she manually rolled cigarettes, five hundred packets

PERCENTAGE OF CITY DWELLERS PER COUNTRY

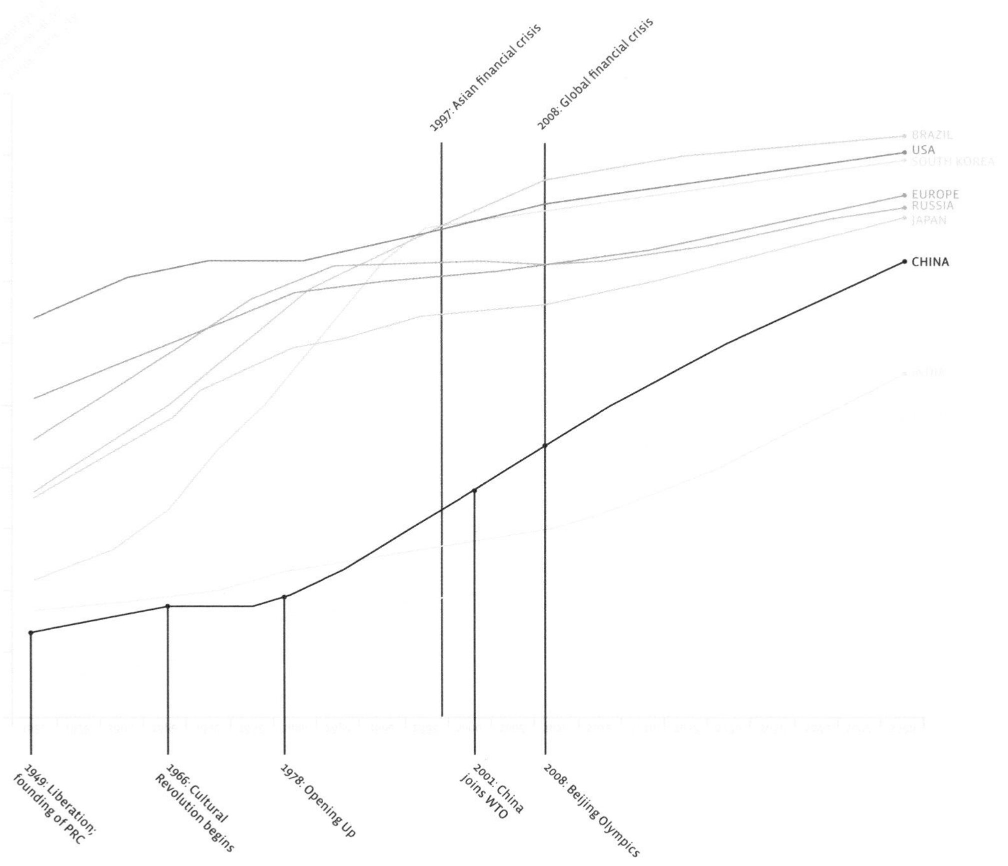

a day. 'She was the fastest in her unit,' says Ying. 'When Mao visited Zhengzhou one day, they took her picture with him.' Like all other workers she lived on the factory premises. Ying's mother had just grown up when the first changes brought by the new economic era could be felt. She became the first female taxi driver in Zhengzhou. 'Her best customers were Taiwanese who came here to invest.' Ying herself took the next step. Before she started her coffee shop, she studied English for a year in Leicester. 'A few years ago it suddenly became very popular among wealthy parents to send their children abroad. I was very proud that I could go as well.' Once back in Zhengzhou she met Brian, her American boyfriend, with whom she has since become engaged. Apart

from her marriage she has another plan for the coming year: she wants to open her own nightclub, near the lake, in the new business district of the town.

Bottles of Ballantines stand on the tables, next to jugs of iced tea and bowls of artfully carved fruit.

In Zhengzhou we see the first contours of a new kind of megacity typical of China. The tightly structured high-rise with plenty of light, air and space reminds of the City of Tomorrow by Le Corbusier, who proposed to replace the entire Parisian city centre with a broad grid of skyscrapers. The abundant neon lighting, omnipresent Roman columns and European themed areas instead are reminiscent of Las Vegas. The city bears the marks of both a dominant state and an unbridled and aggressive market, which replaced as its icon the factory with the skyscraper. In numerous real estate advertisements Zhengzhou presents itself as an idyll where living, working and recreation form a harmonious mix. And above all, it is a city where a strong faith in the future prevails.

On our last evening we visit V8, the hottest night spot of the moment. Even on a Tuesday night the two-storey club is packed. Here the twenty- and thirty-year-olds who form new middle class amuse themselves with dice games. Bottles of Ballantines stand on the tables, next to jugs of iced tea and bowls of artfully carved fruit. The interior of opulent chandeliers, Chesterfield sofas and oak panelling is *Moulin Rouge* meets *Route 66*. A singing DJ, dancers on moving platforms, and music by Snoop Dogg, Beyoncé and 50 Cent warms up the audience. As the evening progresses, more and more customers switch from dicing to dancing. Just after midnight, a Village People classic plays, clearly V8's club song. Everyone jumps up and sings along. *Go West, where the skies are blue. Go West, this is what we're gonna do.*

Journey to the West is the title of one of China's most famous classic novels, about the legendary pilgrimage of a monk seeking holy texts in the 'western regions.' During our

ZHENGZHOU (2010)

journey to the west we describe the transformation of 'provincial' towns in the heart of China to potential global metropolises. How fast things can change, we discover when we return to Zhengzhou in the spring of 2010. Tao Ying has given up her coffee shop and now runs a thriving café in a street full of bars in the old town. Multinationals are now also deploying activities. Louis Vuitton has just opened its first shop in Zhengzhou, with a VIP-lift and a floor mosaic depicting the Champs-Élysées. The Japanese car

manufacturer Nissan has announced it will partially relocate the production of its Qashqai SUV to the city. And the Taiwanese company Foxconn has built a new iPhone factory that ultimately will provide employment for 300,000 people. One third of them have already started work.

The taxi ride from the station to the new district of Zhengdong now takes almost an hour because of the maddening traffic jams. In the Central Business District nothing

remains of the erstwhile silence. People are walking around everywhere, and cars stand parked in front of every restaurant. The hotel tower rising from the lake has reached its apex. Business people are not the only ones frequenting the new district. On the large car park parents are flying kites with their children. Women are selling pineapples from delivery bicycles, while a man grills lamb kebabs over a barbecue. In Vancouver Town the elderly residents sit in the sun. And the first students of Little Harvard have a go on the slide.

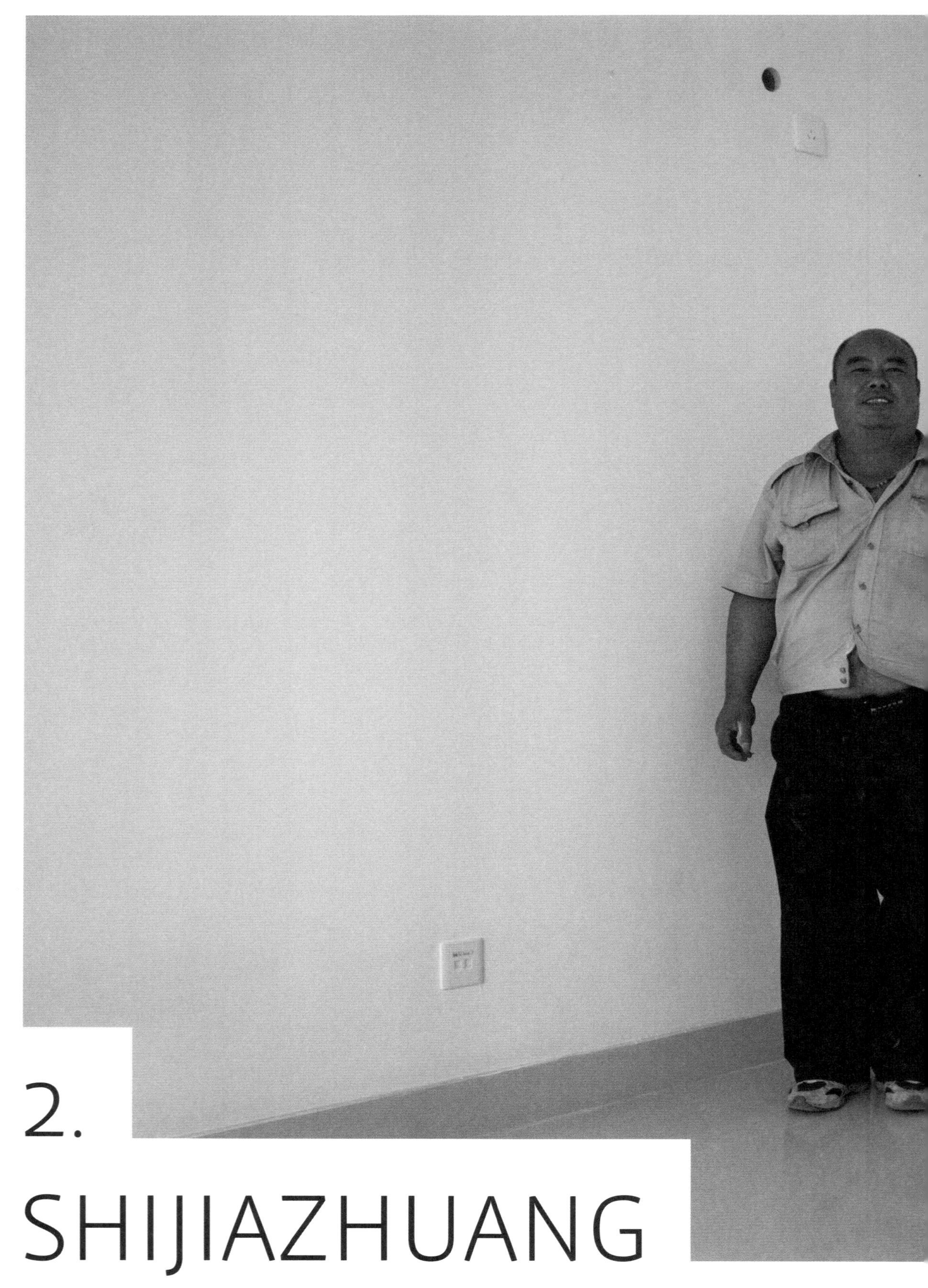

2. SHIJIAZHUANG

SHIJIAZHUANG

HOW THE CITY MOVED TO MR SUN

HEBEI - TURKEY
With 70 million inhabitants, Hebei province has roughly the same population as Turkey

SHIJIAZHUANG

South of the double-decker motorway is a nine-hole golf course. The area immediately north evokes the impression of a ecent bombardment. A few buildings and remnants of structures remain standing amidst enormous mountains of rubble: houses, a small temple, a school. Abandoned objects lie scattered in the debris: toys, an umbrella, a shoe. Laundry dries in the wind from facades of still intact houses. Empty beer crates are piled up in front of a small supermarket. These are the last signs of life in the otherwise mostly forsaken village of Jianling. Right next to the motorway, a nine-step staircase flanked on both sides by large green plants leads up

to the entrance of an untarnished four-storey house. As the front door swings open the smiling face of Sun Huanzhong appears. 'Welcome,' he says cordially. 'You have come to exactly the right place.' He leads us to a capacious living room on the ground floor resembling a surrealist movie set. Psychedelic landscapes and popular fantasy video game avatars completely cover the walls, staring down at the double bed placed smack bang in the middle of the room. 'Until recently I let this to an Internet café,' says Mr Sun by way of explanation of the eccentric furnishing. 'Now I live here with my wife.'
Sun is a sinewy 65-year-old. He sits down at a large table. He rolls a cigarette using paper and tobacco. He has tanned skin and sturdy hands, is frugally dressed in slippers, pleated trousers and a T-shirt. He smokes like he talks: abundantly and dedicatedly. He recites an urban tragedy typical for the Chinese city, a modern parable about peasants becoming city dwellers without moving an inch. It is a story about peasant cunning, creativity and small entrepreneurship, and about how these qualities founder in a system that uncompromisingly equates modernity with order.

In the 1980s Sun is still a simple farmer from Jianling, a village of twelve hundred families. He cultivates corn and keeps livestock: two pigs and several chickens, which he slaughters at Chinese New Year. An unpaved road separates his house from the farmland on the other side. It is a half hour walk from Jianling to the outskirts of Shijiazhuang, the capital of Hebei province. Shijiazhuang is a relatively young city that has come into being at the beginning of the twentieth century from the clustering of a dozen villages at the crossroads of two new railroad lines. In the 1950s and 1960s textile and chemical industries have developed, and as a result the number of inhabitants increased to half a million. But at the end of the 1980s the countryside still remains near. Vast cornfields surround the city, on which tens of thousands of peasants work every summer, protecting themselves from the sun by wrapping white towels round their heads. Nothing suggests that twenty years later Shijiazhuang will be one of China's most turbulent megacities.
At the beginning of the Nineties, Sun senses change. Until then, China's economic growth has largely bypassed his village. Now, more and more migrants are arriving from other parts of the province to work in Shijiazhuang. They come to Jianling seeking affordable accommodation.

At the same time, the expanding city greedily eyes the farmland. Local officials offer compensation, but the amounts are low. 'Growing corn is more profitable.' Together with others Sun submits a petition to the provincial authorities against the expropriations, but in vain. His fields are sold to Century Park Golf Club, which aids a growing upper class in filling the new concept of 'spare time.' The new land owner quickly removes the corn, plants grass, digs ponds and builds bunkers. In an ironical 'transvaluation of all values' rich urbanites now work themselves into a sweat on the former farmland, exchanging the hoe for the golf club.

The authorities coax the sulking villagers with promises. There will be jobs for everyone. For every *mu* (660 square metres) of expropriated land, the expanding chemical and pharmaceutical industry is to create five jobs. The village has 3,000 *mu* of land. Sun quickly does the math and calculates this means fifteen thousand jobs – 'more than enough' for the 7,000 villagers.

The assurances never materialise.

Without land and jobs, the peasants have to rely on their own ingenuity. 'No one took care of us. We had to do everything ourselves.' A new source of income presents itself: letting properties to migrant labourers arriving in Jianling in ever larger numbers from the rest of the province. Sun makes a decision. He invests the 3,000 dollars received as compensation for his lost farmland into a building of his own design. In 2001 this self-made architect sets to work. Without as much as having read a book on architecture, Sun creates a four-storey, 800-square-metre multifunctional building with some interesting low-tech sustainability solutions. His brother, a design engineer, helps him draw the building plan.

Ground floor: built-to-let office space with a shop front. On the right a separate entrance to a stairwell leading to the flats on the second and third floors.

First floor: office space, connected to the ground floor by an internal staircase.

Second floor: a four-room apartment for Sun and his family featuring a natural stone tile floor and a modern kitchen and bathroom. A glass loggia provides access to the bedrooms, and insulation for the house in summer and winter. On the street side lies a two-bedroom apartment intended for letting.

Third floor: six rooms to let surrounding a central patio, with a tree growing from a minimalistically tiled planter in the middle.

SHIJIAZHUANG IN 1934

Village
Railway
Hutuohe River

A number of villages grew together following the construction of a train station and formed the city of Shijiazhuang. Currently the city has ten million inhabitants.

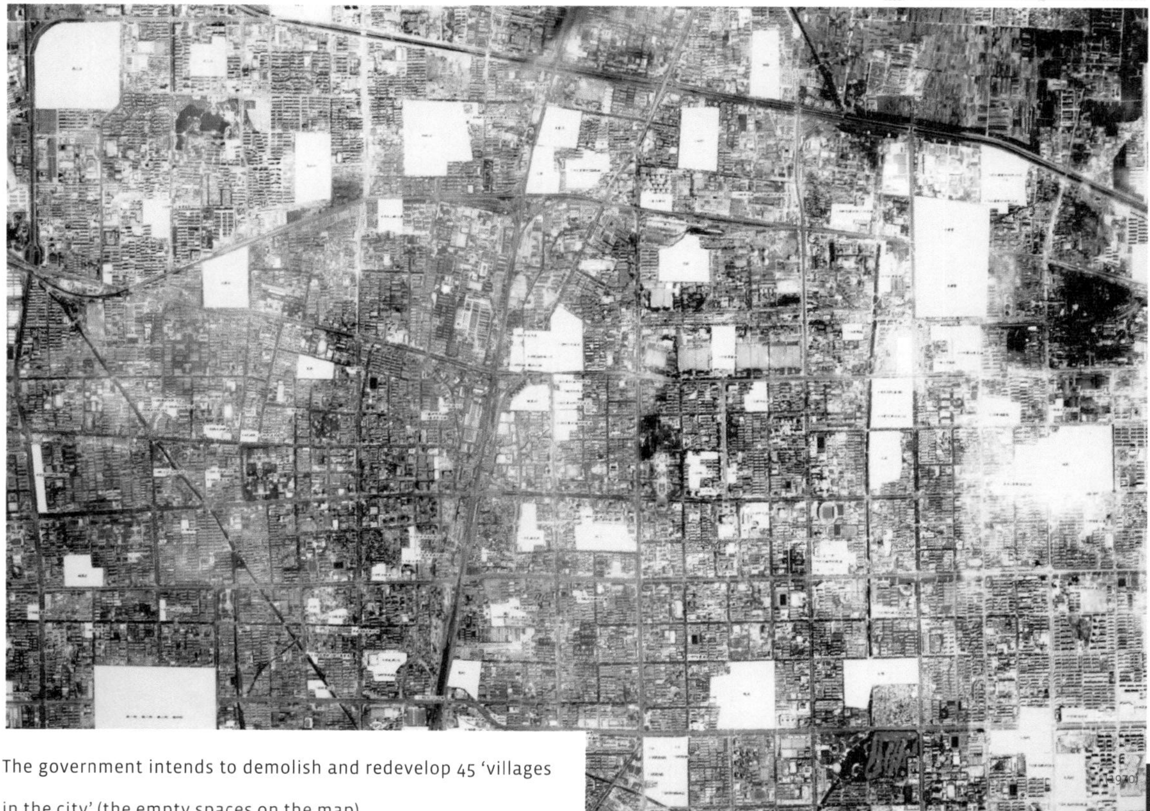

(1970)

The government intends to demolish and redevelop 45 'villages in the city' (the empty spaces on the map)

飞起来

On the roof, accessible through a steel external staircase, is the unique selling point. Here, Sun creates a rooftop field of organic farmland. The thirty centimetres of earth insulates the building and produces food for his family: eighteen different kinds of fruit and vegetables, including cucumbers, aubergines, various types of cabbage and several pomegranate trees. Sun places fish ponds in two corners of his field. 'Architects in Beijing talk about this kind of thing. I have gone right ahead and done it.'
He completes the house in the summer of 2002. For the first time Sun lights the grill on the roof. As he eats the fruits of his new fields, he looks out over his old lands, the golf course.

'We had to do everything ourselves.'

Sun is not the only one in Jianling to design his own home. 'Every family has an architect.' To make as much money as possible, almost all the peasants build apartment blocks. They demolish their farms of clay, straw and pig dung and replace them with buildings of three, four or five storeys made of concrete, with aluminium window frames and chrome railings. The tile patterns on the facades vary in pattern and colour. The placement of windows differs on each floor. Precast tympanums or columns adorn some of the buildings. Like Sun, other former farmers also build roof gardens. This is how Jianling develops into a typical *cheng zhong cun*, a 'village in the city' – a phenomenon linked to the ultra-rapid urbanisation that can be observed in all budding metropolises in China. The villages stand out because of their diversity in form and character. Their skylines form organic wholes of individual expressions. The informal architecture starkly contrasts with the tight uniformity of other new districts, which, by contrast, express strong central control.
The more a 'village in the city' has the opportunity to develop, the less it looks like a traditional village. The buildings can sometimes reach heights of fifteen to twenty floors, which means they far outgrow the usual level of 'informal architecture'. Due to the high density of construction, veritable 'mini Manhattans' come into existence, in a great many different styles and forms. Living, work and recreation are not separate,

but completely mixed. Accommodated beside, above or beneath each of the buildings are supermarkets, poultry farms, hostels, karaoke bars, slaughterhouses, restaurants, warehouses, and clothing shops.

By 2004 thousands of migrant labourers have supplemented the 1,200 original families of Jianling, and the streets start to form a lively spectacle, day and night. The peasants have reinvented themselves as successful entrepreneurs. They form the capitalist upper crust of Jianling. Sun lets the rooms on the third floor to migrant labourers and the business premises on the ground floor to an estate agent. Later an Internet café will move in. And so Sun Huanzhong, who has never owned a mobile telephone in his life, at sixty years of age, becomes the landlord of a room with dozens of computers where Chinese youths play video games, day in day out. Three floors higher he does what he loves best: growing fruit and vegetables.

China's budding metropolises only reluctantly tolerate the urban villages. In the long run there can be no room for the former farmers' handiwork that does not suit the image of modernity envisaged by city administrators. They see demolition on an iconoclastic scale as the road ahead. The struggle takes place against a backdrop of a socio-economic model described by Yasheng Huang, professor in Economics at the prestigious Massachusetts Institute of Technology, as 'capitalism with Chinese characteristics.' He observes a struggle between two Chinas: entrepreneurial, market-driven rural China versus state-run urban China. Huang does not hide his preference for the first China. 'When and where rural China has the upper hand, Chinese capitalism is entrepreneurial, politically independent, and vibrantly competitive in its conduct and virtuous in its effects. When and where urban China has the upper hand, Chinese capitalism tends toward political dependency on the state and is corrupt.' [1]

There is no doubt which China has the upper hand in the budding metropolises. Expropriations are the order of the day. Residents refusing to leave are 'stubborn nails' blocking development. Or, as former mayor of Beijing Wang Qishan expressed it: 'We don't forcibly remove anyone, except those who don't want to go.' [2]

The fate of the 'villages in the city' such as Jianling reflects the power of economic and legal institutions in China, where the individual always loses against the state, and creative peasant capitalism must inevitably yield to developers with the right

THE HOUSE THAT SUN HUANZHONG BUILT

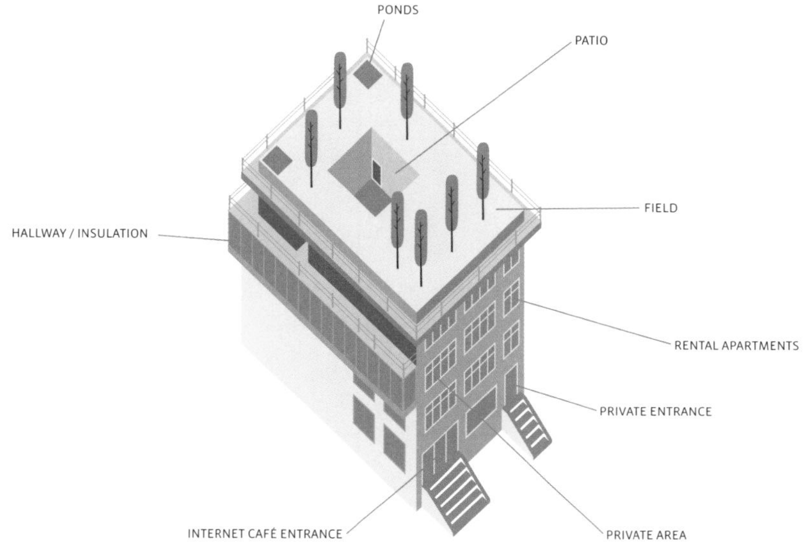

government connections. The vibrant anarchy from below succumbs to a 'harmonious society' imposed by the Party. The eighteenth-century British Prime Minister William Pitt poetically expressed the antithesis to this system: 'The poorest man may in his cottage bid defiance to all the forces of the Crown. It may be frail, its roof may shake; the wind may blow through it; the storm may enter, the rain may enter – but the King of England cannot enter; all his force dares not cross the threshold of the ruined tenement.'
In other Asian countries with similar periods of ultra-rapid urbanisation the swiftly expanding cities also swallowed villages. Their ultimate destiny illustrates the balance between property rights and the power of the state. Singapore knocked down almost all of the villages, but in Taiwan, South Korea and Japan they continued to exist and grew into regular city districts. Taipei's pulsating 'villages in the city' consist of hundreds of self-built blocks of flats, all different from one another. They are a confirmation in brick and concrete of democracy and rule of law.

In China, this system does not exist. One way or another, fair or foul, Sun Huanzhong's house must disappear.

The shaky position of the individual provides China with immense opportunities for

(1985)

the improvement of living conditions of its inhabitants. Few countries in the world pursue a reform agenda so energetically. The unchained cities do not only effortlessly tear down the self-built creations of the farmers, but also the ruins and hovels that could eventually turn into slums. This is far more difficult in democracies such as Brazil, India or South Africa. Many Western politicians and urban planners secretly envy China's possibilities to 'follow through' or 'get things done' that elsewhere would take years to complete.

In 2007 party secretary of Hebei province, Zhang Yunchuan, decides that Shijiazhuang must finally bid its peasant past farewell. Zhang personifies a twenty-billion-dollar project named 'Every Year a Great Step, Three Years of Great Change.' The province aims its plan at all big cities in Hebei, but Shijiazhuang is to lead. The Three-Year Plan has a clear schedule. First year: demolition. Second year: relocating factories to the city outskirts. Third year: commencement of construction projects to give the city a new face.

Shijiazhuang starts with the most far-reaching aspect of the three-year plan. No less than forty-five 'villages in the city', loathed for their disorderliness and uncontrollability, must be torn down, or, as the authorities prefer to say, 'redeveloped'. Expectations about the results are sky-high. An official circular sums up the imagined blessings: 'Redevelopment of the city is not only a way to properly utilise the available land, optimise the city structure and realise the urban development plan, it is also the best way to improve the living environment, to solidify the image of the city, to quicken modernisation, to stimulate internal demand, to hasten economic growth of the city and to stimulate social development. It is a project that will bring results in the present and earnings over the centuries.' [3]

The phenomenal scale of the demolition soon becomes apparent. City dwellers come up with a joke: Prime Minister Wen Jiabao flies in his airplane over Shijiazhuang. He looks out of the window, and shouts angrily at his staff: 'Why have none of you told me about the earthquake?!'

In 2008 rumours start to circulate in Jianling. Some inhabitants whisper that the village has been nominated for demolition. Not much later, real estate firm Wanda opens a sales centre a hundred metres from Sun's house. Inside, a model displays the design for a shopping mall housing Bentley, KFC, Adidas and Motorola. Behind the building,

The diversity of 'villages in the city'

restaurants and cafés with outdoor seating are to line the car-free streets. Apart from shops and a multiplex cinema the plan envisages a five-star hotel, twelve office buildings, and 28 thirty-storey residential towers. The total surface area covers nearly two million square metres, roughly eight times that of the Empire State Building in New York.

Wanda symbolizes China's new urbanism. In all major cities, the company is erecting 'Wanda Plazas': multifunctional complexes many hundreds of thousands of square metres in size. The Wanda Plaza in Shijiazhuang is to become the largest project of the Wanda empire. The Wanda group is a subsidiary of China National United Oil, which again is connected to China's largest state-run oil company. The company prospers: founder Wang Jianling is one of the richest men in China. He is advisor to various provincial and municipal authorities, vice president of the Association against Unfair Competition and president of the China Charity Foundation.

'I have no problems with corruption, but you have to take proper care of your own people.'

In the room on the ground flour, Sun does not hide his anger. The village committee, he says, has offered him and his fellow residents a compensation package: for every square metre of their self-built property, they will receive 1.3 square metres in the residential towers of Wanda Plaza. That means two apartments, or even three. It sounds like a tempting offer, if not for the catch. The maximum compensation is 300 square metres. That will decimate Sun's property, his source of income. 'I have 800 square metres now. And who can assure me I will be able to let these new apartments? What if Wanda goes bankrupt in the meantime?'

Sun focuses his fury on the Jianling village committee. He accuses them of corruption. Officials have allegedly squandered public money on pleasure trips, expensive cars and drunken evenings with women in karaoke bars, accumulating a debt of over three

SHIJIAZHUANG

(2000)

million dollars. They have closed a deal with the Shijiazhuang municipal authorities: in exchange for debt cancellation, they must ensure the participation of the villagers in Wanda's plans. This allows the developer to keep his hands clean, while the village committee takes care of the dirty work.

'I have no problems with corruption,' says Sun, 'but you have to take proper care of your own people.'

A delegation of residents has recently travelled to Beijing to submit a petition to the State Office for Letters and Conversations, to many ordinary Chinese the last resort in disputes with local authorities. An official has told them they are right, and that they can stay. Once home, however, the written statement from the capital does not dissuade the village committee. The villagers simply must leave. Some of the residents have voluntarily accepted Wanda's offer. Their houses have already been demolished. Due to declining patronage, the Internet café in Sun's house has ceased to exist.

With only 300 families left, the atmosphere in the village has hardened. The electricity has been disconnected, and the water has been cut off. Sun Huanzhong beats his fist on the table. All this injustice, he can hardly fathom it. He stands up and makes a tour of his home. Now Sun and his wife are using the former internet café as a home, the second, third and fourth floors are empty. They have moved the furniture to their son's home, so they can leave immediately in case of emergency. Via the external staircase he reaches the roof, where the flowers are in full bloom. He looks out over the mountains of rubble that remain of his village. 'I do not like to come here anymore,' he says, 'all I see is destruction.'

Sun Huanzhong does not wait for the eviction of his village. A couple of weeks later, he accepts the village committee buyout of 75,000 dollars. That may seem like a large sum to a Chinese farmer, but it is not a lot to the owner of an 800-square-metre building near the centre of a speedily growing city of millions. He then moves into his son's apartment at the other side of town.

He is just in time. A few months later, on 30 December 2009, a mob armed with hoes and machetes storms the village. Several days afterward, an eyewitness posts a report and pictures on the popular website Tianya. 'They are breaking into houses, smashing windows and threatening the villagers.' By way of warning the gang beats one of the

Mr Sun's house in September 2009, April 2010, February 2011 and June 2011 (clockwise from top left)

Wanda has ambitious plans for Shijiazhuang

美观时尚
嘉亿
道
宝

villagers so badly that it puts him in hospital. Bystanders phone emergency numbers, but, writes the anonymous blogger, 'police cars simply drive past our village. Nobody is helping us.'[4] The accompanying photographs show various villagers covered in blood. Harassment of residents refusing to leave is the order of the day in Chinese cities. Whether local authorities or developers hire the gangs usually remains unclear. That the topic disturbs many Chinese city dwellers is clear from the popularity of the online video game 'stubborn nail versus gang of thugs,' a hit on the Chinese Internet in 2010. To win the game, inhabitants use a wide selection of weapons to fight off as many property developers, officials and gangs as possible.

Cities do not always assimilate villages through violence or coercion. Some villages orchestrate their own urban metamorphosis. The village of Fangbei, several kilometres from Jianling, has opted for this route. 'Yesterday more than 320 villagers celebrated on the village square as they received the keys to their new homes,' reports the evening newspaper *Yangzhou Wenbao* on 22 September 2009. 'Fangbei is the first village of the Three-Year Plan whose villagers have returned.' The article quotes 53-year-old Wang Shuyan as being 'incredibly happy' with his new home: a spacious apartment on the sixth floor of building seven. The paper also cites Ren Yongjie, CEO of the Fangbei Group. 'The buildings have been completed on time,' he says. 'We have a total of three blocks of flats with 400 apartments each for returning families.'[5]

Like all Chinese villages, Fangbei was a Maoist agricultural commune until 1978. In contrast to many other peasant communities, Fangbei never completely abandoned its collective character. The village administration has fully embraced Deng Xiaoping's masterful distortion of communist doctrine: 'Socialism is getting rich together'. After economic liberalisation the village established one business after another: a printer, a metal factory, a fish market. The village chief adopted the title of CEO, while the villagers became shareholders receiving annual dividends. The names of the enterprises expressed their collective nature. Fangbei Group comprises Fangbei Industry, Fangbei Commercial Enterprise, Fangbei Property and Fangbei Youyou Fish Market. As the growing city engulfed more and more of the village agricultural land, increasing numbers of peasants found employment in village enterprises. In 1994 the last piece of farmland made way for the construction of a major thoroughfare.

The village administrators promptly built a strip of buildings beside the road and let them to night clubs. At the Dance Parlour, the Golden Triangle KTV, the Green Island Friendship Club and various massage parlours, other activities soon supplemented the singing and backrubs. Fangbei gained fame as Shijiazhuang's Red Light District. As in Jianling, the peasants built additional floors on their homes.

In 2002 the village committee led by party secretary Ren took a dramatic decision: Fangbei committed suicide. Village enterprise Fangbei Property was to destroy existing buildings and replace them by more urban construction. The village hoped to keep external property developers at bay with this 'tactic of cultivated Earth.' There was far less resistance to the plans than in Jianling. The villagers had known their village business for years, and knew that as shareholders they would benefit from the proceeds. Property development is one of the most commercial businesses in the world, and communism is the least commercial economic system. Fangbei managed to mix them into an optimal blend.

Fangbei 2.0 consists of a number of light grey tower blocks about a hundred metres high grouped round a tiled leftover space – the town square, with a car park below it. Valuing pragmatism above all, the villagers abandoned any attempt at design: the buildings lack individual detail of any kind. The project has succeeded in the pursuit of optimisation, but at a price. From a distance the extreme makeover has created an impressive skyline, but facial reconstruction has produced an emotionless expression close up. Fangbei 2.0 no longer has dark alleys or prostitutes, or small rooms where migrant workers rent bunk beds. It also has no restaurants, shops, or any pleasant public space. The collective character of the transition appears from the slogan on a red banner hanging from the building: 'Work shoulder to shoulder for a better living environment for our village.'

The day after the delivery of the flats, about a hundred villagers stand in the middle of the empty square. Red snippets of paper on the ground bear silent witness to the opening fireworks. There is a mood of gentle excitement. Yesterday all the families in the village, depending on the number of family members, received one or more apartments in the new blocks of flats, distributed through a raffle. One man is sulking. He did not make it to the draw in time, and to his disappointment has won a penthouse flat. Being a former peasant he prefers to stand *jiao ta shi di*, with both feet on the ground.

In the middle of the square a woman has set up a Formica kitchen. Customers pick colours from a binder with samples. Anything goes, apart from white. 'In a dusty city like Shijiazhuang, that will turn grey in a couple of weeks.' Dozens of street traders sell electric blankets, tiles, curtain rails and anything else a new homeowner could possibly need. Their presence betrays the fact that the informal economy in the village has not yet been completely rooted out. Most activity takes place near the entrances of the residential towers. Men and women with furrowed faces, dressed in cheap jackets and woollen vests covered in embroidered flowers linger around a wooden placard with handwritten adverts. The former farmers have started their new careers as landlords of modern apartments.

On the street side the Fangbei buildings contain a line of shops, where large furniture companies sell Moooi Design and Artemide rip-offs. For the moment they target customers from outside the village. But how long will it take before the first farmer drags a polyester horse by Marcel Wanders into his living room?

'In a dusty city like Shijiazhuang that will turn grey in a couple of weeks.'

At the end of 2009 a farmer lays hundreds of sheaves of corn out to dry on a square between white-tiled residential blocks six storeys high.

It is his last harvest.

Trails of the recent rural past are present everywhere in Shijiazhuang. Modern business districts lie next to hand-tilled farmland. Peasants hold markets under raised motorways. Walking through a new housing estate, you might suddenly encounter a shepherd and his flock. It will not take long before these rural elements disappear from the streets altogether, as will all 'villages in the city.' Sun's self-built multifunctional building will be replaced by a Wanda living/shopping complex, and the peasant village of Fangbei has transformed itself into a high-rise district barely distinguishable from the rest of the city.

All that remains are the local village dialects, rural dress and traditions. The peasants

still bury their dead with processions and lots of fireworks. The rural communities form islands of local culture in an increasingly amorphous sea. They maintain the memories of the peasant past, as long as it lasts.

It is April 2010, and Sun Huanzhong smokes a cigarette in a comfy chair on the sixth floor of a block of flats. He has just heard that his house in Jianling was demolished a few months ago. Sun has not returned to his old village. It is too painful. He and his

SHIJIAZHUANG (2025)

wife do not enjoy living in the modern compound much. 'We don't know anybody here. It's a bit lonely'. There is one redeeming feature of living with their son: they see their two grandsons every day. Ultimately they will get accustomed to their new lifestyle, Sun thinks. 'But there is so little to do here. I miss my fields.' He picks up the remote control and zaps to CCTV10, the scientific channel of Chinese public television. In five minutes, there is a documentary on about dinosaurs.

3.
CHONGQING

SNOW

BUILDING THE LARGEST CITY IN THE WORLD

CHONGQING

CHONGQING - IRAQ
With 32 million inhabitants, Chongqing province has roughly the same population as Iraq

Mr Deng wipes his hands on a kitchen apron that may have been white once upon a time. He rushes out enthusiastically and full of curiosity. He rarely gets to see outsiders here. With sweeping gestures he points to a construction of bamboo, corrugated iron and sailcloth, while welcoming us with the traditional greeting, *huanying guanglin*.

'Liangping Restaurant', claims a handwritten text on a wooden sign above the entrance. From the bamboo poles propping up the roof hang several power metres, connected by a tangle of wires. In the middle of the room stands the cooking island: a table with a two-burner gas stove surrounded by bowls with sliced vegetables, meat and noodles, behind which a woman is cooking. 'My wife,' explains Deng. Sat on low plastic stools, twenty patrons eat at the wooden folding tables, mostly men and one or two women. Their sweaty, tanned faces suggest a life in the outdoors. A curtain in the rear of the business partitions off the sleeping area. Next to it stands a small television set from which a pianist plays Bach.

Deng is a cheerful man of thirty-seven. Under his apron he wears a green polo shirt, jeans and trainers. He sits down on one of the blue stools, while his wife serves platters of peppered tofu and beans. The businessman tells us he named his restaurant after his hometown, Liangping, a three-hour drive from here. Like many men his age, he left for the East Coast aged eighteen, looking for work. He found a position as a house painter in Shanghai. 'The pay was quite bad,' he remembers. But it had its perks: painting the house of a bank director he met his future wife, who worked there as a cook. 'I liked her at once,' he says. His wife throws him a loving glance.

They married and decided to set up for themselves. They quit their jobs, pooled their savings and opened a small restaurant in Shanghai. It was not a success. 'The Shanghainese do not like the spicy Sichuan kitchen,' thinks Deng. 'We didn't have enough customers.' Relatives suggested trying closer to home, in Chongqing. In the meantime, this city in Central China had started on an incredible growth spurt, and there were opportunities everywhere. 'They said we could make enough money in Chongqing,' says Deng. He and his wife heeded the advice, packed their belongings and took the train west. They then rented this temporary structure, for two dollars a day.

For two years now, they have been serving food from seven in the morning to eleven in the evening: spicy meals washed down with tea, Coke, or large bottles of beer. Liangping Restaurant only closes at Chinese New Year and during the October Vacation. Deng and his wife then travel to the other Liangping, where Deng was born and where his fourteen-year-old son lives with Deng's parents.

Liangping Restaurant stands with five similar establishments on the muddy plain forming the centre of an improvised village consisting of dozens of improvised buildings. To the east, the area is hemmed in by a highway overpass, over which cars travel to and from the new international airport. The road doubles as a roof for the daily market where vendors sell vegetables, fruit and meat. The western end of the settlement overlooks a massive construction site, flanked by a row of detachable houses with characteristic blue roofs for construction workers. China's rapidly growing cities have hundreds of these improvised settlements. They can be found anywhere: under overpasses, between office buildings, or even in the central reservations of grand boulevards. A construction site is always near. The large number of construction workers attracts entrepreneurs: restaurateurs, such as the Dengs, but also hairdressers, greengrocers and many others. So the 'floating villages' come into being: informal, temporary settlements inside the city.[1] After several years, upon completion of the construction project, the inhabitants move on.

The settlement is completely isolated from the rest of Chongqing. The main link with the outside world consists of a steep, narrow path that climbs up through the grass past the latrines and the building site, leading to a car park with a McDonald's restaurant. A different world starts here. Inside young parents are feeding their child a hamburger. A beautician fusses over a young woman in a wedding dress sitting at one of the tables next to the ball pit play area. Her future husband talks to the photographer who will soon immortalise the couple in a nearby park.

'The Shanghainese do not like the spicy Sichuan kitchen.'

The Dengs are not the only ones drawn to Chongqing in recent years. Three million migrant workers now live in the city. Most wind up in so-called 3D jobs: difficult, dangerous and dirty. One in three works in a factory. Others find employment as cleaners, waiters, security guards, garbage collectors or prostitutes. A quarter toil as bricklayers, welders or labourers, and help constructing the hundreds of new residential towers, bridges and government offices popping up all over the city.[2]

Due to its tempestuous growth, journalists all over the world almost exclusively describe Chongqing in superlatives. 'The fastest growing urban centre on earth' *(The Guardian)*, 'Chicago on the Yangtze – the largest city you have never heard of' *(Foreign Policy)* or simply 'the mega metropolis' *(Der Spiegel)*. The city overwhelms or repulses – there is no middle ground. Chongqing is best described as a mixture of Fritz Lang's *Metropolis* and *Blade Runner's* Los Angeles. On the mountainsides at the intersection of the Yangtze and Jialing rivers stand hundreds of tower blocks connected by walkways. Between them dart monorails. Motorways in two or three layers meander through the landscape like roller coasters on stilts. Above them float gondolas transporting passengers from one end of the river to the other, over the tops of the tower blocks. The illuminated night-time skyline equals that of Hong Kong or Shanghai.

Pinpointed precisely to the day, this tumultuous growth began on Friday 14 March 1997. Then the Fifth Session of the Eighth National People's Congress in Beijing adopted a resolution detaching Chongqing from Sichuan province. Like Beijing, Shanghai and Tianjin it became a municipal province under direct control of the central government. On paper, this turned Chongqing into the largest city in the world. With thirty-two million inhabitants, the population of this metropolis rivals that of countries like Uganda, Iraq or Canada. At 82,000 square kilometres, the municipal province is as large as Austria. In reality, however, Chongqing consists of thirty smaller cities interspersed by countryside. The actual urban centre has merely an estimated eight million inhabitants. By developing Chongqing, the authorities hoped to divert the continuing mass migration to coastal cities such as Shanghai, Beijing and Guangzhou. The global financial crisis lent a helping hand. Driven by spending cuts, more and more companies moved their production inland, where wages are lower than on the coast. This created hundreds of thousands of jobs, which means that many villagers from the interior of China no longer have to travel to the coast when looking for jobs. As in all the rapidly growing cities in the interior, migration to Chongqing is a local affair. The overwhelming majority of migrant workers come from the countryside around the city itself. Most of them dream of one day having enough money to buy a house in their hometown.

Once his customers have finished lunch and left, Deng clears the tables and walks to the communal tap near the fence of the building site for water to do the dishes. The improvised village under the motorway has 800 inhabitants at the moment, he says. Seven hundred construction workers populate the container houses, a hundred self-employed workers camp out in the structures of corrugated iron. 'We are one big family. We all know each other through and through.' Almost all the members of this family

belong to China's *liudong renkou* (literally: 'flowing population') of peasants traversing the country in search of paid employment. Depending on the numbers you choose to believe, China has between 70 and 300 million of these migrant workers, or between ten and 40 per cent of the urban population. Just how many people are involved becomes clear at Chinese New Year, when most of them return to their villages. According to the ministry of Railways, in 2009 a record number of 188 million people bought a train ticket at the turn of the year, though admittedly the Chinese love for lucky number eight could have influenced this estimate.[3] During the New Year festival the dependence of the cities on the former countryside dwellers becomes obvious: hairdressers, karaoke bars, restaurants and numerous shops forcibly close, no one collects the garbage, and construction grinds to a complete standstill.

A clear administrative boundary runs between 'real' city dwellers and migrant workers. Though Deng has worked in Shanghai and Chongqing for years, the authorities still register him as a peasant from the village of Liangping. The likelihood he will ever become a townsman is small, due to the *hukou*, a system of registration dividing all Chinese into two very distinct categories: city dwellers and peasants. Mao introduced the system in the 1950s precisely to avoid migration to the cities. Farmers were supposed to till the soil, while city folk worked in factories.

A clear administrative boundary runs between 'real' city dwellers and migrant workers.

The *hukou* functions in practice as an internal passport binding all inhabitants of China to their birthplace. Citizens only have rights to health care, education and pensions in the areas they were born in. The *hukou* passes from generation to generation. Even after ten or twenty years of blow-drying hair, selling socks or lugging around bricks in the city, the vast majority of migrant workers remain registered as peasants. This is the seed of the most important social division in China: only city dwellers can access good education and affordable health care. Farmers moving to the city are not allowed to use them. They have few rights. Their status is strikingly comparable to that of illegal Africans in the European Union or Latinos without green cards in the United States, with the only difference being that the Chinese migrant workers legally reside in the city.

Deng stands at the bottom of the social ladder, but compared to those left behind in the countryside he is rich and successful. The average annual income in Liangping is 600 dollars, an amount that a small entrepreneur in the city can save in several months. All in all, Deng and his wife manage to save almost 7,000 dollars per year. 'Business is going very well,' he laughs, as he wipes the eating bowls one by one with a cloth. He has bought a large motorcycle from his savings, which he has parked ceremoniously in front of the restaurant. It is his pride and joy.

After lunch, Wen, a composed man in his fifties, walks past the latrines to the construction workers' housing, consisting of two layers of white containers. He carries a fresh newspaper under his arm and a bottle of cold tea in his hand. His tidy clothes show that he does not pour concrete himself: he manages 120 workers. Wen is doing well even by city standards: as foreman he makes an annual rural salary each month.

Washing hangs out to dry from the railing above his container, beside which a man is brushing his teeth. Wen opens the ground floor door. His home has two rooms. In the front, a meeting room, with walls covered in drawings and work schedules. Behind it is a bedroom with four bunk beds, two of which look slept upon; the rest are covered in clothing, plastic bags and paper. Wen is privileged as a team leader, he says. 'I share this shack with one colleague instead of eleven others, like the rest.' Wen has bought an apartment in his birthplace, Wanzhou, a three-hour drive from the centre of Chongqing. It is a spacious and modern home of more than a hundred square metres in an eight-storey building. 'My wife lives there already,' he says. 'Of course, I miss her. She visits me several times per year, and I visit her a few times. But the visits are always too short.' He is looking forward to retirement. 'Then I can finally go back to Wanzhou.'

Wen proposes having a look at the construction site. He leaves the shack and returns with a couple of white construction helmets. Moments later, a creaking construction

RURAL POPULATION MOVING TO CITIES (Source: National Bureau of Statistics.)

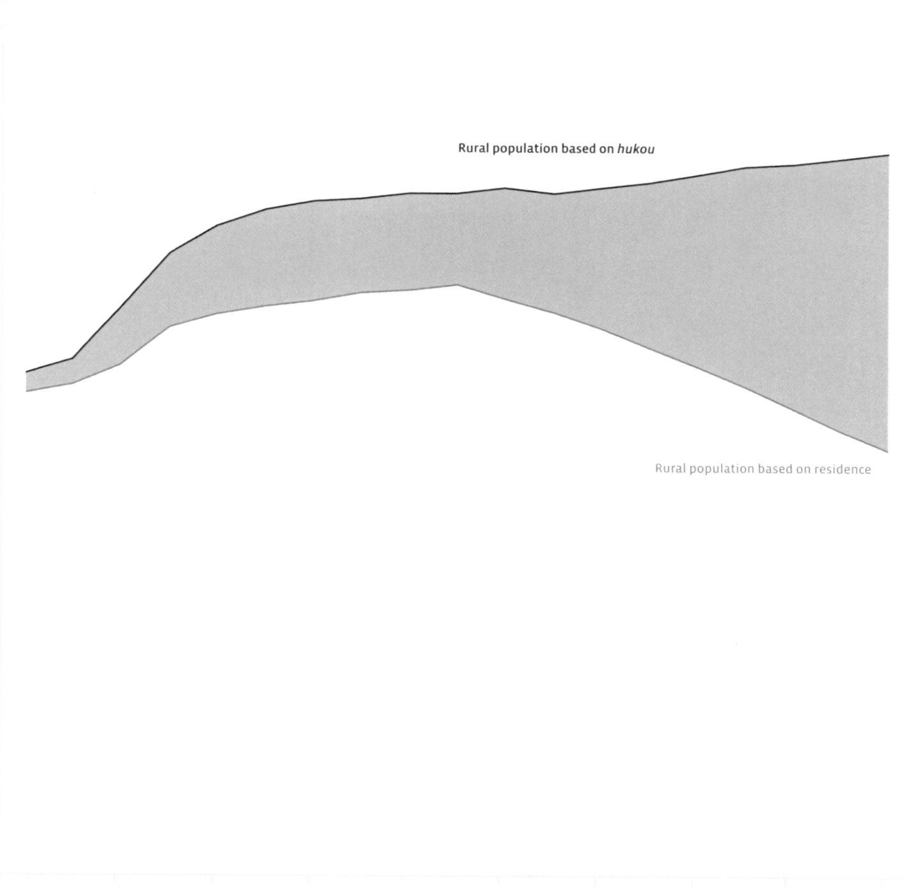

lift rises to the twenty-sixth floor of one of the uncomplete tower blocks. In the lift about ten workers stand smoking or playing with their mobile phones. They carry wheelbarrows full of bricks. The number of women is remarkably high. They do not only do the lighter jobs, such as operating the lift, but also perform heavier tasks, such as hauling sand, cement and bricks. High above the ground Wen's unsecured colleagues perform daredevil feats. Forty metres from the floor, three construction workers

THE VILLAGE OF MR DENG, May 2009

July 2010

Market Stalls
Security
Health Centre
Barber
Pub
Supermarket
Fresh Market
Restaurant
Mahjong Area
Offices & Housing
Restaurant
Dump

dismantle part of the scaffolding they are sitting on. Others balance on the twentieth floor to fill the last holes on the outside of the building. The spectacle is reminiscent of the famous 1920s New York photograph, with construction workers having lunch on a beam floating in nothingness, several hundred metres above ground. 'It is impossible to suffer from vertigo,' Wen lectures. 'You just start on the ground and build higher week after week. Once you get high up, you're used to it'. Accidents must happen regularly here, though Wen vaguely mumbles that 'it could be worse.'

The toiling workers are barely visible to drivers passing on the motorway. All they can see are the billboards announcing the rising district: Star City, a gated community of twenty-eight towers of twenty-five storeys on average. According to the advert an eighty-square-metre flat here will cost 90,000 dollars. The workmen will never be able to afford a sum like that. By the time the first families receive the keys to their dream homes, the workers will already be living in a new container near the next residential area, railroad or business centre under construction.

Daily routine around the construction site under the overpass follows a clear pattern. The restaurant owners get up at five thirty and start preparing breakfast. At seven the first builders start eating their meals and at eight the first construction lifts go up. Workers take a longish break for lunch and perhaps a nap between eleven thirty and one. With the onset of dusk the working day comes to an end and dinner is served. By ten o'clock most of the residents are in bed. This pattern repeats itself seven days a week, fifty weeks a year. The villagers rarely leave the construction site. They do not visit the new restaurants or coffee houses of Chongqing, go to the theatre or shop in the countless new malls arising everywhere. They work from dawn to dusk, and there is enough to do in their temporary village in the evenings. The informal economy flourishes. The settlement has two mobile and six covered restaurants, a bar, a mahjong area, a small supermarket, a greengrocer, a hairdresser, two arcades, three cinemas and a clinic.

A young doctor has set up his surgery in a tent of blue plastic sailcloth. He sits behind a desk with a stethoscope, some infusion bags and a reflex hammer. Two large cabinets on the left side of the tent contain an extensive stock of drugs. The doctor studied medicine in the southern city of Nanning, he says. He prefers not to mention his name, as his clinic does not have the required permits. He also remains hazy about whether he attained his degree or not. This much is clear: the doctor is not working here out of mere philanthropy alone. 'I make good money here,' he says. 'I just built a tent and started work.' For the uninsured labourers, his cheap medical care – less than a dollar for a bandaged finger – offers a way out. Common complaints are colds and diarrhoea, says the doctor. 'And, of course, construction accidents.'

A barn just beyond the improvised surgery houses an arcade with scrapped slot machines and arcade games. Movie lovers attend the cinema beside it. An old fashioned blackboard announces today's films and series: *The Sixth Sense*, *Desperate Housewives* and the documentary *An Unlikely Weapon*, about war photographer Eddie Adams. Tickets are one yuan, just over ten US cents. Inside, twenty-odd builders sit on low wooden benches watching a TV set connected to a DVD player. They watch in complete silence. The owner of the cinema is not exactly proud of his business. 'Such poverty,' he says. 'It is a disgrace to China.'

One in three city parents does not want their child to play with migrant children.

The Chinese city consists of a class of recognised citizens inhabiting permanent locations, and a group of residents circling around it, constantly seeking employment. Millions of construction workers live in temporary settlements cut off from daily life. So do many millions of factory workers living in dormitories on the factory premises. Closer to city life are the many waitresses, hairdressers, shop assistants and cleaners who rent shared rooms from the former peasants in the 'villages in the city'.

'Migrant workers lead miserable lives. They live in makeshift shelters, and eat the cheapest tofu with cabbage. They have no insurance, and often receive their salaries too late. On top of this the city dwellers discriminate against them.'[4] This is how Wang Yuanchen, member of the National People's Congress, describes migrant life. Wang,

himself a migrant, has succeeded in life with a flourishing business in computer courses. According to research conducted by the Chinese authorities, almost half of all migrant workers have no labour contract. One in six interviewed migrants did not even know what a labour contract was.[5] This has predictable results: very long workdays and low wages, paid late. Things are not much better as far as health care is concerned: less than ten per cent of migrants in Chongqing have insurance.[6] Chinese law prescribes that all children must follow – free – education for nine years, but practice is different. State schools in the city demand exorbitant fees for migrants, arguing that they do not receive a budget for students who officially reside elsewhere. Migrant schools specially set up as an alternative usually offer substandard education. Out of necessity, three quarters of migrants leave their child with relatives in the countryside while they work in the city. According to the *Chongqing Daily* around two million *liushou ertong*, or 'left-behind children', live in the villages around Chongqing city.[7] For China as a whole the figure is sixty million.[8]

Yin is an exception. She sits next to a pile of empty beer crates in Liangping Restaurant. She wears a black dress and trainers. A colouring book and some felt tip pens lie on the table in front of her. The ten-year-old is one of the few children in the provisional village. She clearly enjoys the attention all the adults shower her with, and cheerfully recites a phrase by Confucius she has learnt in school today. Her proud mother sits knitting beside her. 'I couldn't do without her,' she says. 'School fees are higher here than in our village, but it's worth it.' Yin stands up to play with her best friend, a red-eared turtle she feeds scraps of food from the palm of her hand. If Yin later wants to take her high school exam, she probably will have to return to her grandparents' village, where she still lives according to her *hukou*. If she does well there, she might be able to go to university – one of the few ways in which peasants can also officially move to the city and obtain an urban *hukou*.

Every resident of the builders' village knows the story of lift operator Shi Tong. At 180 dollars a month she has one of the worst paid jobs on the construction site. But her daughter has made it: she studies computer engineering at the University of Chongqing. As the number of migrant workers swells, the question about what kind of urban society China wants to create becomes more and more acute. Their trek to the city has given millions of rural residents the opportunity to flee the poverty and hopelessness of the countryside. The city has reaped economic benefits from the influx of cheap labour lacking medical insurance, right to education or permanent contracts. It has led to a lively mix of enterprising people all pursuing a better life. The last, crucial step in this emancipatory machinery is, however, still missing: the elevation of peasants to urban status. If the present system does not change, the number of second-class citizens in China will grow to 500 million migrants, each and every one of which will not be a fully accepted inhabitant of the city. Inevitably, such apartheid will create unbearable tensions between insiders and outsiders.

On 2 March 2010 thirteen newspapers and magazines throughout China published an editorial demanding urgent measures. 'China has suffered for too long from the *hukou* system,' wrote the papers. 'We believe that people were born free and have the right to move freely. Citizens today still suffer from the bad and untenable policies from the time of the planned economy.' The editorial appeared just before the largest political event of the year, the meeting of the National People's Congress, and struck a nerve. One of the authors, Zhang Hong of the *Economic Observer*, was sacked immediately. 'I have never heard of Chinese newspapers jointly publishing a leader before,' said vice

(2005)

dean Yao Yang of Beijing University. 'It is highly unusual.'[9]

That something must change is obvious to the party leaders in Beijing, but what? In 2007 they appointed Chongqing as one of the cities permitted to relax the *hukou*, with limited results thus far. Most of the migrants do not meet the requirements: a labour contract or evidence of tax payments. Other migrants are wary of the consequences. If they discard their rural registration, they also abandon their safety net, the farmland they posses in their villages.

Following the call in the media, Huang Qifan, the mayor of Chongqing, admitted the necessity of a transitional arrangement. Migrants should be able to temporarily hold on to their houses and land in the villages. 'We can't send farmers naked into the cities.'[10]

He proposed to grant ten million people in Chongqing an urban *hukou* between 2010 and 2020 – more than double the present number. Huang suggested starting with the 1.2 million migrant workers that had lived in the city for over ten years already. The mayor of Chongqing gave an extensive and passionate interview to the *Farmer's Daily* to clarify his motives. 'The existing *hukou* system obstructs more than 200 million migrant workers from integrating into cities in China. They are like migratory birds, moving back and forth between their hometowns and cities. This causes lots of social conflict. Migrant workers come into cities, work diligently for two or three decades and yet have to return home and feed themselves without a pension for their old age. During this period, if their kids go to school, they have to pay extra fees. This is quite unfair. We cannot treat farmers like second-class citizens. They deserve basic public services, because they help create those services with their own hands.'[11]

City dwellers show very little support for plans like these. They fear their own social services will be put under pressure if millions of 'peasants' can use them 'just like that.' Besides, they look down on the farmers. One in three city parents does not want their child to play with migrant children, a large government survey showed.[12] The word *nongmingong*, literally 'peasant worker,' has such a negative connotation that some city administrations now soothingly have started to speak of *xinshimin*, new city residents, instead.

At nine in the evening darkness covers the building site, but the village is still full of life. Workers play mahjong in a room lit by fluorescent lamps. The losers sulkingly place a small amount of money on the table and make way for the next player. It is a noisy

蜕变重庆

game. The last customers of Liangping Restaurant drain their plastic beer cups, while outside a group of heavily made-up women in short skirts and high heels walk into the area over the muddy path. Restaurant owner Deng smilingly describes them as 'the workers' girlfriends.' Around eleven, after all the customers have left, all the restaurant owners pull up a stool. They drink beers and pass round cigarettes. The women pick up their knitting, while Deng and his colleagues talk about their homelands. One day they will all return, they say. Mr and Mrs Deng have already bought an apartment in Liangping. It is eighty square metres in size, they say proudly. They are saving the rest of the money for their son's education and for their retirement.
They have hardly gotten to know the city in recent years. 'I only know the old Chongqing at the intersection of the rivers, not far from here,' says one of the cooks. 'That is where the temples and old houses are. It is the most beautiful part of town.' The others nod in agreement. They do not realise that several months ago the wrecking ball flattened all the old buildings in that area. What remains is a barren plain. Chongqing's new Central Business District will arise on the riverbanks in several years. Here and there the first containers that will house the thousands of builders hired to complete this monumental task have already been put in place.

Less than a year later a grassy park has replaced Liangping Restaurant. The cinema and arcade have disappeared. A tennis court inhabits the site of the doctor's tent. The muddy field is now tiled and serves as the outdoor seating area of a café. Dozens of Star City residents eat at tables shaded by parasols, cooled by large fans. The towers of the new district stand in a fenced-off garden filled with ponds. The atmosphere is calm, the fragrance of blossoming plants fills the air. The new shops of Star City can be found on the ground floor of one of the towers. The abundance of estate agents is particularly striking: fourteen in total, besides a dentist, a shop for baby clothes and a lingerie store. Executive and luxury cars fill the car park in front of the buildings. The area inhabited a year ago by second-class urban residents has been taken over by its permanent inhabitants: those with a city *hukou*.

4. WUHAN

(1950)

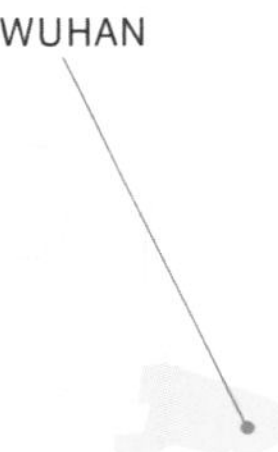

HUBEI - ITALY
With 57 million inhabitants, Hubei province has roughly the same population as Italy

CANARY WHARF IN CENTRAL CHINA

Two guards sit on wooden stools outside an aluminium shack, looking at a barrier. It is not completely clear what exactly they are protecting. On the other side of the enclosure, a road runs into the emptiness, straight as a ruler, with barren terrain to the left and right. A single structure towers above the guard hut, a giant billboard exclaiming 'height is the future.' The guards suddenly look up when a car closes in at high speed. It stops just in front of the roadblock. Two men with tangled hair jump out. One of them carries a film camera with a logo identifying them as journalists of a local television station. He lifts the camera onto his shoulder, walks to the barrier and starts filming the vast nothingness in front of him. 'We are shooting an item on the beginning of construction,' explains the other. The two finish their work in several minutes, and get back into the car. They turn round and tear away, stared at by the guards.

'It's good they moved the military airport,' says Yu Yiding. 'It was dangerous in the middle of town and caused noise pollution.' The deputy director of the planning authority draws on his Red Golden Dragon cigarette, a local brand. 'Besides,' he says, 'the airport's departure provided Wuhan with an immense opportunity.' Yu has an archetypical academic's office. Papers and reports cover his desk. The cabinet is crammed with books. A wooden globe stands by the door. Cardboard boxes containing bottles of mineral water litter the room.

In the Nineties, when Yu worked as a professor at Wuhan University, the first voices in favour of moving the Wangjiadun military airport could be heard. Due to the incredibly rapid growth of the city, the runway and control tower had ended up within the Wuhan urban area. After a while, residential areas completely encircled the air base. In 2002 Yu swapped the University for the Planning Authority. His timing was excellent. Less than a year later Wuhan's People's Congress decided to get rid of Wangjiadun completely. It was every city planner's dream: the sudden materialisation of an empty zone seven square kilometres in size, twice as large as New York's Central Park, in the centre of a fast growing city of millions. Few urban planners ever have the opportunity to put their ideas into practice on such a scale. No wonder that Yu felt privileged. 'I really wanted to lead the project. Until then, the airfield had been isolated from the rest of the city. Now we had the chance to open up the area for the inhabitants of Wuhan.' His time came after the city administration reached an agreement with the People's Liberation Army, which owned the land. During the closing ceremony on 25 December 2007, Yu observed a Russian-made Sukhoi SU-30 jet making its symbolic last flight from Wangjiadun.

Yu had spent the preceding five years figuring out what to do with the enormous swath of land. He spreads out a map of Wuhan on the low wooden table in his office, and points at the strategic position of the former airfield: only a few kilometres from Wuhan's Central Station, and close to Financial Street, where HSBC, Société Générale and more than ten other banks keep their regional headquarters, including the China Construction Bank, the Bank of Communications, the China Merchants Bank, the Guangdong Development Bank and the Shanghai Pudong Development Bank. Yu remembers the lively debates at the planning authority. 'How should we use the area? We could turn it into a residential district, a park, or perhaps even a forest. But none of these ideas seemed quite right. The local authorities had spent a lot of money on shifting the airbase, and wanted to recover the costs. It soon became clear we would have to do something else.'

The name 'Wuhan' refers to three cities at the junction of the Han and Yangtze rivers. The first part of the name alludes to the ancient city of Wuchang on the eastern bank of the Yangtze, the second part to Hanyang and Hankou on the other side of the river. The three cities united into a single administrative unit in 1927. With an urban core of seven million people, out of a total of ten million, Wuhan is a large city even by Chinese standards. It is the capital of Hubei province, which has the same population as the United Kingdom, but is slightly smaller in size: just about that of England and Wales put together.

Like many Chinese metropolises, Wuhan has an ancient history. The construction of the famous Tower of the Yellow Crane in AD 223 marked the establishment of Wuchang, the largest of the current three city districts. Tang Dynasty poet Cui Hao sang an ode to it that all Chinese schoolchildren learn by heart: '*The Yellow Crane has long since flown away/ All that remains is the Yellow Crane Tower*'. The city with its famous tower blossomed into one of the most important inland ports of China. Around 1850, the three cities that later formed Wuhan counted one and a half million inhabitants, making it one of the largest conurbations in the world.[1] International trade developed from 1858, under foreign compulsion. After losing the Second Opium War against the British and the French, the victors demanded the opening of several ports to foreign shipping, including Hankou. Subsequently Great Britain, France, Germany, Russia and Japan each built their own 'concessions' in the city, business districts under foreign dominion subject to different rules than the rest of China.

Such concessions were not new in China. Following defeat in the First Opium War in 1842, the vanquished Qing emperor opened five 'treaty ports' to trade with Europe: Guangzhou (Canton), Ningbo, Xiamen (Amoy), Fuzhou and Shanghai. Their number would eventually increase to more than thirty, from Harbin in the north to Kunming in the south-west of China. Despite its dubious justification, international trade led to great economic prosperity. As a result of the opening to international commerce, many of these cities developed explosively.

Wuhan underwent a transformation. In 1925 American traveller Harry Alverson Franck

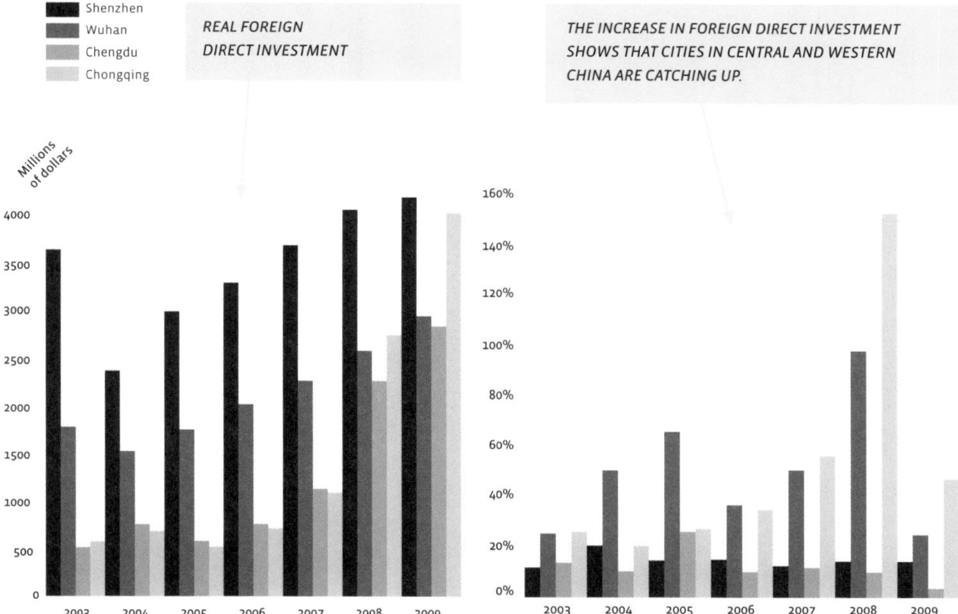

found himself '... dumped suddenly in a bustling city wholly Western in its architecture and layout, even though completely surrounded by China, among buildings looming high into the air ...' Dodging 'automobiles dashing their imperious way up and down the river-front,' an astonished Franck noted 'several theatres' that 'offered only American movies.'[2] Franck was staying in the international concession that gave Hankou its un-Chinese appearance. Banks with classicist facades lined the river; colonials spent their cash in restaurants and bars, at the tennis club, the golf club or at the races. 'Hankow is largely a foreign creation,' wrote the famous American journalist Freda Utley in 1939. She described the Chinese trading cities as 'foreign towns on Chinese soil administered by foreigners in the interest of foreigners.'[3] Western hegemony lasted for several decades. Germany left its concession during the First World War, in 1917. Russia abandoned her share in 1920 by voluntarily renouncing 'imperialist rights and privileges' in China. In 1927 the British fled furious workers taking over their district. The French stood their ground longest, and quit Wuhan only in 1942. Their departure marked the conclusion of a period in the history of the city as an important centre of international trade.

市新空间
提升城
城
The City

A closer look reveals that the two guards at the former military airport are not just protecting empty space. Road cleaners in orange safety waistcoats are sweeping the tarmac of the brand new roads traversing the immense area behind the barrier. The tidily planted greenery on the central reserves of the roads seems especially out of place. Plants and flowers grow between young trees standing at ten-metre intervals. Streetlamps line the roads. The traffic lights even turn from red to green, even though lorries drive by only occasionally.

All new Chinese districts offer this anomalous spectacle of fully completed roads in an otherwise empty area. It is standard procedure to fully form the public space before placing the first stone of the first building. At the north end of the former airport hundreds of trees grow closely together, a green gauze protecting crown and roots. A small sign reveals this to be a future park. Cyclists or motorcyclists drive past occasionally, but human activity here focuses on a collection of site huts in the centre of the empty plain. There, builders are smoking cigarettes, awaiting the start of construction.

Wuhan is a large city even by Chinese standards.

After decades of isolation under Mao Zedong, a new period of internationalisation commenced in 1978. By carefully introducing market policies, Deng Xiaoping, the new leader, hoped to bring similar economic prosperity to his country as Japan, Taiwan, South Korea and Singapore had experienced. He believed that, like the Asian Tigers, China had to focus on economic growth through a combination of exports and foreign investment. Initially, this only happened in the Special Economic Zones (SEZs): government designated areas with liberal economic regimes. The most famous Special Economic Zone is Shenzhen: a fishing town near Hong Kong that, boosted by local market forces, bloomed into a thriving metropolis in twenty years' time. In 1984 the government gave fourteen similar 'open coastal cities,' including Guangzhou and Shanghai, permission to focus on foreign trade. Interestingly, the 'open coastal cities' are almost identical to the treaty cities from the colonial period. According to urban researcher Thomas Campanella, Deng turned the symbolic significance of the trading cities inside out: 'The old outposts of foreign exploitation would now be agents of Chinese renewal, fuel injectors of foreign capital that would prime China's economic engines.'[4]

Wuhan followed at a later stage, when economic openness moved inland. To draw foreign investment, the city established three special 'development zones.' The car industry, including companies such as Citroën, Nissan and Honda, settled in the Economic and Technological Development Zone of Hanyang. Nokia and Foxconn perched in Optical Valley, a name referring to its Californian example and the fibre optic industry it was designed to attract. The city lured potential Taiwanese investors with a specially tailored district in Hankou: the Wujiashan Taiwanese Businessman Investment Zone. Since then, over a thousand Taiwanese businesses have set up shop in Wuhan. The zones and the former concessions show conspicuous parallels. Both are demarcated areas where different rules apply, with a concentration of activity as a result. The greatest difference is that the Chinese themselves set the conditions in the post-1978 economic zones, rather than governments in Paris, London, Berlin or Moscow.

New openness provoked a thousandfold increase in foreign direct investment in Wuhan, from ten million dollars in 1990 to ten billon dollars in 2006. Over ninety per cent of that money is invested in one of the three business areas. Because the investment zones form about a third of the entire municipal territory, this means foreign capital has a significant impact on city structure. Over time, the appearance of apartment blocks, shops, hospitals and schools beside businesses blurs the physical frontier between special economic zone and 'ordinary' city.

In an office on the thirty-sixth floor of New World Plaza bearing the inscription 'VIP Room,' a relaxed Feng Song sinks into a giant brown leather armchair. A model of a Russian-built fighter jet stands beside him on the thick yellow carpet. The window overlooks the old airfield runway.

'If Wuhan wants to develop any further, it needs a Central Business District,' says Feng. 'That is what McKinsey told us.' Feng is deputy director of the Wuhan CBD Investment & Development Company, the business in charge of redeveloping the former airport.

Like professor Yu, he has been involved in the development of the area since 2002. 'Before that I worked in Australia,' says Feng. He points at a blue rugby shirt bearing the logo of the Dennis Family Corporation from Melbourne, one of the largest property developers in Australia. That McKinsey's consultants proposed building a Central Business District on the site of the airbase was hardly surprising. Ever since Shangai constructed its Pudong business district in the early Nineties, every ambitious Chinese city wants its own 'CBD': a district with an impressive skyline of high-rise office blocks containing the regional headquarters of multinationals, banks, legal firms, investors, insurers and consultants. Beijing built the new Chaoyang CBD, Guangzhou established Tianhe CBD, and Tianjin developed Binhai CBD. The concept is so popular that the abbreviation CBD has become a word in the Chinese language.

'In the whole world there are only two cities using this method: London and Wuhan.'

Feng: 'East Coast cities are a few years ahead of Wuhan. But we have prime land at a top location at our disposal. That is the first thing you need when you want to build a CBD. Not people or technology.' The logic behind the Central Business District is simple. Now China has transformed itself in the last decades from a country of peasants to a nation of manufacturers, it is time to improve the high end services industry. As the SEZs stimulated industrial development, the CBDs must now encourage growth of the financial sector. Administrators see a business district as the crowning achievement in the transformation of their town to a modern metropolis. 'A CBD speeds up the pace of development,' says Feng, citing from the McKinsey report commissioned by the city. Like other consultants, the agency is increasingly taking over the role of architects and urban planners. 'And I'll tell you something,' sighs Feng, 'McKinsey is so expensive!'
The consulting company studied thirty different business districts worldwide for

Wuhan, from Tokyo's Shinkuju to La Défense in Paris, from the Frankfurt Bankenviertel to the Chicago Loop. A delegation including Feng and urban planner Yu visited several European business districts for inspiration. McKinsey finally proposed to use London's Canary Wharf as an example, and advised not only to follow a similar master plan, but also to use a comparable approach. Feng: 'that means a business will be responsible for developing the district, rather than the government'. His hand taps firmly on the armrest of his chair. 'In the whole world there are only two cities using this method: London and Wuhan.'

The local army and local government established the Wuhan CBD investment company in 2002 jointly with Ocean Wide, an enterprise trading on the Shenzhen stock market. After a transitory phase both state companies sold their shares to Ocean Wide. The authorities hoped this commercial setup would prevent some of the problems experienced by other cities. 'Look at Zhengzhou, where the government took charge of the development of the new CBD. The lack of occupancy is enormous. That will not happen to us. We are a business, we conduct market research before we start building.' Enthusiastically, Feng sketches the ambitions for the former airport. 'A financial centre, China's Frankfurt, that will attract two thousand companies, mostly Chinese and predominantly in the financial sector. But we also want to draw foreign multinationals.' Apart from offices, the new CBD will offer housing to 'Wuhan's elite,' foreign and domestic businesspeople. 'We want exceptional people. Look at London, where you see the same thing. The most expensive houses in town are in Canary Wharf, where the business elite live.' The former military base will not provide cheap housing, let alone social housing. 'The area must have a grand allure, and as a company our goal is to make a profit. It is not our responsibility to build inexpensive housing. Anyway, we will be creating a lot of jobs.' The developer sums up: five to eight hundred jobs in the new hotel, another 1,000 in the mall. 'That is a contribution, too.' Then he leaps up. 'Shall I show you the scale model?'

On the other side of the floor, an empty office illuminated by neon tubes functions as a provisional promotional area. Drawings of the new CBD hang on the walls. A model of the master plan stands in the middle of the room. Apartment blocks occupy a large part of the area. The actual business district takes up about a square kilometre at the southern tip of the former runway. The new business district will provide Wuhan with

A model says more than a thousand Excel spreadsheets

JOHN M SMYTH CO

an impressive skyline of its own. On a table in the corner stands a model of Ocean Wide Plaza, the luxurious mall being built at the moment. The night markets popular in other areas of Wuhan do not fit the image of a modern business centre, and will have no place in the new district. 'That is obviously not the intention,' Feng laughs. This is where the elite live. This neighbourhood will be completely different from other parts of town. We will only allow shops selling top brands.' He then walks over to the most remarkable scale model in the room: a tower so huge it touches the panelled ceiling of the office. 'This is another lesson from London,' says Feng. 'A tower like that provides a reason to put other buildings around it. Wuhan Tower will put the area on the map and stimulate development.' As the Yellow Crane Tower symbolises the history of the city, Wuhan Tower expresses ambitions for the future: 428 metres of glass and steel, almost twice as high as One Canada Square in Canary Wharf.

Wuhan hopes not merely to emulate London's business district, but strives to overtake it. Feng smiles broadly as he rattles off a sentence he has clearly used before. 'New York built Manhattan in a hundred years. It took Paris fifty years to complete La Défense. London started with Canary Wharf in 1984 and Shanghai with Pudong in 1994. I think we can be faster. This CBD will be completely finished in ten to fifteen years.'

Shanghai and Beijing make significant marks on global politics, economy and culture, and can justifiably call themselves global cities. As China strengthens its position in the world and develops its interior, a number of cities in Central China will also make the list of world cities. This has not happened yet, but city authorities have huge ambitions. By attracting foreign companies and multinationals they hope, firstly, to create jobs and money, and, secondly, to raise the international profile of their cities. Administrators have a personal interest in success. China may not be a democracy where politicians answer to their constituents in elections, but the ruling party does hold mayors and other senior officials to account based on performance. 'Officials holding government posts, such as governor or mayor, are rated according to an impressively lengthy list of numerical indicators, which look like they were drawn up by management consultants,' writes Richard McGregor in his revealing book, *The Party*. 'Economic growth, investment, the quality of the air and water in their localities, and public order all theoretically count in benchmarking performance.'[5] The most important criterion by far is that of economic growth. Directors able to show the prettiest school report can count on promotions to larger cities or national politics. Cities compete in all sorts of ways for the favour of foreign investors, who are among the main drivers of economic growth.

Cheap labour, free land or tax incentives are no longer enough to win the battle. Mayors increasingly turn to urban development and architecture to lure potential investors. This happens in so-called urban planning centres, which depict the future global city in scale models. Every ambitious Chinese metropolis has such a specially designed arena for the seduction of foreign delegations. Wuhan's urban planning centre lies on the top floor of the municipal conference centre. Visitors first pass photographs of senior officials, followed by panels exhibiting the history of the city and maps of the area. They then enter the holy of holies: a hall with a giant model depicting Wuhan in 2020. After taking seats on a special VIP balcony overlooking the model, the lights dim and a slick sound and light show commences, astonishing the visitors with the sheer expression of ambition. The spectator can observe with his own eyes that Wuhan is swiftly becoming a city of global importance, with all the investment opportunities that will provide. A model and a 3D animation say more than a thousand Excel spreadsheets. As *pièce de résistance* of the presentation, the skyline of the future business district appears.

Wuhan is one of the many Chinese cities developing plans for a Central Business District in the hope of attracting foreign companies. Zhengzhou, Chengdu, Chongqing, Shijiazhuang, all want their own skyline of office blocks. According to researchers Li and Chibamba of the University of Geosciences in Wuhan, the 'megaproject' of the new CBD 'must be seen as evidence of stiff competition between Chinese cities for foreign capital.'[6] This is significant. In the struggle for the dollar and the yen China is probably building more CBDs than it needs. Deputy director of the provincial planning institute in Guiyang city Shan Xiaogang purposely avoids joining the craze. 'A real CBD is a commercial area with headquarters, supported by financial institutions and consultancies. As a city you can copy the buildings, but not their content.' Most Chinese cities have not yet reached that level of development. Let's put it this way: if you wanted to start a management consultancy firm, I would still advise you to do that in Shanghai.'

The battle to establish the most successful banking district of China's interior brings readily to mind the competition between the airports of Dubai, Doha and Abu Dhabi

(2005)

Map and model of the Wuhan CBD

CBD

to become the main hub on the Arabian Peninsula. It is clear there will be a winner; the question is who that will be. Wuhan feels encouraged by the participation of international specialists such as McKinsey and Jones Lang La Salle, and the outlook is sunny: in April 2010 financial consultant Deloitte opened its first office in Central China in Wuhan. Ernst & Young's accountants were already there. PricewaterhouseCoopers, however, sticks to its offices in Chongqing and Xi'an for the time being.

To create a CBD of international appeal, Wuhan sought advice from large international design and planning companies, and asked the American SOM, the British Atkins, the German Obermeyer and the Chinese Academy for City Planning in Beijing all to submit proposals. This happened by what is known as plan selection, a typical Chinese phenomenon in which several parties are paid to submit designs. The client then picks the best liked elements and forges them into a single whole. This kind of pragmatism is completely absent from Western urban development. 'In plan selection the quality of the final master plan depends on the quality of the client,' says Samuel Huang, who submitted a proposal on the Wuhan business district for US architectural firm SOM. 'Our proposal consisted of a lake in the south and a hill in the north. That excellently suits the Chinese concept of *feng shui*. The trick is to excavate a hole for the lake and use the surplus soil for the hill.'

Huang, an easygoing thirty-something-year-old of Taiwanese origin, sits in the coffee corner of his office on one of the top floors of a skyscraper on People's Square in Shanghai. His mountain and lake ended up in the final CBD master plan. 'The Wuhan planning authority used our suggestion as a basis and added a couple of ideas from the other agencies.' The Chinese are used to this unconventional cobbling together conflicting ideas. The most striking example is of course China itself, which sells the inclusion of capitalist and freer Hong Kong into the mainland with the slogan 'One country, Two Systems.'

Huang in the meantime has moved to HOK, another US company, but is still involved in the Wuhan project. 'The planning authority has asked my present employer to flesh out the details of the plan.' According to Huang, Wuhan has learnt from past errors. Normally a city auctions large parcels of land to various property developers, who then design the buildings themselves. They have to abide by a limited number of

安全在心中
浙建集团
汉江国际金融中心
INTERNATIONAL
FINANCE
CENTER

preconditions, such as maximum height, maximum density and minimum amount of greenery. 'The planning authority only draws the road grid.' The consequences can be seen all over China. Huge roads separate individual blocks that lack any relationship to each other, as in, for instance, Shanghai's Pudong business district. As a result pedestrians avoid large parts of the neighbourhood, giving it a gloomy and desolate aura.

Wuhan hopes to learn from the mistakes of cities that already built financial districts, and that its late start may now prove to be an actual advantage. Huang fishes out a book with detailed maps, cross-sections and street profiles of the future CBD. 'We have made a detailed urban design for each separate piece of land. That is completely normal in the West, but I don't know any other city in China that has gone about it in this way.'

'The Wuhan CBD is a Chinese business district,' says professor Yu in his cluttered office at the planning authority. 'It has to have a couple of typical Chinese elements, it cannot be otherwise.' He taps a new Red Golden Dragon from his packet and lights up. 'We have a central axis in our plan, but it is not completely symmetrical. That was a conscious decision. One of the architectural agencies proposed a completely symmetrical master plan. I immediately rejected it. It looked like it was designed by an emperor! You can't build something like that nowadays.' Completely abandoning tradition was impossible, says Yu. 'The Chinese like a show of force, and we have rules for *feng shui*. You need support in the back, as you look in a mirror. The mountain in the north and lake in the south reflect this.' As client, Yu composed the ultimate master plan from the various proposals. 'I had some vague references in mind: New York, Chicago, Paris, Seoul and London. We consulted a panel of professors from Wuhan on various aspects, such as transportation, environment and architecture. We took the best elements from every plan and mixed those.'

The urban planners hope the solidity of the approach will become evident when the first pedestrians walk through the area. 'Most Chinese cities in recent years have copied Western business districts with buildings around enormous squares where no one wants to come. People prefer to walk in streets with shops. In Wuhan we don't want a second Pudong, like in Shanghai. I really don't want that. The scale of that district is inhuman. And for pedestrians it is almost impossible to cross the roads in Beijing's CBD, that's how massively wide they are.' Yu sketches what he thinks a modern CBD should look like. Much of the neighbourhood will be car-free, with large underground parking garages. There will be pedestrian-only shopping streets, but also lively roads with both shops and traffic. The buildings built by various property developers and designed by different architects still need to form a consistent whole. Yu hopes to achieve this by selling every plot of land with Samuel Huang's design guidelines as a precondition. The urban planner is not afraid the extra rules will deter developers. 'This will only make the area more valuable,' he says. 'I expect them all to be satisfied.'

The large towers evoke the feeling you have seen them somewhere before.

Though pedestrians will find Wuhan's CBD more pleasant than similar business districts in the rest of China, in other respects it is not so unique. The first designs of the large towers evoke the feeling you have seen them somewhere before, in another business district in a different large town, in Asia or somewhere else on the planet. The Wuhan CBD will have the same expensive offices, shops, hotels and houses as countless other business districts all over China and in the rest of the world. Like everywhere else, a conference centre and a large theatre must attract the first visitors to the area. That local party functionaries intentionally encourage a copy and paste job appears from the meaningless brief they formulated for the area. 'High starting point, high standard, high efficiency and high level.' The fact that the same global architects operate worldwide further produces conformity. SOM also makes plans for CBDs in Beijing, Chicago, Tianjin, and – not completely coincidentally – drafted the master plan for Canary Wharf in London.

All over China, authorities invite the same architects to submit designs, even for iconic buildings such as the highest tower, the museum or the theatre. The Frenchman

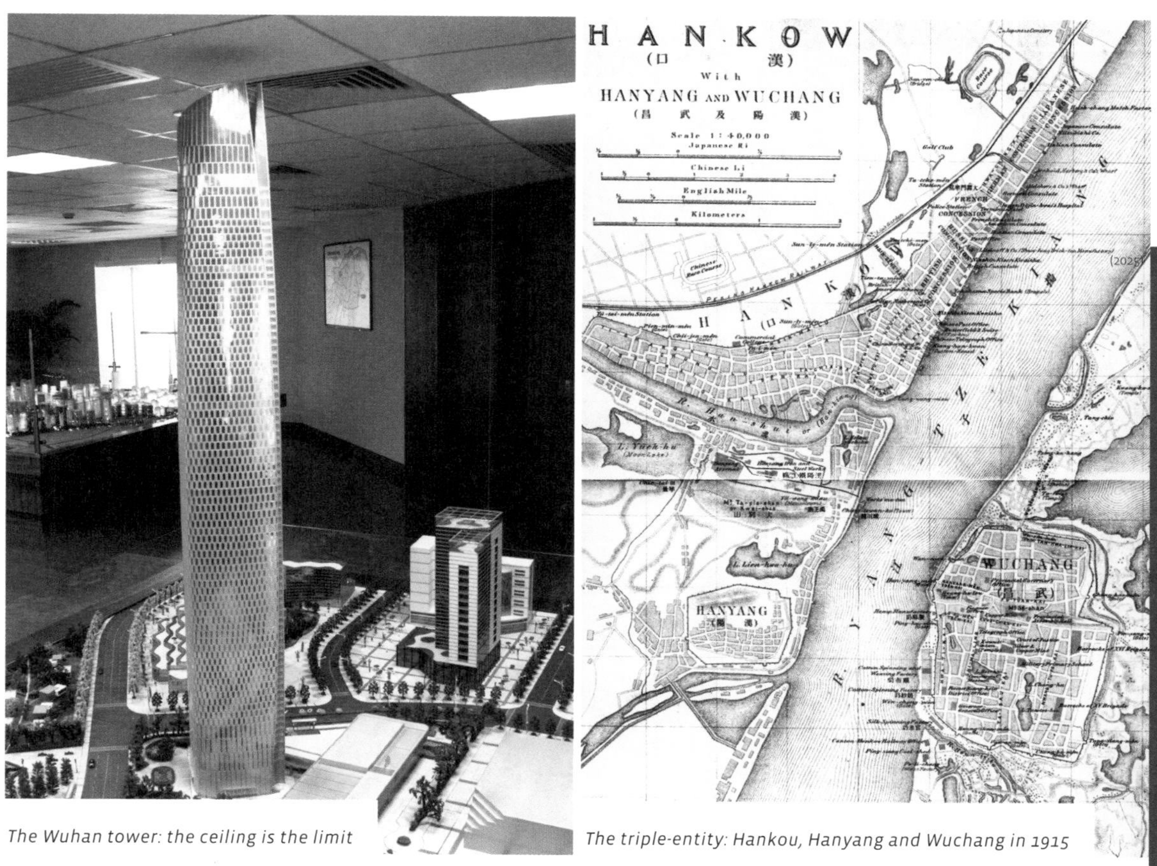

The Wuhan tower: the ceiling is the limit

The triple-entity: Hankou, Hanyang and Wuchang in 1915

Paul Andreu has made cultural buildings for business districts in Beijing, Shanghai, Jinan, Suzhou, Chengdu and Taiyuan. As he consistently uses globes in his designs, Chinese architects say that Andreu 'lays an egg in every Chinese city.' In its desire to radiate professionalism, Wuhan has eliminated all distinctiveness from its CBD. A line of billboards by the former airfield encapsulates the conformist dreams of the city government in a giant poster on which the skylines of New York, Paris, Hong Kong and Shanghai smoothly assimilate into that of future Wuhan.

5. XI'AN

‘HEAVEN FOR YOUNG LEADERS WHO ENJOY LIFE’

SHAANXI - ARGENTINA
With 37 million inhabitants Shaanxi province has roughly the same population as Argentina

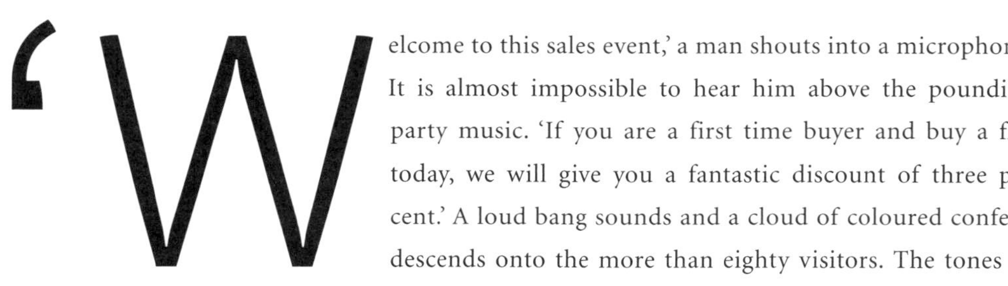

‘Welcome to this sales event,’ a man shouts into a microphone. It is almost impossible to hear him above the pounding party music. ‘If you are a first time buyer and buy a flat today, we will give you a fantastic discount of three per cent.’ A loud bang sounds and a cloud of coloured confetti descends onto the more than eighty visitors. The tones of *Hotel California* fill the room – ‘*and I was thinking to myself, this could be heaven or this could be hell*’. The crowd throngs around a scale model of twelve identical 32-storey residential towers in the middle of the sales centre. Men with cameras are filming the spectacle. Estate agent site Soufun has hired them to record the hunger for houses for a promotional video. In the corner of the hall a man places a thick wad of 100-

yuan banknotes on a table, an amount of roughly 4,500 dollars, a down payment on an apartment in the new neighbourhood. The meeting is not only chaotic, but also extremely short. Within twenty minutes everyone has returned to the two luxury coaches from which they appeared. On this rainy Sunday morning, Soufun's buses make stops at five new districts: first Sun City and City Garden, followed by Holiday Garden and Leisure Garden. The collective hunt for housing ends around lunchtime with a visit to today's most expensive *xiaoqu* (literally: small neighbourhood): the Maple Forest Luxurious Garden.

The participants are in a cheerful mood. Like anywhere else in the world, buying a house in China is an emancipatory act: by signing the deed, the buyer joins the propertied classes and attains the state of 'little comfort,' *xiaokang*. The passengers know that those who sit in this bus have made it in life. Twenty-five-year-old Wang Lei nonchalantly browses through the pile of gleaming leaflets he received upon entering the bus. Wearing a sporty fleece sweater, jeans and trainers, he looks as though he has prepared for a long walk in the outdoors. To the question what kind of house he his looking for, he has a clear answer: 'cheap.'

His friend Li Yujuan, a young woman, sits beside him. Like the other home hunters on the bus they belong to China's emerging middle class. Wang Lei is a computer programmer with a Chinese company; Li Yujuan works as a chemical engineer for a multinational corporation. She: 'He's buying a house for the first time, so it is quite difficult to make a choice.' He: 'I want a flat with a living room, bedroom and study.' She: 'And preferably an extra room, right?' He: 'Yes, with an eye to the future.' Li Yujuan starts to laugh. 'Yes, exactly! For when you will have a large family.' Wang Lei hastens to prevent misunderstandings. 'We don't have a relationship, actually. We are just good friends.'

Today's new construction projects are all in the High Tech Development Zone in the south of the emerging metropolis of Xi'an. 'It's an up-and-coming neighbourhood,' says Wang. 'The company I work for will probably move here next year, too.' The furious pace of construction becomes clearly apparent during today's trip. For miles on end, the coach passes nothing but new apartment blocks and construction sites – an impressive scene. All along the way real estate adverts alert passersby to the latest construction projects. As the coach drives into the Holiday Garden car park, the Soufun tour leader stands up and addresses the passengers from the aisle. 'Don't forget to show your membership card if you make a down payment today, otherwise you will not receive a discount.' She speaks quickly and casually, as if she is touting watermelons rather than houses. The prospective buyers then leave the bus and walk to the entrance of a specially built sales centre. Here, another ritual plays out befitting a market with a high supply and even higher demand, where the point is to sell *lots* of houses in a short period of time, and where there is little opportunity for tailored solutions.

The home seekers walk in, grab full-colour brochures from the hands of sales girls, and crowd around a scale model of the district. Dozens of salespersons present well rehearsed sales pitches on security, the prime location and special facilities in Holiday Garden. But they especially emphasise the finances.

'Everyone who decides today will receive ten square metres extra surface space – that is an extra room.'

'With a Soufun membership card you receive a one per cent discount.'

'Those who now pay a down payment of 10,000 RMB get a 10,000 RMB discount, plus electric appliances worth 6,888 RMB.'

This unrelenting fixation on price is no accident. Architecturally speaking, Leisure Garden hardly differs from Sun City or the Maple Forest Luxurious Garden – or indeed, from any new housing estate in any Chinese city. In contrast to what the name implies, even the Maple Forest Luxurious Garden consists of tidily stacked apartments, from sixteen to twenty-seven floors in height.

The five building projects are each examples of *compounds*, a modern Chinese housing model so successful that it has seemingly made all other forms of housing superfluous. The fast-growing cities use this type of mass construction in answer to the huge demand for housing. A compound typically is a themed landscape garden containing a number of cloned residential towers, cut off from the outside world by a fence, wall or shopping area. Uniformed adolescents guard the dividing line – though usually displaying little conviction. You can find compounds anywhere: at the city limits beside a meadow, near a six-lane ring road or in the middle of the business district. Wherever 'villages in the city,' farmland or old city districts disappear, these fenced-off apartment block neighbourhoods materialise, targeting an urban middle class seeking peace and security in China's heaving metropolises.

It would be easy to cynically dismiss Holiday Garden as a petty bourgeois dream. But it is much more interesting to unravel the idyllic enclosure by examining its spiritual mothers and fathers: the academics, property developers and architects who conceived it. The historic roots of the compound lie mostly in Xi'an, the birthplace of Chinese urban construction.

'Everyone who decides today will receive ten square metres extra surface space.'

Wang Lei looks a little lost in front of the enormous scale model in the Holiday Garden sales centre. He seems overwhelmed. 'This is the second time I am on the Soufun housing tour,' he says. 'I can't make up my mind.' Holiday Garden is like any other Chinese compound. The neighbourhood lies on the boundary of Xi'an's High Tech Development Zone. Its dimensions are typical. The model shows an area of 500 by 500 metres in size surrounded by wide motorways, with a total of forty towers in different heights: ten, fourteen, nineteen and twenty-six storeys. The flats stand in neat rows facing south, a result of legislation on natural lighting and *feng shui* conventions. You can observe this phenomenon everywhere in China, in the northern half of the country even more so than in the south. This is linked to differences in climate: in the colder north it is more important that the low afternoon sun can warm living rooms.

In the world of Holiday Garden, property developer Jintai has built everything: housing, shops, parks, roads, and all amenities. Residents pay a monthly service fee to the Holiday Garden management team, which tends the greenery, sweeps the streets and keeps lifts and communal areas clean. After the sale of the last apartment, Jintai will transform the sales centre into a clubhouse, a not uncommon procedure in China. In the new Holiday Garden Sports Club, the residents can use basketball courts, ping pong tables, the fitness centre and tennis courts in exchange for a monthly fee. As befits a compound

of this magnitude, Holiday Garden offers its inhabitants a plethora of additional services. These will include, among others, a Holiday Garden Library, a Holiday Garden Elementary School and a Holiday Garden Health Centre. Supermarkets, hairdressers, DVD-shops and restaurants will line the main shopping street. Pupils can take the Holiday Garden School Bus to schools outside the compound. And if both parents work, Holiday Garden employees take care of lunchtime childcare. In effect, Holiday Garden is a privatised piece of the city. The local government has even stopped taking care of security. A private firm will patrol the streets of Holiday Garden twenty-four hours a day, seven days a week. Most new compounds in China employ such unarmed security personnel, mostly young migrant workers, recent arrivals from the provinces, who have not been in the city for long. The fluctuation is huge: compound security guard is a badly paid and unexciting job.

Wang Lei pops another one of the cherry tomatoes into his mouth that property developer Jintai has put down everywhere in white plastic bowls as a healthy snack for potential customers. Wang shrugs as his friend chats with a salesperson about all the facilities in Holiday garden. 'You have to pay for all those extras,' he says. 'I just want the largest apartment for the lowest price.'

Though Holiday Garden lies close to Xi'an's new business district, the compound purposely displays no urban ambitions. The name itself suggests an ideal world where no one needs to work and the residents laze on the beach all day long – the antithesis of a bustling metropolis. The dislike of the city, with its swarming masses of humanity, noise and unending flow of traffic also speaks from texts on notice boards placed everywhere in the sales centre. Here Wang reads that, despite its 'central location,' Holiday garden offers a 'safe and quiet home.' 'You live in a prosperous city while you enjoy your own courtyard.' The announcements cleverly package the *dolce far niente* by referring to the lifestyle of China's pre-communist aristocracy. 'You feel the constant charm as you walk past the trees and bamboo. Beautifully designed paths, rockeries, plants, pavilions and arches create a traditional Chinese garden culture.' It is a modest marketing strategy. Most developers in Xi'an sell their compounds using abstractions such as 'international,' 'successful,' or 'upper class.' This morning, Sun City advertised a 'North American atmosphere:' 'Obama makes history, Gates is still a youth idol everywhere in the world. Under the blazing North American sun, the country creates scores of young leaders (...) Sun City is heaven for these young leaders who enjoy life and shopping.' Numerous estate agents present patently impossible claims: snow white beaches with swaying palm trees in the heart of China. Writer Adrian Hornsby described the Chinese compound as an 'abtopia,' a place that 'will by necessity try not to be part of the thing which it is in fact extending. It is a dream of self-denial which cannot give itself up.'[1]

The flight into the compound displays strong similarities to the last century's trek of American and European families into suburbia. The motive is the same: the middle class leaves the busy, chaotic, but above all unsafe city in masses to perch in green and safe havens of peace and quiet. There are differences, too: the Chinese haven lies in the middle of the city and is hundreds of metres high.

Even before the collective housing tour leaves for the next compound, Wang Lei decides to scrap Holiday Garden from his list. 'I can only buy a small apartment here,' he says. He strongly leans toward a house in cheaper Sun Garden. 'I think that a lot of young people will go and live there.' Then the voice of the tour guide echoes through the enormous space. The hunt for houses continues. Visitors quickly cram leaflets into plastic bags before the crowd moves to the exit of the sales centre like a swarm of lemmings, on the way to the bus. This was Holiday Garden. On to Leisure Garden.

With an urban core of more than six million inhabitants, and a metropolitan area of about nine million, Xi'an is the capital city of Shaanxi province. The city is famous for housing one of China's most celebrated tourist attractions: the army of 9099 terracotta statues in the mausoleum of China's first emperor, Qin Shi Huang. Less well known is that the urban planning typical of the Chinese imperial period also originated in Xi'an. Or, more accurately put: in its illustrious predecessor Chang'an, the city of 'Eternal Peace,' that for twelve hundred years was the capital of the mighty Middle Kingdom.

Professor Xiao Li of the University of Architecture and Technology in Xi'an draws a direct line from the imperial city via the twentieth Century communist live/work unit to Holiday Garden. One urban planning tradition especially stands out as an element of continuity: the wall, used by the Chinese for centuries to fence off houses, neighbourhoods, city districts, cities, and even their entire country.

Professor Xiao Li is a petite woman used to expressing herself carefully and thoughtfully.

HOLIDAY GARDEN: TWENTY-FIVE STOREYS OF SUBURBIA

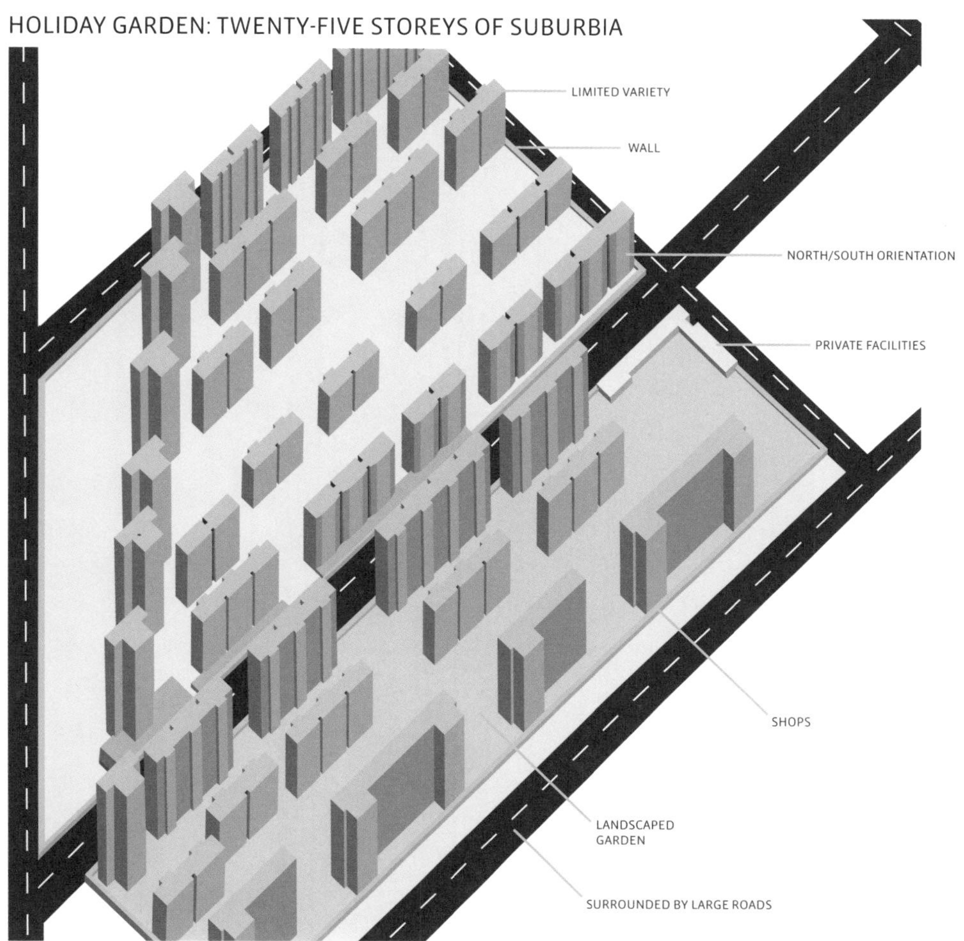

She has taught an entire generation of architects in Xi'an on the history of Chinese urban planning. Her former students now populate the architectural agencies and design institutes, where they draw compounds such as Holiday Garden for a living. The professor has her office on the second floor of the faculty building. Hundreds of statues stand on her conference table, in cupboards, on the windowsill, varying from Indonesian warriors to terracotta soldiers, both authentic ones and touristic replicas. Her statue collection displays a frivolous side of Xiao that starkly contrasts with her passionate analysis of China's urban planning concepts. 'Everywhere I go, I buy a statue,' she laughs. 'And nowadays I receive many as gifts.'

置业计划书

In the sixth century AD, the imperial city of Chang'an occupied the location of present-day Xi'an. The city consisted of a collection of palaces without a clear urban structure. 'Some experts believe that astrology determined the placement of buildings,' she says. 'But this is not at all certain.' Legendary city planner Yu Wenkai resolutely put an end to the irregular city structure. He devised a master plan for an area larger than Manhattan, which displayed an aura of totalitarian power and order dwarfing Hitler's plans for post-war *Germania*, the new world capital that he wanted Berlin to become. Xiao calls it a 'clever and comprehensive plan,' that still forms the basis of Chinese urban development. Yu started on the construction of his magnum opus in AD 582. A rectangular earthen wall with a length of thirty-seven kilometres formed the city wall. The 158-metre-wide Heavenly Boulevard ran from north to south, and formed the symmetric centre of the all-encompassing city grid, made up of 113 blocks of 500 by 500 metres, up to 500 by 800 metres, in size. Walls enclosed all these blocks, named *fang*, which were separated by impressive streets of superhuman dimensions.

Xiao Li stands up and walks to an adjacent room. She returns with a colossal book that she carefully places on the table and opens on a map of ancient Chang'an, with its chessboard-like street pattern. The city was strictly zoned, explains the professor. 'The imperial palace lay in the north, and living quarters for civil servants and the market for the imperial family in the east. The Silk Road ended at the market in the western area.' She quotes a stanza from a Tang Dynasty poem. '*The people in the east of the city have respect / but the people in the west of the city are rich.*' At its peak, Chang'an was the most powerful city in the world, comparable to Rome and Athens at their height. According to a AD 742 census, 1.9 million people lived in the urban area.[2] Mediaeval Chinese authorities governed the city like a military camp. At night, all inhabitants had to return behind the walls of their own *fang*, to be permitted out again only in the morning. Huge pomp accompanied this daily operation. Three hundred drumbeats sounded the opening of the gates, eight hundred their closing. Public life took place on the markets, but not in the streets. 'Street trade was strictly prohibited.' Every block had two to four small entry gates in the wall. Like modern compounds, each *fang* had its own name: Golden City, Eternal Happiness or Eternal Sunshine. Contemporaries considered streets inferior. Apart from the Heavenly Boulevard, they did not have names.

Later dynasties relaxed the reins, and broke down *fang* walls, but the symmetrical city with broad boulevards, large plots of land and a palace in the north continued to exist. Imperial cities such as Beijing and Luoyang continued the tradition. The model even travelled overseas to Japan, where rulers used the same structure for, among others, Kyoto. In the following centuries, senior civil servants and wealthy merchants everywhere in China built their own miniature versions of the city. They structured their courtyard houses like the imperial palaces: symmetrically around a central axis, with a garden in the middle. On the northern side stood the owner's house, while the rest of the family lived in buildings to the east and west of the garden. A windowless wall divided the courtyard houses from the outside world. The principle of an inward-looking walled garden with houses has been the foundation of Chinese housing for more than a thousand years. These elements from the imperial age can be seen in houses built during the communist period, as well as in the modern compounds arising everywhere in China.

In the 1950s the new communist regime introduced for the first time the concept of mass housing to China. The state could swiftly provide large groups of workers with good and affordable housing by using standardised design and prefabricated elements. Chinese architects almost immediately started to work with colleagues from the Soviet Union, which had over twenty years' experience in building multi-storey blocks of flats. 'The Russians designed almost all the buildings in Xi'an,' lectures Xiao Li, who in the meantime has opened the big book of maps on a different page. 'The architectural education at the university also completely followed the Russian example.'

Nationalised enterprises followed the Soviet model of living and working in communes. Behind the factory gates, live-work units called *danwei* contained high-rise housing for workers and included all necessary amenities. After a discussion, urban planners decided on a uniform structure of parallel housing blocks, oriented from north to south, a practice still followed in modern residential building. The names expressed the industrial ideals of the time. Workers lived in the New Star Isolation Materials Factory, the Lightning Rod Factory or the National Self-improving Factory. Labourers worked together, ate together, lived together and spent their spare time together in the communal courtyard. Their children went to the same schools, which provided them with the prospect of a job in the same *danwei*. The architecture displayed equal uniformity. Houses were built in series and partially prefabricated. Apartments had four standard sizes: 90, 70, 60 and 35 square metres. 'The standard designs all came from Beijing.' Only the details of residential buildings differed regionally. 'In the south of China buildings had staircases on the outside of the buildings, here in the north on the inside.'

The similarities between *fang, danwei* and compound are striking: closed, inward-looking, largely self-sufficient units built in an extremely limited architectural variation. These elements, employed in both imperial and communist times, are still in use today. In both imperial Chang'an and in communist Xi'an, the public space between blocks played a limited role. As in the modern compound, the houses do not lie directly on the street, but in a protected, semi-public area. If colleagues in communist times forcibly shared neighbourhoods, residents of modern compounds have very different backgrounds and occupations. The question is, whether this collective mould has enough to offer an increasingly individualising Chinese society in the long run. As she closes the book of maps, Xiao Li speculates on the future of Chinese housing, which she believes will, in time, adapt to an ever more pluralistic society. 'There are so many different Chinese people, with so many different lifestyles. Soon they will not want to live in the same type of homes.'

The modern Chinese metropolis largely consists of an archipelago of walled neighbourhoods, divided by a dilapidated public space. In the West critics attack similar developments as tendencies towards a 'prison state'. If inhabitants retreat behind the barriers of their neighbourhoods, so the argument goes, then the urban space loses its role as the area where people from all walks of life meet and exchange ideas in public, a principle from Western urban construction dating back to ancient Athens. The American theorist Mike Davis even sees in the rise of gated communities in his country 'the destruction of the democratic urban space.' Turning the argument upside down, the segmentation of residential units seems to perfectly fit China's current political system.

The advantages of living behind the gates of Holiday Garden are obvious: the compound is in fact a small, closed community, a guarded buffer zone between the individual home and the anonymous metropolis of Xi'an. Those who do not know better could think that the strong emphasis on security means that murdering and pillaging armed gangs are running amok, targeting the property and lives of Chinese citizens. Numbers contradict this. Compared to South American or African metropolises, cities such as Xi'an, Chongqing or Zhengzhou appear extremely safe. Though the comparison of international crime statistics often collapses because of differences in definition, the Chinese murder rate is one of the lowest in the world. Nor do Chinese cities have the no-go areas found in many other developed countries. At the same time the fear of crime in Chinese cities is great, and often linked to the presence of large groups of migrant workers. 'The stereotype of rural migrants is that they are uneducated, ignorant, dirty, and also have high propensities to be criminals,' write researchers Wang Feng and Zuo Xuejin.[3] In a major study in Shanghai, 81 per cent of the respondents felt that the decrease in security was the largest problem connected to the presence of migrant workers in the city.[4] Whatever the case, it seems plausible that China's urbanisation will lead to a gradual increase in crime, not least due to the ever growing income gap in the cities.

'Soon, Chinese will not want to live in the same type of homes.'

Two days after the Soufun housing tour's visit to the compound, Mrs Li gets off the bus at Holiday Garden. Together with her husband she has her own interior design studio in the south of Xi'an. Half a year ago they bought a home in Holiday Garden. Li is 'delighted' with her new flat. 'The quality of the homes is very good,' she says. 'It is a safe, clean and quiet place to live in.'

From the motorway to her own front door Li progresses through several levels of increasing isolation. She enters Holiday Garden on a dusty six-lane motorway, flanked by a petrol station, DIY stores and other walled compounds. The only reason for pedestrians to be in this area is to get on the bus. From the motorway a shopping street cuts through the heart of Holiday Garden. Halfway down the street she passes a barrier allowing access to Holiday Boulevard, a semi-public green zone. The guards

CHANG'AN, LARGER THAN MANHATTAN AND EXUDING TOTALITARIAN POWER

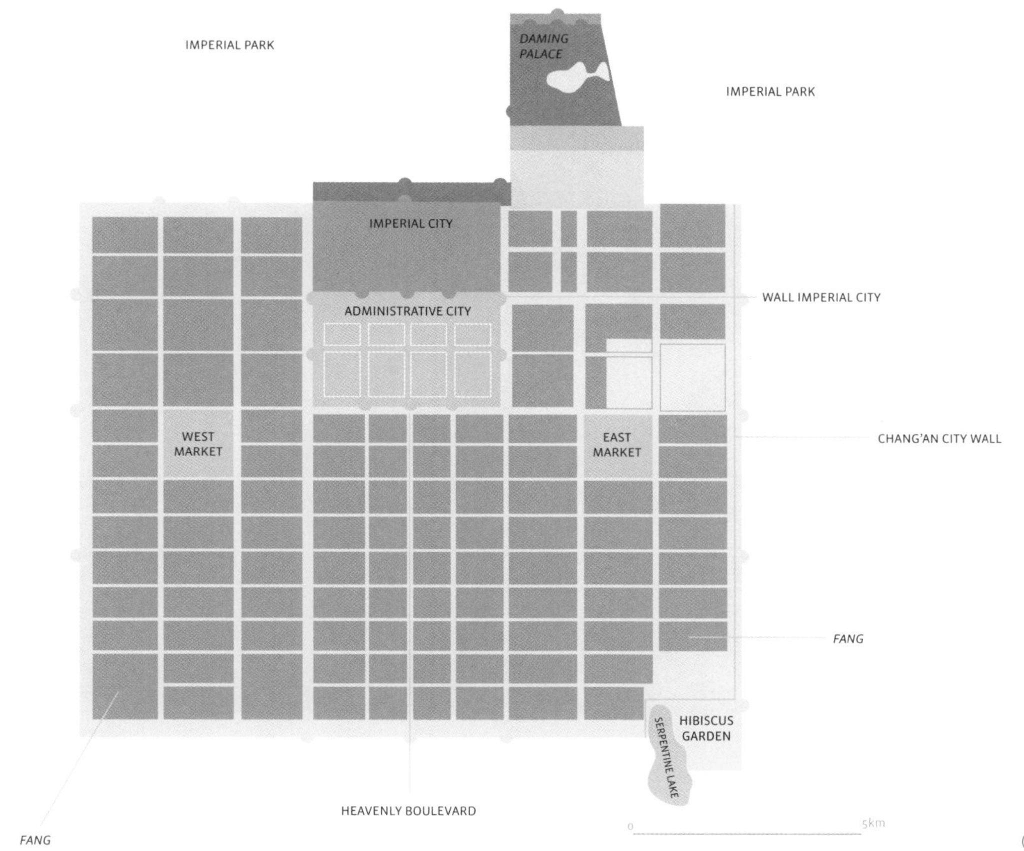

standing here keep beggars, street vendors and other less harmonious elements outside the walls of the compound. Li passes Joy Garden and Jade Garden before she arrives at Prosperous Garden. She swipes her smart card through an electronic card reader and enters the courtyard she shares with 500 other residents. Here, her ten-year-old daughter can play to her heart's content, safely and unsupervised, with the girl next door. 'That the garden is closed gives me a safe feeling,' she says. 'Not just anybody can come here.' She meanders towards an elevator on a winding path past shrubs and

bamboo, where she once again swipes her card through a scanner to bring her to her destination.

On the third floor she arrives at Holiday Garden's unique selling point: a flat with a private garden, a two-by-two-metre balcony covered in earth. She takes the key from her pocket and opens the front door.

Home at last.

For the up-and-coming Chinese metropolis, the compound seems the ideal solution to a combination of different problems. The lack of building land in Chinese cities explains the high density of construction, and the demand for speed the endless repetition. Finally, the compound with its enclosed courtyard presents fulfilment to

(2005)

millions of urbanites looking for green, quiet and, most of all, safe housing. For Jintai director Ma Yapeng, everything revolves around one aspect: *sellability*. The property developer receives his visitors in a VIP area of Holiday Garden, a glass box in the corner of the sales centre with a red carpet and red couches along the walls.

Ma is a pensive man, but not a formal one. He wears bright shirts and velvet jackets, and enjoys handing out cigarettes, preferably by lobbing them through the room, followed moments later by a lighter. His employees have become expert catchers. Trained as an architect, Holiday Garden's property developer switched to real estate years ago. His background expresses itself in a persistent habit of bolstering his words by making little drawings. The ground rules of his trade are simple: Ma buys land at the lowest price possible, on which he builds properties he sells at the highest price he can. The

西安房地产

difference he calls profit, and that keeps him in business.

Like his competitors, Ma is realistic and pragmatic enough not to tamper with the demands of the market – that is playing with fire. He does not see the isolation of compounds as a matter of tradition, but as a result of persistent customer demand. 'Chinese people want safe areas for their children, they don't like the idea of strangers walking into their compound.' The same goes for the relentless north-south orientation. 'The market pays 30 per cent less for buildings facing east or west.' His message is clear: it would be madness for a businessman to build those.

The determining factor that limits variety in types of housing, that sets the margins in which a property developer can operate, is the price house buyers are prepared to pay. 'Better designs are more expensive. In richer provinces on the coast you see more and more different designs, but the market can't handle that here.'

One of the variations on the compound is the SoHo housing type. This acronym does not refer to London's fashionable entertainment district, but to 'small office, home office.' SoHos are towers with units useable both as offices and homes. The floors are higher than usual, offering owners the possibility to build mezzanine levels for making combined live/work studios. The space between the towers is usually public, with shops and restaurants on the ground floor. The result is much more urbanity and dynamism than the protected quiet of Holiday Garden or Sun City. If the compound aims at the family, the SoHo primarily attracts an urban class of young entrepreneurs. The residents have to cope with the relative turbulence and commotion that are part of life in business premises. Ma also admires projects such as 'Linked Hybrid', by architect Steven Holl, in Beijing, a complex of eight residential towers connected by sky bridges. 'But the building costs of that project alone were 20,000 RMB per square metre. The highest sale price possible in Xi'an doesn't exceed 10,000 RMB.'

On top of this, the most expensive projects in Xi'an target those who have become rich from one day to the next. 'They usually don't have good taste, and don't care about design. Even famous property developers who build radical projects in southern China, construct very average complexes in Xi'an.'

Ma is proud of Holiday Garden. He feels it explores the boundaries permitted by the Xi'an market. Its design tries to create social cohesion in a neighbourhood with blocks of flats of around 4,000 families by dividing them over eight separate courtyards,

SAVOUR THE COURTYARD

At That Time, Light Become Able To Think Of The Sweet Years Story, Would Have Been Memorable

南北通透的板式三房、让每一个空间宽阔、舒适、合理

BETTER CITY
城市理想
3G时代的社区

当建筑插上信息的翅膀，建筑就有了理想......

让北城风尚起来

13年来，深植沃土，与古城共经风雨，不离不弃。
13年来，用数十个精品人居奉献西安，
13年，近十万人的居住因此不同，焕然一新。
不断追求卓越品质的紫薇地产，
将未来人居风尚带到北城，
一个汇聚科技力量的节能示范社区，
一席改变生活方式，调整生活态度，升华人生境界的居住领地。
紫薇风尚，风尚北城！

经典蔚蓝，璀璨西城

天朗地产四大城系—蔚蓝城 勾勒西城美丽天际

天朗地产起家力作，8年雕琢大器已成，开发面积过百万平米，市场高度认可，名门血统一脉相承，沿袭经典，突破创新！
曾经沉寂的西城，今天已经被天朗蔚蓝经典系列产品焕发出璀璨的城市光芒！

蔚蓝城三大项目 2009率先启航

天朗 · 蔚蓝花城

建筑面积约60万平米，绿化率约40%，社区由纯板多层、小高层和高层组成，园区内保留众多的原生树木，环境幽静空气清新，尽享都市内罕有的宁静。

天朗 · 蔚蓝领寓

总建筑面积73550平米，绿地率42%。户型面积45-128平米，毗邻蔚蓝印象大社区，尽享成熟生活配套！

天朗 · 蔚蓝观园

西城 · 公园里 · 一等大宅，从社区内一步即入公园，3万平米自然绿脉铺设的公园已然成为了社区的后花园。110-180平米轩阔大宅，户户均设空中花园，宽庭阔院修为宅邸！

天朗拓疆

天朗地产四大城系

踞守中央 百万平

XI'AN

instead of creating one large, anonymous district. 'Studies have shown that a group of 250 households can form a social unit. If you want everyone to know each other and to relate to one another, the groups should not be larger.' That ideal scenario unfortunately was not possible. 'It appeared that the units had to be twice as large for us to make a profit.'

Ma presents himself as a property developer subjected to the whims of the market. As long as homebuyers do not want to pay more, variation will stay limited. He complains that his only source of salvation is failing him: the designers. 'We give the architects we work with all the space they need, they can make suggestions. But they don't present any new ideas, either.'

'Traditionally, the Chinese like extensive dinners. Now we eat fast food every day,' says Zhao Zuanchao, head architect and director of Northwest Design Institute. With his metaphor Zhang describes a property market stampeding out of control. 'Developers want to make as much money as possible in as little time as necessary, and the government just wants quick progress. Of course, as architects we would love to build masterpieces, but we don't have time for that at all.'

'That the garden is closed gives me a safe feeling.'

Zhao and co-directors Zheng Zhenhong and Qu Peiqing sit at a long conference table. This threesome is the board of the Northwest Design Institute, with 900 employees one of the largest design agencies in China. Every large city has one or more of these institutes that emerged in the 1950s through the forced amalgamation and nationalisation of architectural firms. Private architectural firms have started to re-emerge in China since the 1990s, but the role of the design institutes is still highly influential, as they are the only ones permitted to produce official construction plans.

The architects of the Northwest Design Institute together devise about half of all new districts in Xi'an, which makes the institute largely responsible for the 'happy meal' of urban housing. Zhao: 'Five years after graduation, an architect in Xi'an has built on average more than 100,000 square metres. Rem Koolhaas once said that a Chinese architect is 2,500 times more effective than a western one.' The three directors are part of a system they themselves detest. Zhao does not mince his words. 'I know it is ironic for me to criticise,' he says. 'We are members of that mob of gangsters ourselves.' He thinks architects have too little influence on housing. 'If you do not concede to the property developers, they will just ask someone else. That is the reason why we are still making the same kind of designs for compounds.'

The eldest of the threesome, Qu Peiqing, aside from being a director is also a professor of architecture. He characterises the development on the housing market of the last thirty years as frothing, eager and immature. In the beginning of the 1980s property developers built their first flats in Xi'an, he says. 'Those were simple buildings of concrete and brick, without too much architecture.' They sold out fast. At the end of the 1980s the first adverts appeared, which meant that property developers had to distinguish themselves from one another to draw customers. The state issued the first design competitions. Everybody was tired of the communist *danwei* and wanted to make something new. 'The projects weren't very good, but that didn't matter, the market was eager.' Housing developers did their best to evoke an international atmosphere, mainly by placing an abundance of columns and Roman statues. That trend has been reversing in recent years, says Qu. 'With the growing influence of China in the world, you see a return to more traditional Chinese elements in housing design.' Holiday Garden is an excellent example – the compound has no Roman columns, Tuscan tile roofs, South American haciendas or Canadian rockeries, but Chinese bamboo gardens.

The third director, Zheng Zhenhong, was responsible for the design of Holiday Garden. In a calm tone he explains why he only had limited influence on the final design. 'When the government offers new building land, developers want to know two things: what is the maximum number of homes we can build, and what are the construction costs?' Based on state construction rules (such as maximum density, height and ratio of greenery), Zheng and his colleagues make a volume study showing how many homes can be built on a piece of land. Based on this the developer decides his maximum bid. 'During the bidding, money is the only criterion.'

The developer organises a design competition only after a winning bid. Based on the volume study, he sets all variables: height, spacing and location of the flats. 'The developer even provides floor plans, based on the buyer profile.' This reduces the task of the architect to inventing a 'concept.' This is not a comprehensive plan, but a theme deciding the design of the garden and the materials used for the façade. Zheng: 'Developers constantly want something new: "music", "education", "holiday." And that is an improvement on the past. In the Eighties and Nineties you had concepts such as 'one garden in the middle, four gardens around it.' The designers dismissively call this 'four dishes and a soup,' an expression referring to a wholesome but dull Chinese meal without any extras.

The architect believes that in Holiday Gardens he has tested the margins of what is presently possible in Xi'an. 'We have introduced a green zone that people from outside the compound can access. That is quite something.' Most new compounds are hermetically sealed from the outside world. Another suggestion by the Design Institute, to build in lower densities, did not make it. Zheng: 'Holiday Garden is the result of

difficult negotiations. Our worst disagreement was with the developer. He wanted maximum profits, we wanted the best result.'

Director Zhao compares the developments of the compounds with the *danwei* from the heyday of communism. 'Those were small, isolated societies, built by the state. Now property developers build these small societies. Some compounds are so large and have so many amenities, you could call them small cities. We are doing some research into the design of these compounds, but all of it is very superficial. We have no time for serious studies. Real estate companies are holding architects hostage, and not just us, but the government too.' Then, playing it down: 'This is a phase we need to go through. Maybe there will be more room for new ideas when the market cools down a bit.'

6. KUNMING

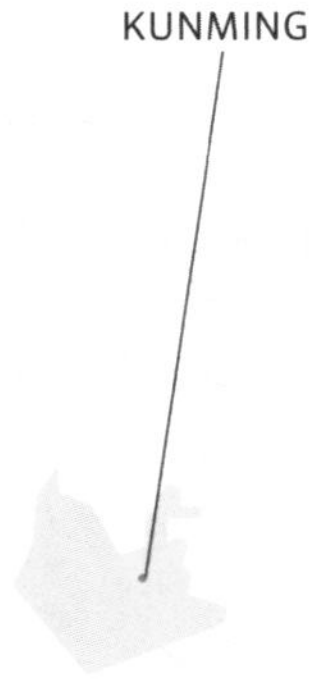

A NEW FUTURE FOR OLD CIVILISATION STREET

KUNMING

YUNNAN - SPAIN
With 45 million inhabitants, Yunnan province has roughly the same population as Spain

Stunningly beautiful students in traditional close-fitting high split *qipao* dresses reverently bow their heads as they open the doors for the guests. They hand white flowers to visitors, who pin them to their lapels as corsages. Long tables filled with drinks and bowls of fruit await them. Everywhere in the villa members of the military, senior civil servants, artists and journalists converse in hushed tones. This Friday morning the Kunming urban elite travels back in time to pre-communist China. They are attending the opening of the completely restored 'General's House,' once owned by Jiang Zonghan.

According to the placards on the wall, this illustrious military leader and businessman of the Qing Dynasty built an impressive trade empire in food and textiles with what is now Myanmar. The newly renovated traditional Southern Chinese two-storey house looks better than ever. Restorers have refurbished the wooden structure, replaced the tile roof, painstakingly repaired decorative carvings and covered them in shiny black varnish. Nothing betrays the neglect the house suffered in recent decades. Today's inauguration of a gallery for traditional art strengthens the villa's nostalgic atmosphere. Paintings and pen drawings on rice paper by local artist Lao Wei cover the walls. He has drawn calligraphic poems from distant centuries, for instance by the famous seventh-century poet, Wang Bo. '*The evening clouds fly with the lonely bird / The colour of the autumn river blends with the sky.*' The beaming artist accepts congratulations as the guests attentively examine his work. He considers it 'an honour' to be the first artist to exhibit in this special location.

At the end of the morning the visitors leave the General's House crossing a red carpet, and re-enter the unvarnished reality of an early twenty-first-century Chinese city. A historic neighbourhood in an advanced state of decomposition surrounds the restored courtyard house. Decaying shops with upstairs apartments and characteristic grey-tiled roofs line the narrow streets. Residents and shopkeepers have mostly abandoned the area. Bricked-up doors keep trespassers out of empty buildings with smashed first floor windows. Red and green paint is flaking from the facades, and plants grow from the rooftops. 'Dangerous house! Danger! Do not come closer!' warns a sign in red characters on a house that is clearly still inhabited. High whitewashed walls screen off the area from the outside world.

In one of the ramshackle shops a woman waits in vain for customers for her Sony Playstations. Apathetically she watches protagonists in the soap *A Village in March* frequently exchanging meaningful glances. 'You can't imagine how terrible it is to live here,' she complains. 'The woodwork is rotting, mice and other vermin run around, and the ceiling collapses when it rains. Left by themselves, these old buildings will simply fall over. So it goes. All good things must come to an end. Eventually something new will come along. It would be better just to tear everything down. What a mess.' Diagonally opposite her shop a row of houses has been demolished. Construction workers are building a deep basement. In the bottom of the pit steel benders tie reinforcing bars together with pieces of wire. Thirty metres further on, carpenters present an anachronistic spectacle. Armed with chisels and smoothing planes, they are carving traditional ornaments into wooden beams. Elsewhere, colleagues have just erected the skeleton of a brand new 'historical' building.

On the fence surrounding one of the building sites hangs an image made with Google SketchUp, a free 3D modeling programme, that depicts the future of the neighbourhood. It shows platinum blondes in dark sunglasses and men in suits passing in front of cafés where loving couples are seated in Arne Jacobson butterfly chairs. It is hard to judge to what extent the original buildings will be incorporated into the visions of the future. The accompanying slogan by property developer Zhi Jiang drops a clear hint: '*Reproduction of the past to make a bright new future.*'

This is *Wenming Lao Jie* (Old Civilisation Street) in Kunming, the capital city of Yunnan in the far south-west of China, a province the size of Iraq with 45 million inhabitants. Due to the pleasant climate, Kunming bears the nickname Spring City. Called Yachi in ancient times, it was a trading post on the Southern Silk Road. In his thirteenth-century best-seller, *Description of the World*, Venetian trader Marco Polo described Yachi as a 'great and noble city' with 'countless tradesmen and craftsmen' selling rice and eating raw meat. He especially praised the open sexual mores in the city. 'They do not see it as a problem if a man is intimate with another man's wife, as long as the woman herself agrees.'

As is the case with most cities in China's interior, the economic rise of Kunming only commenced recently, around the turn of the millennium. Until the 1990s, this was a relatively small and underdeveloped town with housing dating back to the late nineteenth and early twentieth centuries: one- or two-floor buildings with sloping tile roofs, and wooden decorations covering the facades.

This has changed rapidly. In ten years' time the number of inhabitants in the city proper increased from one million to roughly three million. Seven million people now live in the entire Kunming conurbation, and there is no end in sight to this turbulent growth. New skyscrapers keep popping up everywhere. In the south of Kunming tens of thousands of construction workers are building the huge new district of Chenggong: endless compounds and colossal government buildings along wide roads. As elsewhere, inhabitants are the notable absentees in these expansion districts.

The Old Civilisation Street

During its growth spurt Kunming demolished most of its historical construction, apart from a few isolated buildings scattered around town. Wide motorways slashed through the narrow nineteenth-century neighbourhoods. Labourers hauled the rubble away in Dongfeng lorries and countless handcarts.

Old Civilisation Street is the largest single obstacle standing between Kunming and a city without a memory. Considering the shoddy state of the buildings, the question is, for how long.

The destruction of historical neighbourhoods takes on even more radical form in Central and Western China than on the East Coast. In recent years cities such as Shijiazhuang or Xi'an have destroyed their built history with astonishing speed. At the same time, a rapidly changing society shows an increasing longing for 'traditional' Chinese neighbourhoods. This paradox expresses itself in a remarkable set of affairs. While almost completely destroying history, cities construct 'ancient' buildings. In the south of Kunming lies an example of such a historically themed district. On the site of an old hamlet run traditional village streets reconstructed in concrete, with wooden

beams forged from steel. The shops are still empty, but if the fate of similar districts in Chengdu and Chongqing is anything to go by, thousands of tourists will soon be tramping through the streets, munching snacks, past modern townsmen dressed in folk costumes performing traditional crafts, such as basket weaving or jewellery making. Writer Ian Buruma labelled such mock historical districts a 'sanitised version of the past, safe and clean, with nice things to do for the kids,' preferred above the 'real historical diversity.'[1] All Chinese metropolises have these areas. Xi'an has the most far-reaching plans, with proposals to reconstruct within the historic town walls the ancient nine-square-kilometre imperial centre.

'You can't imagine how terrible it is to live here.'

The story of Old Civilisation Street mirrors the fate of thousands of similar streets in China's new megacities. It plays against a background of Chinese history reinvented for the second time in a hundred years.

When Wang Shishun, a young English student from Beijing, moves to Kunming in 1928, Old Civilisation Street still bears the name New Civilisation Street. Most of the buildings are only several years old, and painted in cheerful colours: red, green, yellow, blue. Wang finds a job as a teacher at a Christian school. Several years later he marries, and with his wife he opens a business in New Civilisation Street: The Oriental Book Shop. It is a welcome addition to the existing assortment of porcelain dealers, pharmacies, restaurants and hairdressers. The Wangs move into the tiny apartment above the premises. First they have a daughter, and then a son. When she is only a few years old, daughter Runshang sees how every evening the street 'fills with market traders selling cheap clothes and cotton,' as she writes years later in an account.[2] Behind the shops run grand houses with multiple courtyards, in which wealthy officials and businessmen reside.

Problems start at the end of the 1930s. Because of the war with Japan the supply of literature from the Chinese East Coast falters. To secure his turnover, Wang starts to sell pots and pans made from warplanes that have crashed all around Kunming. An American army doctor stationed in the area takes a colour photograph of New Civilisation Street. Sixty years later the framed picture provides Wang's daughter with a tangible memory to a 'prosperous street less than hundred metres long where I was born. I saw people do business and learnt all kind of things you don't learn in school.'

After the communist takeover in 1949 the atmosphere in the street changes permanently. With the introduction of a new ideology, old beliefs are scrapped. At the beginning of the 1950s the Kunming city administration brands the Kunming city wall as 'imperialist, outdated and an impediment to progress.' Thousands of youths tear it down, and use the stones for a new road. In 1956 the Party expropriates all enterprises in Civilisation Street as part of the nationwide elimination of the private sector. The state puts Wang Shishun and his wife to work in their former company as ordinary employees. 'Co-operation they called that. In practice it meant they took our shop away from us,' says his son Xulun more than fifty years later, still bitter about the events.

Civilisation Street changes with the times. The 1920s shops with upstairs housing become small state factories. The city villas, once symbols of money and power, are now hateful reminders of capitalist exploitation of the working class. The government redistributes them among the people.

The Wangs have to move from their shop home to a courtyard house shared with eight families. The new tenants do not treat the former aristocrats' buildings gently. They build kitchens in the stairwells, divide the former salons into multiple dwellings with thin partitioning walls, cover the richly decorated courtyards and fill them with improvised sheds. Pulverising the Four Olds (old habits, old customs, old ideas and old culture) will eventually culminate in 1966 in the Cultural Revolution. Red Guards destroy temples and statues everywhere in and around the city. They imprison the Wangs in a remote village, who, having run a business, are 'class enemies'. Like millions of others their son and daughter leave for the countryside for an 'ideological re-education' by peasants.

The era ends with Mao's death on 9 September 1976. 'Then it all quite suddenly stopped.'

Though damaged, most buildings in Civilisation Street survive the excesses of thirty years of Maoism. The second twentieth-century revolution will leave a far larger trail of

People's Street autumn 1996

People's Street spring 1997

People's Street autumn 1997

People's Street spring 1998 *(Photos: Carl Fingerhuth)*

(1990)

destruction: the embracing of market economy from 1978 onward. It is not symbolic *devaluation* which now threatens the historic buildings, but the financial *appreciation* of the land on which they stand. The young real estate market has much to gain by replacing cheap low-rise by lucrative high-rise.

In the 1980s Civilisation Street once again turns into a thriving shopping area. The surrounding streets form the backdrop for the Kunming Flower and Bird Market, loved by the local population for the wide range of cheap products. Growing streams of foreigners find satisfaction for a touristic yearning for the 'authentic' China in the historic buildings. A guidebook from this period describes the street market as Kunming's 'largest, most attractive shopping area, where it is always spring.' Still, the residents can sense that the new times will take their toll. The street is the geographic centre of a shrinking historical island, surrounded by a swelling sea of compounds and shopping centres where the new middle class feels itself more at home than in the draughty, damp shops and houses from the 1920s. The duel between innovation and consolidation can only have one convincing winner.

'The style of the shopping centre isn't Chinese, foreign, or modern. I call it a fake.'

Critics of the new developments are scarce, but they work in influential positions. In the 1990s Kunming's Planning Authority protests in vain against the complete eradication of architectural memory. In 2002 one of the staff members, who will later be promoted to the directorship of the authority, reflects on the period in an article. 'Because of conflicting interests,' he writes, 'we at the urban planning department are regrettably forced to witness the results of insufficient protection of public open spaces, natural landscape areas and, above all, the historic urban scenery.'[3]

The destruction of old symbols and buildings considered useless, outdated or simply undesired in the new period is, of course, not a purely Chinese affair. Nineteenth-century Paris demolished large parts of the mediaeval centre. Almost nothing is left of pre-twentieth-century New York. In the 1960s, Amsterdam knocked down a third of its seventeenth-century housing stock, draining disused canals for parking spaces. There are also more recent examples of the dismantling of history in the West. After the fall of communism, Berlin not only destroyed the Berlin Wall, but also the Palace of the Republic, the former East German parliament. In 2008 the last load of steel from the idiosyncratic building left by boat for Dubai, to be incorporated in a contemporary icon, the Burj Khalifa, the highest skyscraper in the world. On the empty space a replica is to arise of an eighteenth-century city palace, apparently more valuable in the present age.

The airbrushing of too much history almost inevitably evokes a response. After the French Revolution of 1789, the new order introduced the notion of *patrimoine* (heritage) as legal concept to protect art and buildings considered an insult to republicanism. It meant authorities had to choose between 'objects that would be melted, pulverized, or burnt' and those that should be preserved for future generations.[4] Even during China's Cultural Revolution, individuals attempted to protect cultural heritage. Prime Minister Zhou En-Lai used the army to prevent Red Guards from venting their anger on the Forbidden City in Beijing. This was never followed by adequate legal protection. China's budding metropolises might be a lot older than their European counterparts; little of that past remains visible nowadays.

When the Kunming Planning Authority employees receive no response to their conservation agenda, they seek help from foreign contacts. In 1996 an airplane lands in Kunming with experts in heritage conservation: a team of Swiss architects and urban planners. A long-standing city twinning between Kunming and Zurich forms the background to the visit. 'The Zurich experts were our big hope, as the opinions of urban planners from developed countries are highly rated in China' writes the future director in his retrospective. The delegation, led by Swiss architect and urban planner Carl Fingerhuth, finds itself in a construction site of astonishing proportions, dwarfing anything in their homeland. 'The quick tempo, with which old, small wooden houses are replaced with new, up to 100-metre-tall glass and steel skyscrapers is breathtaking for

Europeans,' the architects write. They observe that 'a tendency to dismantling prevails.'[5] The Swiss document Kunming's transition in a revealing series of four photographs of old People's Street that crosses Civilisation Street in the north. Within two years, People's Street changed from a busy pedestrian area with market stalls and historical houses (autumn 1996) into a barren sixty metre wide area (spring 1997), and then into an eight-lane motorway (autumn 1997) with modern offices and residential towers more than twenty-five storeys high (spring 1998). Fingerhuth attributes the cause of the systematic destruction of memory to the fact that 'trust in the usefulness of the existing building stock has been lost.' He observes a basic conflict in all urban societies. 'How much of the existing building stock must be preserved for the city to keep its identity and to prevent its inhabitants from becoming homeless?'[6]

In joint sessions, Chinese and Swiss architects warn that Kunming will lose its character. They want to save the 'structures and buildings in the old city' because they 'are more important and necessary for residents, for a common city identity and for cultivating Western and Chinese tourism than steel and glass skyscrapers that look exactly like those in Singapore, Bangkok or Frankfurt.' The desire for nostalgia and striving for profitability meet each other in a new use for the last remaining small historic neighbourhood surrounding Old Civilisation Street: tourism. That is a 'political argument' to convince the city administration. The Swiss propose a system of legal protection of monuments.

The notion that a certain dose of history can increase the recognisability of the city appeals to the local authorities. The idea that history must be based on concepts such as authenticity or veracity takes longer to take hold. Despite a strong lobby, the 'old, narrow north-south axis, lined with trees and decorative two-storey wooden houses,' south of Civilisation Street makes way for 'a faceless highway. Instead of a winding district of small houses between the two pagodas, there is an immense boulevard with pseudo-historical palaces and a massive, fortified city gate where before there was none,' writes one of the disappointed Swiss architects.

In 1997 the defenders of the historic city achieve their first major result. The Kunming municipal authorities officially establish the 'Civilisation Street Conservation Area,' a half-a-square-kilometre district in which demolition of existing buildings and construction of new ones is forbidden. The decision turns Civilisation Street into

New history requires details

Kunming's official memory, albeit a very small one.

The Swiss-Chinese team look on the result with pride. 'Kunming is one of the few cities in China that is prepared to use such zoning measures, not only for individual historical monuments, for example temple complexes, but also for larger continuous areas of houses and commercial buildings.'[7]

They have saved the buildings in the Civilisation Street Conservation Area from demolition, but not from natural decay. The real work starts only now. Two Chinese urban planners fly to Zurich for a heritage conservation course. The planning authority writes a manual and sets up a new department to fulfil the ambitions: the Kunming Historical Street, Block and Building Protection Office.

In the summer of 1998 the Swiss and a local planner jointly make an inventory of all the buildings in the area around Civilisation Street. They pay particular attention to the most striking facades in the narrow alleys, because 'daily markets are held in the streets and a scenic background helps highlight tourist attractions.' To Kunming officials this aspect is 'of first priority.'[8]

The final plan aims at maintaining the most important cultural historical elements in the district. All narrow streets, alleys and courtyards should remain. Then, it earmarks all facades as protected, and declares twenty-six city villas as monuments. The other buildings in the area may only be changed providing 'scale and typology' can be maintained. Only a line of former workers' flats from the communist period may be demolished, to be replaced by new housing 'in accordance with the historic construction.'

In April 2000 Kunming presents a scale model of the completely restored neighbourhood to its residents and puts it to a vote. The result would not be misplaced in Pyongyang: 95 per cent of the participants vote in favour. Two years later one of the Swiss urban planners, Werner Stutz, looks back at the cooperation with the Chinese. He concludes that the 'long and continuous collaboration' seems to be bearing fruit. 'Today, no one speaks of demolishing houses in the "Civilisation Street Protection Area" anymore.'[9]

They forgot to count on market forces.

The Kunming municipal administration wants a property developer to execute the renovation plan, and selects Zhi Jiang, a company that constructs shopping centres,

普洱茶
13759162522
普洱茶厂家直销
精致生活
EXCELLENT LIFT STYLE
多彩时光

supermarkets and pedestrian shopping areas all over China. Kunming awards the redevelopment of Old Civilisation Street for a low price, in exchange for compliance with the strict rules in the protection plan. When the property developers first walk through Civilisation Street, they chiefly see a 'disgrace' for the city. 'Many houses lack electricity or toilets. The neighbourhood is densely populated, thirty or forty people live together even in small buildings.'[10] The company starts with the easiest part: the demolition of the communist flats. The developer decides to build a five-storey shopping centre, which will provide the money to restore and redevelop the rest of the area. Shopping centre Justice Gate becomes a potpourri of modern glass house fronts with here and there clichéd references to an indistinct historical building style. Shops by Calvin Klein, Tissot, Adidas, Levi's and a Pizza di Rocco restaurant ('Italian home style cooking') populate the ground floor. In Kunming's spring climate, the third floor indoor skating rink provides a haven for skating enthusiasts. On the roof, a pedestrian area with restaurants and outdoor seating offers vistas of the historic area. While the construction of the shopping mall continues unabated, the developer starts his work in the rest of the neighbourhood.

'We have to take care of our history for future generations.'

Meanwhile, in Old Civilisation Street, an old acquaintance has made a comeback: the Oriental Book Shop. The new owner is Wang Xulun, the son of Wang Shishun, who established the shop in the 1920s. Wang junior picked up his father's trade in the late 1990s, after the factory in which he worked went bankrupt. Instead of literature he sells computer books. 'Those sell better nowadays,' he says decisively.

At the end of 2003 the busy daily market is closed down. The property developer orders the semi-permanent market stands to close shop. The traders leave, and take most of their customers with them. The shopkeepers can linger on for a while. The evictions do not begin until two years later. As most houses belong to the state, this causes few

problems. The authorities direct Civilisation Street tenants into modern apartments twelve kilometres from the city centre. After that, the housing developer negotiates buyouts with the remaining owners. He also approaches the Oriental Book Shop. Wang Xulun, who has bought the building, thinks the sums offered are too low. He doubts that the developer will really restore the street to its former glory. 'Look what they have built: a shopping centre. The style isn't Chinese, foreign, or modern. I call it a fake.' Wang has not lived in the toiletless home above the shop in years, but in an apartment a few kilometres away. 'These buildings are unsuitable as modern homes.'
The developer builds a wall around the area and starts demolishing a number of houses in Old Civilisation Street. Wang: 'They promised to restore the buildings, but they are not doing that. They are breaking them down and replacing them with something else.' The bookseller refuses to become the victim of a radical upheaval the second time in his life. 'They shouldn't cheat me. I have offered to open a shop after the renovation selling books on the Cultural Revolution. I think that this will interest a lot of young people and foreign tourists.' The property developer responds with little enthusiasm to the proposal. The company wants expensive clothes shops, famous restaurants and bars to fill Old Civilisation Street version 2.0. 'If you are not a famous brand,' says an estate agent, 'you can forget it.'

It is clear: property developer Zhi Jiang sees little advantage in simply restoring Old Civilisation street. That will only cost money. To understand what the company does want, we have to travel to Shanghai, to the prime example of historical redevelopment in China, Xintiandi. After reconstruction in 2002 this decrepit neighbourhood changed in a few short years to one of the most expensive and popular entertainment districts in town.
Cities demolishing their historical buildings and filling the resulting hole with fake history – it is a schizophrenic condition that only someone capable of uniting such apparent contradictions can solve. Someone like that is Ben Wood, a flamboyant American architect with a past as both a peace protestor and fighter pilot, who abandoned the United States because of George Bush, exchanging it for Hu Jintao's China. Wood not only owns a bar in Xintiandi, he also has an office in the district.
Xintiandi's success consists of downplaying the value of history as such and rejecting

Historically-themed district (left) opposite the Xintiandi model (right)

the notion that buildings can be restored to their 'original condition,' says Wood. 'A preservationist finds a magic date in the past and says that that the building should look the way it did that day. He sees everything that appeared later as bad. I prefer to believe in the idea of constantly changing buildings.'

Wood permits himself the liberty to demolish parts of old buildings, merge, expand or rebuild them, as much as is necessary to make them suitable for modern use. He judges the historic components only by their utility and whether they can appeal to a nostalgic, romantic feeling that modern architecture can never offer. 'All new things need at least fifty years to radiate romance. I want to create instant gratification. If you show the general public a modern work of art, they won't understand it. Show them a Renoir, and they will like it. If you want to serve the masses, you must give them Renoirs.'

With the transformation of the former houses into expensive wine bars, luxurious international restaurants and coffee chains, Wood has adapted the old buildings to suit modern China. His detractors regularly accuse him of pastiche, mostly because they see a lack of authenticity and good taste in the commercial exploitation of historic buildings. Wood himself is 'not the type to have sleepless nights if people call what I do pastiche.' In present Chinese conditions, the Xintiandi model may be the only viable conservation method, because of the simple fact that it is commercially highly successful. No wonder that numerous Chinese cities now build similar districts. Wood believes his project has contributed to better protection of the remaining historical buildings in Shanghai, because 'people now better recognise their qualities.'

Almost eight years after property developer Zhi Jiang landed the Kunming contract, the project finds itself in an almost complete deadlock. The property developer ascribes the standoff to homeowners refusing to leave. The company claims to have spent 200 million dollars on buyouts and relocations. A spokesperson considers it 'incomprehensible' that people are still protesting. 'They should make a sacrifice and think of other people for once.'

The delays are also a setback for Gao Xuemei, who administers the Kunming Historical Street, Block, and Building Protection Office. She guards the correct implementation of the protection plan. Gao is a tall woman with a powerful personality, and not afraid of voicing strong opinions. But against market forces she, too, has few defences. 'We find ourselves at a crucial stage in the process. The developer has been able to make money out of the shopping centre. Now the company has to show it is committed to the preservation of the historical neighbourhood.' In her central Kunming office, Gao doodles on a piece of paper what she considers to be the problem. She draws a row of historical houses in Old Civilisation Street, and points out the dimensions: they are all five metres deep and two and a half metres high. The former shops and homes are too small to create an expensive nightlife district like Xintiandi. The low ceilings, steep stairs and lack of space for toilets, kitchens or storage areas make it impossible to let them to pricey shopping chains or trendy clubs. 'The high-ceilinged buildings in Shanghai Xintiandi are better suited to modern use.'

Gao Xuemei sits down. 'The property developer,' she says, 'is looking for possibilities to make the houses higher and larger. The company proposed to demolish everything, dig basements, and rebuild the buildings in modified form, with an extra floor on top.' With a few lines, Gao sketches the result: the same buildings, supersized. 'According to the agreement, the developer must repair and renovate, but the company would prefer to demolish and rebuild.'

She believes the city administration has lost all interest in the neighbourhood. 'The government prefers to spend its attention on fast train links and the new business district in the south of town.' Gao has worked for ten years on the Civilisation Street protection plan. 'All that time we have mainly focused on the design, and paid too little attention on how to achieve it.' Time ticks by in favour of the developer. Once the buildings are too fragile to be saved, they will have to be demolished. It would not be a first if a mysterious fire put an end to an old city quarter. 'There are few Chinese cities with an intact historic area,' says Gao. 'We have to take care of our history, not only for ourselves, but also for future generations.'

As in nature, architecture also knows its Darwinian survivors: buildings that can easily adapt to historical change. The twenty-six spacious villas in Old Civilisation Street have held up exceedingly well in the ideological roller coaster of the previous century. In the 1920s they served as small city palaces for the aristocracy, under Mao as factories or communal housing for the proletariat.

Capitalist Kunming also has uses for the roomy buildings. In contrast to the cramped

【菊翁劳伟先生书画展】
JU WENG LAOWEI CALLIGRAPHY AND PAINTING EXHIBITION
开幕暨“初月集”首发剪彩仪式
主办单位：云南省文学艺术界联合会
承办单位：昆明市之江置业有限公司
展览地点：昆明老街钱王街腾越总兵府（小银柜巷八号）
展览时间：2010年1月8日–1月22日

shops with upstairs housing such as Mr. Wang's Oriental Book Shop, the historical courtyard houses are perfect for contemporary use. Developer Zhi Jiang restored the old houses 'in original condition' and put them to use. He found a number of new tenants, varying from television studios to teahouses, from restaurants to nightclubs. And so, on a Friday morning in January 2010, the Kunming elite gazes at traditional oil paintings in the fully restored General's House in Old Civilisation Street. However, this involves a little white lie, as becomes apparent several days later from a blog post on the popular Sina website.

'They have restored the Jiangs' house,' said my father. 'When you have time, you should take a look."

'Have they done a good job?', I asked

'Yes. But they call it "The General's House". That's wrong! However could the general's house be in Kunming? Ridiculous! I have told the supervisor to go to the library and read a history book.'

The blogger reveals himself to be the great-grandchild of Jiang Zonghan, the distinguished Tang Dynasty general, and presents the basic facts of his family history. The general who founded an international business empire never set foot in Kunming. It was his grandson who moved the company headquarters in 1924 to a new courtyard house in Civilisation Street. By that time, the general had been dead for more than twenty years.

7. CHANGSHA

(1950)

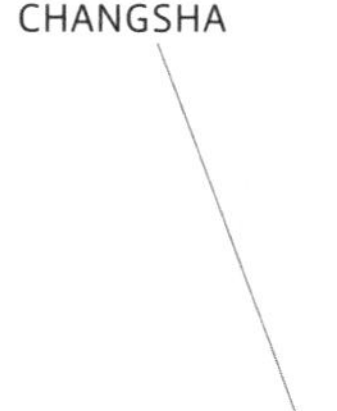

HUNAN - FRANCE
With 64 million inhabitants, Hunan province has roughly the same population as France

MILLIONAIRES IN LITTLE VENICE

In a suburb of Changsha stands the famous *Pont Neuf*. It is flanked by two white victory columns topped with golden statues of Pegasus, the winged horse from Greek mythology. On the other side of the water looms the Phoenix Hotel, an immense neoclassical building with an imposing facade, apparently constructed from sandstone, surrounded by a palm tree garden. Four black Audi A6 cars with blinded windows are parked in front of the entrance. They belong to local party officials amusing themselves in the hotel's luxurious karaoke bar. The hotel's furnishing can best be described as eclectic. The entrance leads to a domed hall with an enormous gold chandelier. From there run marble-tiled corridors decorated with paintings of Italian urban scenes. The vaulted ceiling depicts frescoes with angels that look as if they have flown in straight from the Sistine Chapel. A thick carpet with Chesterfield sofas covers the lobby.

The Phoenix Hotel is the opening act for an even greater spectacle. Just past the car park the road veers to the left and ends in a road block reminiscent of military checkpoints in the Gaza Strip. The four grim sentries guarding the double barriers wear green camouflage uniforms. All that is missing are automatic weapons. Behind it starts the habitat of Changsha's well-to-do: Little Venice, an artificial island containing 2,000 detached villas and townhouses with gardens, designed in a 'European Style.'

Her dog, Coco, barks as Mrs Chao gives the guards a friendly nod before she enters the villa district. After a morning walk through the Phoenix Hotel garden, she returns to her home in the protected zone of Little Venice. On her free Saturday Chao wears a blue tracksuit and comfortable trainers. Though small in stature, her forceful presence suggests that, as director of an energy company, she is used to issuing orders. In 2007 Chao moved with her husband, a manager in the car industry, and son to Little Venice. She still works in her old home of Laodi, a three-hour drive from here. During the week she lives in an apartment there, and spends her weekends in Little Venice. Chao belongs to a growing group of affluent people not satisfied with an apartment with a tub of earth on the fifteenth floor of a compound. In Little Venice she can afford her own private piece of the planet.

She walks along the street with her dog on a leash and explains what she enjoys about her home. 'We used to have a flat on the seventh floor in the city. Now we live in our own house with a garden. The air is cleaner here, there is no noise, and we have plants, flowers, fish and a dog. I think that is what many Chinese dream of.'

Changsha is the capital of Hunan, the birth province of Mao Zedong. More than six million inhabitants live in the metropolitan region, of which three million reside in the urban core. Changsha lies about a thousand kilometres north of Guangzhou in the Pearl River Delta. Since the opening of the new high-speed train line that is a journey of about three hours.

For a long time, the city was known as the place where Mao started his political career. Nowadays young Chinese associate Changsha especially with Hunan TV, China's most talked about TV station, whose talent competition *Super Girl* and dating show *Take me out* captivate the entire country. The city administration takes numerous measures to enhance its reputation as China's 'Entertainment City'. One of the most remarkable initiatives was the declaration of 'special entertainment zones' in 2009: three narrow, long pedestrian streets in the centre where entrepreneurs starting bars could operate tax-free in the first two years. With predictable results: in no time at all scores of cafés, eateries and live music bars opened their doors to the public, making the policy a massive success.

As in all Chinese cities, the introduction of a market economy encouraged the establishment of growing moneyed elite. Research by the Hurun Institute from 2010 shows that the province has an estimated 11,000 inhabitants owning over 10 million yuan (1.5 million dollars). For China as a whole the number is over 960,000. A vanguard of 400 super rich Chinese even possess more than 1,5 billion dollars.[1]

Villa districts such as Little Venice testify to the wealth of the happy few. In all burgeoning megacities you can find similar 'European areas,' where Big Ben or the Campanile di San Marco toll for hours on end. There is nothing so strange it can't be found: Dutch canals, German Riegelhäuser, Canadian mansions, Italian palazzi and French chateaux. One of the most prominent things in Little Venice is the universal emphasis on security. The walkie-talkies of patrolling guards sound everywhere. Chao and her dog pass guard huts every fifty metres or so. From lampposts CCTV cameras record everything and anything that moves. Large signs warn residents that the enemy does not just lurk outside. 'Be careful with gas! It can be dangerous!' Chao chuckles at the patronising message. But she sees the 'military cordon' around the villa district as a necessity. 'As soon as people know I am a rich woman, they might want to steal something from me.'

Since former leader of the communist party Deng Xiaoping famously appropriated moneymaking as a socialist strategy by quipping 'Socialism is getting rich together', differences in income have increased to huge proportions. The richest one per cent of the Chinese population own 41 per cent of the nation's wealth, a situation comparable to the United States.[2] This makes the differences between rich and poor in China so huge that, for the time being, there is absolutely no question of 'getting rich together.' The effects of the unequal distribution of income can be seen in the barbed wire and 24-hour patrols in Little Venice. Just outside the gates of the villa district, tucked away under an exit of the Pont Neuf, the Hotel Phoenix staff sleep on dozens of bunk beds in a dark warehouse.

Chao accepts the inconvenience of living in a panopticon. During her afternoon walk

400 people own assets worth more than 10 billion yuan/ 1.5 billion dollars.

CHINA'S NEW RICH

4,000 people own assets worh more than 1 billion yuan/ 150 million dollars. Average age: 50.

60,000 people own assets worth more than 100 million yuan/ 15 million dollars. Average age: 43

960,000 people own assets worth more than 10 million yuan/ 1.5 million dollar. Average age: 39.

Source: *Hurun Wealth Report 2010 and 2011*

the guards regularly ask her where she is going and Chao answers them patiently. Like the Xi'an compound Holiday Garden, the residential island consists of several sectors accessible only to residents. Chao accepts these restrictions to her freedom of movement without grumbling. While Coco disappears into the bushes wagging her tail, Chao explains how visitors can reach the island. Friends or relatives present themselves to the guards at the Little Venice entrance, the guards phone a checkpoint further down the neighbourhood. A second guard then walks to Chao's house and rings the doorbell. 'He asks if we are expecting visitors, what their names are, what kind of car they are driving and what the license plate number is.' After she has answered all the questions correctly, the guard returns to the checkpoint to signal the all clear. Then she can turn on the water boiler.

Little Venice and the real Venice may both be islands, but that is where the similarities end. Changsha has no canals with gondolas, but instead large family cars driving along narrow, winding asphalt roads. Each villa has a small plot of land, with a parking space in front of it and a garden at the back. The 'European style' manifests itself in red roof tiles, decorated flowerpots and the abundance of symbols referring to European architecture, such as balcony bars resembling classical pillars. Although the villas are made of concrete, natural stone tiles and plastered columns aim to convince that the houses have been built brick by brick.

Workers are still building the last part of the area, due to be completed next year. Close to the barrier stands a model home for potential buyers. The fully furnished villa shows them how to decorate their new homes according to latest fashions. The furniture follows international trends in domesticity, directly taken from magazines such as *Jia Zhuang Jia Ju* (Home and Interior) or the Ikea catalogue. Classics like Charles Darwin's *The Descent of Man* and Franz Kafka's *The Trial* adorn the bookshelves. The table has been laid for a French five-course meal, with cutlery for fish and meat and two wine glasses per seat. Pasta and plastic croissants stand at the ready in the kitchen.

You can hardly describe Little Venice as a faithful copy of a European neighbourhood. The houses contain a profusion of elements from classical European architecture, but districts or villas such as these are nowhere to be seen in Verona, Basel or Amsterdam.

CHANGSHA

The French philosopher Baudrillard would describe the houses in Little Venice as bearing 'no relation to any reality whatever: it is its own pure simulacrum.'[3] In the same way that Starbucks is not a copy of an Italian espresso bar, but a typically American coffee chain, Little Venice is not an imitation of an island in the Laguna Veneta, but an authentic Chinese villa district.

'We live in our own house with a garden. I think that is what many Chinese dream of.'

Many critics dismiss this type of decorative layer as tasteless kitsch. 'Who pretends to be more elevated than he is, is a fraud and subject to general contempt, even if it harms no one. But what if someone tries to achieve this effect with fake stone and other imitations?,' wondered architect Adolf Loos.[4] He was not speaking about Changsha in 2010, but about the houses of the Viennese petty bourgeoisie in 1898. The preferences of the upper middle class in the nineteenth-century Habsburg Empire seem very similar to those of Changsha's upper crust more than a hundred years later. 'If it were up to the speculators,' writes Loos, 'they would plaster the facades from top to bottom. That is the cheapest option. It would also be the most truthful, most correct and most artistic solution. But no one would want to live there. To be able to let his property, the speculator must nail down facades that look like this and no different. Indeed, nail them down, because even the materials from which these Renaissance and baroque palaces have been made are not what they seem.'

Architectural historian Li Xiangning of the Shanghai Tongji University is less of a moralist. He compares China's themed neighbourhoods with those in the United States and sees many parallels. 'Europeans perhaps consider this kind of architecture as historical imitation,' he says, 'but Chinese and Americans mostly see something exotic, something foreign. Home buyers will sooner buy a house that has something special,

WHERE DO CHINA'S MILLIONAIRES LIVE?

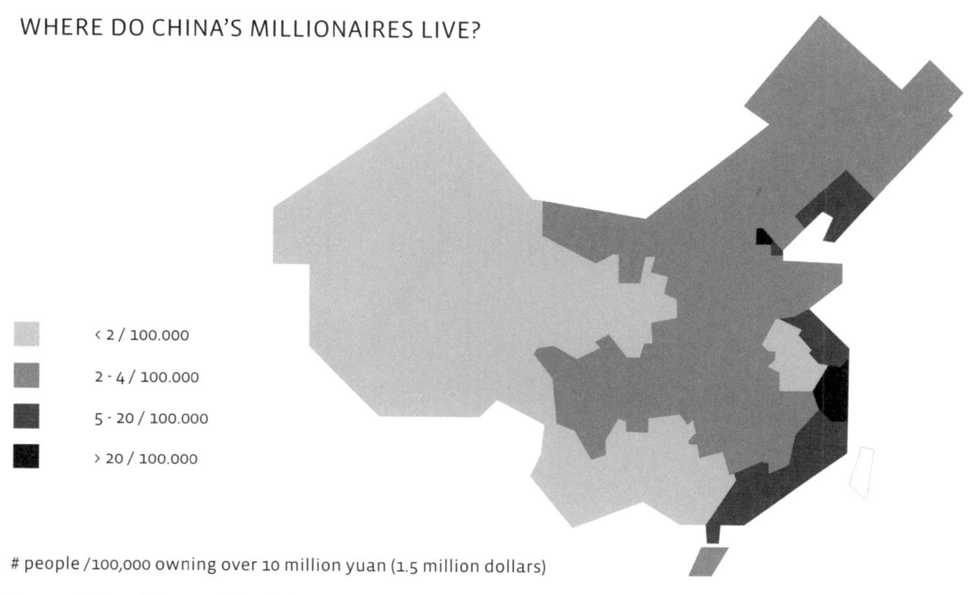

people /100,000 owning over 10 million yuan (1.5 million dollars)

Source: National Bureau of Statistics, 2007

and property developers are well aware of that.' In the United States Li visited Alpine Village near Santa Monica and Solvang, a Danish theme town near Santa Barbara. 'Venice near Los Angeles is the most famous example. It was built as a mock-up with an Italian theme. A hundred years later it is one of the most pleasant neighbourhoods in L.A.'

With their desire for symbols Changsha's new rich celebrate the end of enforced uniformity, which held the country in its grip for thirty years. Between the 1950s and the 1980s communism in China stripped ornamentation from Chinese architecture. The modernist housing blocks, factories and government buildings were indeed 'plastered smooth from top to bottom,' a representation of communist ideals cast in concrete.

With every column, caryatid or fountain that millionaires add to their villas, they move further away from that policy of equality. Lacking contemporary Chinese symbols of wealth, they choose elements from other countries or other ages, and preferably both. In their search for new symbols of wealth and status they are setting the trend for 1.4 billion Chinese. Their extravagance finds followers in malls, restaurants, offices and government buildings all over China.

The result is a hyper-reality where anything goes, without the heavy burden of a discussion on good taste. A Chinese temple on an eighty-metre skyscraper? Fine! The Villa Savoye, but upside down? Great idea! An Egyptian sphinx in a Chinese city park, a Louis XIV chateau with a gold leaf façade, the reconstructed birthplace of Salvador Dali, a concert hall shaped like a grand piano and a transparent guitar? Go for it!

Mrs Chao's house stands at the end of a short street. An earthenware Alsatian in the front garden guards the parking space. A gravel path leads to the back garden, containing a set of rattan furniture with a parasol. The cast iron fence with decorative lions enclosing the property continues behind the neighbour's backyard. 'We chose it together', says Chao.

The quality of construction only partially corresponds to the illusion of grandeur, something observable more often in China. Even though they are at most three years old, the villas on the island show signs of decay. Rusting fences, peeling paint, loose tiles, leaky air conditioning, the layer that provides the districts its identity is not only shallow, but fragile as well. The fact that 40 per cent of the houses are empty enhances the crumbling atmosphere. Chao: 'Many of our neighbours bought it as an investment. They live somewhere else and hope it will be worth a lot of money in a couple of years.'

Little Venice suffers not only from visible degeneration. Constant plumbing leaks forced Chao and her family to live in the Phoenix Hotel for two months last year, and they are not the only ones, even though Chao had selected Little Venice because of Guangdong property developer Country Garden's good name. The company, established in 1997 by former construction worker Yang Guoqiang, successfully builds similar villa districts throughout China. When the founder transferred most of his property in 2007 to his 29-year-old daughter, Yang Huiyan, Forbes promptly declared her the wealthiest woman in Asia, with assets worth 16 billion dollars.

'We had only heard positive stories about Country Garden,' said Chao. Behind her glasses her eyes spit fire. 'But what can you do?' she asks, 'something like this can happen to anyone.'

If the villa is the dream home for the nouveau riche, then the SUV is their vehicle of preference. The two are engaged in a fierce battle for the position of 'status symbol number one.' If the villa represents a piece of the planet, an SUV allows you to wander the earth in unlimited freedom. A car has the advantage that the owner can take his treasure anywhere to be admired. In China an expensive automobile provides at least as much 'face' as a villa.

Toyota, Mercedes and BMW have branches in the Changsha car sales strip not far from the residential island. Porsche opened its doors in January 2009, to cater to the growing market of the super rich. The least expensive vehicle in the showroom goes for 112,000 dollars, and the priciest for 500,000 dollars. At around 150,000 dollars, the Porsche Cayenne is the local bestseller.

While Nora Jones sings through the loud speakers about kissing on a mountain top, three men enter the sterile showroom. They are in their late thirties and wear blue jackets, faded jeans and muddy loafers. They walk in a straight line towards a coffee-coloured Cayenne and start opening and closing the doors, all the while talking loudly. Sales leader Liu lets them do as they please. He knows that the super rich are not always identified by their clothing. Liu describes his average customer as 'a man between forty and fifty years old with his own company.' Almost all of them own one or more cars already. 'Usually a BMW or a Mercedes. They buy a Porsche only to impress.' The sales figures form and indication of the size of the upper class in Hunan province. Liu says he sells a Porsche every three days. The national trend is showing a marked increase. Porsche expects to sell more cars in 2012 in China than in its home market of Germany.

It is not difficult to predict where many of these Cayennes will end up: on the driveways of villas such as those in Little Venice. That irritates chief engineer Wang Huifang of the Changsha planning authority. If an increasing amount of car-owning townsfolk pursue the dream of detached houses with private gardens, planners such as her will simply run out of space. Wang, a woman in her late thirties, sits in a typical Chinese meeting room on the ninth floor of Changsha City Hall. Six heavy armchairs surround an oval table, with a second ring of chairs for the lesser gods. The walls are bare. The only decorations are six giant ashtrays partially filled with cigarette butts. Wang opens a city map and explains the problems facing the city: within six years the number of inhabitants of the city core has to increase from three to six million, without changing the city borders.

'At the moment we calculate hundred square metres of land use per person in Changsha,' she says. 'That includes everything: living, working, recreation, but also hospitals and infrastructure. We have to, because we cannot expand indefinitely.' This is the consequence of a strict national policy prescribing Chinese self-sufficiency in food supply, no simple task for a country with 22 per cent of the world population and only 7 per cent of the planet's arable land. The government in Beijing has ordered that China must hold on to at least 210 million acres of agricultural land, a 'red line' almost reached because of rapid urbanisation. In March 2010 Prime Minister Wen Jiabao once again insisted that 'we have to maintain the strictest possible system to defend agricultural land.'

The Changsha planning authority has little choice, says Wang. 'We discourage the building of villa areas because they use too much limited urban space.' It means that only a small, affluent group can afford to live in low-density areas in the city.

Wang distinguishes another group with this privilege: farmers. 'They have their own land, and can build villas on it with the money they make in the city as migrant labourers.' This can be seen everywhere, especially near the large East Coast cities, where farmers with city jobs are building villas increasingly resembling the homes in Little Venice, covered in pillars, fountains and statues. With only the super rich and former peasants being able to afford villas with gardens, the situation is ironic. Wang does not expect rich urbanites to flock to the countryside en masse in the future for spacious detached homes. That is not permitted

'City dwellers may not own property in the countryside.'

But it happens anyway.

Many village administrators try to attract property developers. The Changsha rich are also moving to the country. Little Venice lies just inside the urban core, but someone with serious money gets into his flashy car for the half-hour drive to Dragon Lake, which is the next step in low-density urbanisation. Here, a builder is constructing homes in both English and Tuscan country style and completing a ten-storey pink castle. The most expensive dwelling in the area is a mammoth villa, with an asking price of approximately seven million dollars. Residents can practice their space-intensive hobbies to their hearts' content. When it opened in 2002, the hilly 27-hole Dragon Lake golf club was the only one in the entire province; now it is merely the oldest. The club is almost always open. The Chinese rich have improved on this international elite sport by inventing night golfing, preferably after a sumptuous dinner including plenty of drink.

Pastiche or exotic architecture?

Overlooking Dragon Lake from the clubhouse, the area might be Wales, with white golf carts driving between rolling green hills and grand mansions. Even the caddies dress in style, wearing tartan trousers, green jackets and chequered caps. Twenty cream-coloured Roman columns with golden lions surround the car park. Judging by the number plates, the Volkswagen Touareg and Audi Q7 belong to the elite, who purchase 'pretty' plates such as AAA555 or S89999 at auctions in Changsha.

The rise of the nouveau riche has changed Changsha beyond recognition over several years. Large billboards show expensive hotels with golf courses. Various five- or even six-star hotels have opened their doors, as have luxurious shopping malls with stores including Zegna, Salvatore Ferragano, Bang & Olufsen, Stelton, Rolex, Cartier and Omega. Every Friday night on the fifth floor of the Sheraton hotel around 200 urbanites throng around oysters, goose liver and scallops in 'Feast – a world of flavours'. Louis Vuitton, Prada and Gucci lure shoppers everywhere.

Those getting lost among all these icons can stop for a chat with 27-year-old styling advisor Eleven in beauty salon Ni Hao Piaoliang (Hello Beauty) on May One Square in the centre of Changsha. 'People who have gotten rich quickly often focus solely on brands,' she says. 'They rarely pause to consider whether something suits them or not.' In the Ni Hao Piaoliang foyer stands a pink grand piano beside the white Mercedes Coupé new customers can win in a raffle. The music system plays preludes by Chopin interspersed with a pan flute rendition of Simon & Garfunkel's *Sound of Silence*. The

salon offers its clients luxurious haircuts and a spa. Eleven, who specialises in clothing advice, sports a trendy haircut, and dresses in a simple T-shirt and comfortable tracksuit bottoms. Her customers consist mostly of women between twenty and forty. They live in villas or luxury apartments and drive expensive European cars. Among them are actors and presenters known from Hunan TV, she says. 'Unfortunately, I can't tell you any names.'

The young styling consultant frequently visits her clients at home. The women put on all their pieces of clothing one after another, and Eleven takes pictures. 'Then, I

CHANGSHA

(2005)

establish a diagnosis. That means I tell them what they should throw away. She laughs. 'Usually, that's most of it.' Because of her job, Eleven has the opportunity to peek behind the facade of status symbols. She observes a depressing mixture of emptiness and relationship problems. 'The most important reason for women to come here is that they hope that a change in wardrobe will improve their relationship with their husbands. They may have a lot of money, but they often have troubled minds.'

The tragedy of the hedonistic world discussed by Eleven differs little from that appearing in European or American tabloids. China has its own editions of lifestyle magazines such as *Vogue* or *Elle*, as well as gossip magazines like *Sunday* and *Easy* that extensively depict the lives and misfortunes of celebrities, their extra-marital affairs, weight problems and overall mental well-being.

'One of my customers is a girl my age,' says Eleven. 'She is extremely bored. The only thing she does is shop.'

Porsche expects to sell more cars in 2012 in China than in its home market of Germany.

The businessmen, TV stars and government officials populating Little Venice have one thing in common: they all started out poor. Thirty years ago, Chinese cities had few wealthy inhabitants.

Yi Weiming, a thoughtful man of 46, grew up in Mao Zedong's birthplace, Shaoshan, not far from Changsha. He shared a thirty-square-metre apartment with his father (a doctor), his mother (a nurse) and his grandmother. 'An average home in those days.' As a boy he wanted nothing more than to become a soldier, which brought high social status – the only criterion of distinction. 'The rest did not matter. All salaries were the same.'

Political changes ended dreams of military glory. After a ten-year witch-hunt against academe, the state restored university education to its former splendour at the end of the 1970s. A high school teacher advised Yi to study Tea Sciences at the Agricultural

URBAN HOUSEHOLD INCOME IN CHINA

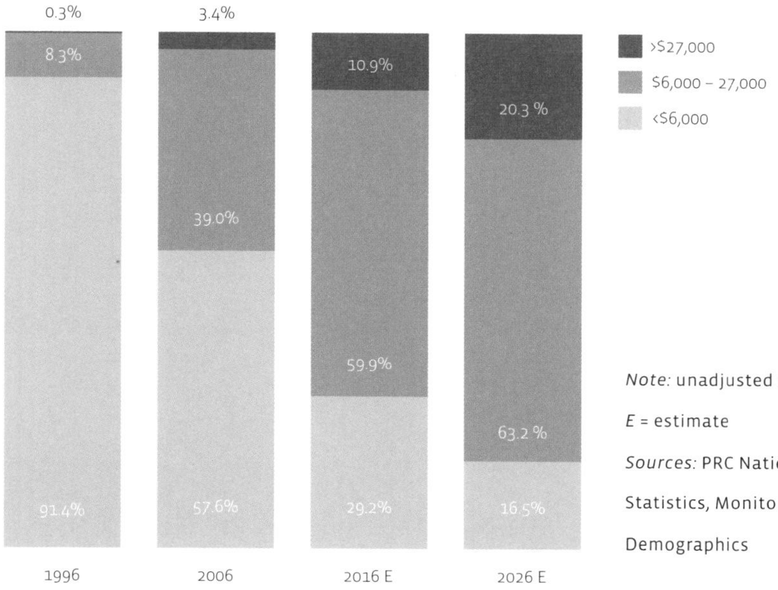

0.3%
8.3%
91.4%
1996

3.4%
39.0%
57.6%
2006

10.9%
59.9%
29.2%
2016 E

20.3 %
63.2 %
16.5%
2026 E

>$27,000
$6,000 – 27,000
<$6,000

Note: unadjusted for inflation
E = estimate
Sources: PRC National Bureau of Statistics, Monitor, and Global Demographics

Academy. The successful completion of this course guaranteed a job with one of the many state companies, and in 1985 he landed his first job at the China Tea Import and Export Corporation in Beijing. Working for the state hardly came as a surprise, as there were few independent entrepreneurs. 'The only businessmen in Beijing where the spring roll sellers,' he sniggers.

At the beginning of the 1990s the government relaxed the rules for starting businesses. Yi waited until 1996 to start a company with three friends in Changsha, or 'jumping into the sea' *(xia hai)* as it was called then. Like most businessmen in those days they traded in anything that made money. They bought clothes in Guangzhou that they sold in Changsha. They imported wood from Africa, and sold it to furniture factories in South China. In the meantime Yi remained active for the tea company.

In 1997 he managed to buy a piece of land in Changsha with his business partners that was to form the basis of his present fortune. With the contract in his pocket he went to the bank. 'That was enough for a loan,' he says. They used the money to build their first

development: a 5,500-square-metre office building. 'The sale was a big success,' laughs Yi. Within two years they made 300,000 dollars. That felt good.

China's accession to the World Trade Organisation boosted the property market and in 2003 Yi and his partners built three new developments: a 5,000 square metre office, another office block 38,000 square metres in size, and a thirty-storey residential tower. The young property developer had no home of his own yet. He still lived with his parents. For success on the property market good relations with local officials were a must. 'Exhausting,' Yi found those to be. 'You had to spend a lot of time with them. And all those contacts could be dangerous.' Yi experienced this for himself when he ran into trouble at one of his construction projects. A contractor with good government relations tried to extort him. When Yi refused to pay, he was thrown in jail following accusations of underworld contacts. It was a month before he came out. 'Believe me, a Chinese prison is not good for you.'

Yi made a drastic decision. He completed his last projects, sold part of his possessions and left the property trade. 'It was becoming too dangerous,' he says. While he meditated on his future, he met his wife, Zheng Chan, in 2005, a hydraulic engineer working for the government.

Four years later, the couple lives in a four-floor villa built on a hillside, with a Toyota and a Buick in the ground-floor garage, and an SUV in the driveway. On the first floor are the living room, kitchen, and Yi and Zheng's parents' quarters, who follow Chinese tradition and live with their children. The couple themselves sleep on the second floor, with an enormous wedding photograph above the bed. On the same floor are a study and a room for their three-year-old son. They use the attic as a laundry area.

The villa is sparsely furnished. Apart from the large orange skai leather sofas and a basketball-shaped side table, the house is quite empty. There is no strategy of minimal design behind the paltry furnishings.

Yi says he has little patience with the lifestyle of Changsha's new rich. 'Many wealthy Chinese care only for status symbols. Luxury brands, expensive bags, watches. They provide "face". Many people waste their time with useless things. I don't care about those much.' His home is all the luxury he needs. 'It wasn't cheap, but now we have our own piece of land under our own piece of heaven.' From the sofa in the living room he looks out over the Bavarian Schloss Neuschwanstein in the adjacent *Window of the*

TUDOR
卓越于心 精致以形
TUDOR
艺术摄影
13755032013

World amusement park, with copies of iconic buildings from around the globe.

The family holidays four times a year, in China, Thailand, the Philippines and Korea. 'Then the three of us have barbecues and go swimming,' says Zheng. She enjoys shopping trips with friends in Hong Kong, a one-and-a-half hour flight from Changsha. Their son is already attending the international nursery, where he learns English, music and painting. By Chinese standards, Yi and Zheng are extremely well off. Psychologist Abraham Maslow would say that the couple is standing at the top of his famous pyramid, where the only desires left to attain are knowledge, freedom and fulfilment. Yi and Zheng believe they will not be able to satisfy these needs in Changsha, or anywhere else in China. They have serious plans to emigrate to the United States. That makes them part of a growing group of rich people willing to trade their Chinese citizenship for a foreign one. Countries like the United States and Canada hand out passports to people willing to make big investments.

A small exodus is taking place. In 2007 China became the largest contributor to world emigration.[5] Some academics fear that China will not only lose large sums of money this way, but also the cleverest and most capable of its inhabitants. Of the 275,000 Chinese students at foreign universities, only an estimated 25 per cent will return.[6] 'China is losing the talent it needs the most,' Wang Huiyao, director of the Centre for China and Globalisation, told BBC News.[7]

The reasons for this elite emigration are varied. Yi and Zheng say they are mostly interested in their son's future. 'Education in the United States is much better than in China,' says Yi. 'In sixty years of communism China has not won one Nobel Prize for scientific achievements.' Financial security plays an important role in their considerations. Yi has personally experienced just how fragile wealth in China can be. A Western passport brings a degree of certainty and liberty unavailable in China.

Zheng cites China's one-child policy as an important motive. 'We would like a second child. But that is not possible here.' Several friends have preceded her. 'Our former neighbours at number thirteen now live in Canada. They have three children.'

Yi and Zheng's parents do not seem completely adjusted yet to villa life. They walk around in winter coats. It is November, and seven degrees centigrade outside, but turning on the heating would be a waste of money. While they play with their grandchild and his stuffed crocodile, the maid prepares their favourite winter meal: braised dog meat. 'That's the best thing against the cold,' says Yi's father resolutely.

8. LANZHOU

(1950)

'IF THE FACTORY PROSPERS, I PROSPER'

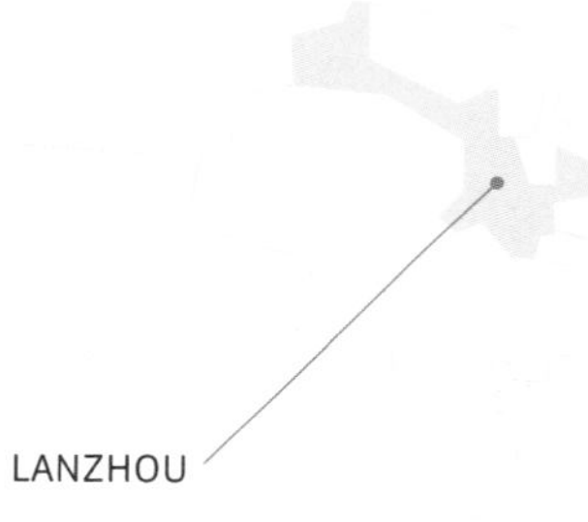

GANSU - SAUDI ARABIA
With 26 million inhabitants, Gansu province has roughly the same population as Saudi Arabia

On the top of the hill the sense of hopelessness mixes with the smell of blood. Four muscular men push a convulsing sheep to the ground, as the ditch beside them slowly colours red. Three hundred metres of slaughterhouses line the disused railway track. Scattered between the sleepers lie decapitated sheep heads and bowls of entrails. The slaughterers, young women and girls in headscarves, sit on low stools by the roadside. Live chickens sit on top of each other crammed in cages, with freshly butchered relatives oozing their last drops of blood on top of them.The butchering is is repetitive. Take chicken from cage. Place on floor with head towards Mecca. Cut throat. Bleed out in tub of hot water. Pluck, remove entrails. Place on top of cage and done. Repeat as above. There are no dustbins, or running water for washing hands. A group of bearded men are talking to each other in front of the mosque. One of them looks at a two-year-old child playing at his feet among the offal, and smiles.

Teacher Wu shakes his head as he walks past. He has lived in Little West Lake district for forty years, and saw the transformation unfolding under his very eyes. Once, this was an industrial area on the outskirts of Lanzhou, a model of the communist worker ideal. In dozens of state factories employees worked shoulder to shoulder, producing electrical appliances, bicycles and clothing sold throughout China. They lived in walled *danwei* divided by small specks of peasant-cultivated farmland. The introduction of the market economy heralded decline. After the year 2000 Wu witnessed the bankruptcy of one company after the other, as the sluggish state companies failed to compete with new private manufacturers. In the following years poor migrant workers from the countryside flooded the neighbourhood, mostly illiterate Chinese Muslims escaping persistent drought. The native farmers of Little West Lake demolished their farms and rented out the new houses they built to the migrants. Once a relatively prosperous industrial suburb, it is now one of the worst districts in Lanzhou, says Wu, with high unemployment and large number of people surviving on subsistence level income. He worries especially about the hundreds of children growing up in poverty. 'All my life the state provided me with a steady job,' he says. 'Now I have retired, I want to do something for society in return.'

Lanzhou is the capital of Gansu province, a mountainous and dry area that forms the link between Central China and the far West. Lanzhou has more than two million inhabitants; the entire urban conurbation more than three million. In the city live more than 150,000 Muslims of the Chinese Hui minority, their presence advertised by the more than seventy mosques, some with imposing golden domes and tall, slender minarets. The city stretches for miles along the Yellow River, itself squeezed between the two mountain ranges that give Lanzhou its distinctive stretched shape, seen in maps available everywhere: long strips of paper folded like accordions. The skyline of skyscrapers against a backdrop of steep mountainsides illustrates the city's progress, monuments to Lanzhou's impressive economic growth of over ten per cent per year between 2000 and 2009.

The fruits of new prosperity are not divided equally among the city's inhabitants, with the richest living in villa districts, the middle class in the countless new compounds, the builders in containers on construction sites and the workers in large dormitories in the factories. But the real losers of China's economic miracle wash up in industrial suburbs such as Little West Lake: the redundant employees of bankrupt state companies, supplemented by young migrant workers who failed to grasp the hoped-for city opportunities. The mixture of these two population groups closely resembles the composition of troubled immigrant neighbourhoods in major European cities.

Wu halts by a rickety house at the end of a short muddy path. 'A former student of mine lives here', he says. He knocks on the door and enters a minute, barely lit room. On a bed occupying half the space sits young couple in their early twenties holding a newborn infant. It is clear from their torn clothes and unwashed faces that they cannot afford to miss a yuan. 'Look at that,' says Wu, 'to think that conditions like this still exist in this country.'

On the brick wall of the former electronics factory pale characters spell the motto 'If the factory prospers, I prosper.' It is an ominous slogan, with the factory now serving as a coop for hundreds of chickens, tended by a man and his two teenage sons who live on the factory grounds in a self-built wooden shack. You can divide China's former state companies into two categories: those which successfully survived China's transition to a market economy, and those which did not. Companies in the first category are China Mobile, China Eastern Airlines, China National Petroleum Corporation, Baoshan Steel, and countless other established names. Little West Lake contains only examples of the second category: small- and medium-sized manufacturers that lost out in the competition with the enormous private enterprises on the Chinese coast.

In his third-floor living room, Mr Ma sits on a worn three-seater sofa, under a large portrait of Mao Zedong. The workers' homes are well past their prime. Ma has lived here since 1974, and worked as a driver for the factory for almost thirty years. 'After the bankruptcy many of my colleagues left,' he says. Mr Ma's electronics plant is not the only *danwei* in decline. Of all the former proud state factories in Little West Lake, only the steel delivery tricycle manufacturer is still operational. Considering the sense of comprehensive misery on the factory grounds, it will not be long before this plant, too, will have to shut it gates permanently. 'The atmosphere in the neighbourhood has

THE POOR VS. THE RICH

changed completely. Everybody used to know each other,' remembers Ma. 'If someone had a problem, we would all rush to help. That has changed altogether; everybody lives their own lives now. Different kinds of people live here now, all doing their own thing, and the number of people from ethnic minorities is growing. They have a completely different way of life. Come to think of it, we are the minority now.'

Ma no longer feels at home in Little West Lake, he says. 'People call this place little Afghanistan. It isn't safe, and most of the new residents have no education. Their children don't even go to school, and if they do, their teachers can't handle them. Parents don't even show up at parent-teacher meetings. Minorities treat their children differently. We don't let our kids out on their own at night like they do. As soon as their children can walk, you see them roaming the streets deep into the night.' Ma's own sons, who have grown up a long time ago, still live in the countryside outside Lanzhou. 'That is better for them, if you don't have any skills, you won't survive in the city.'

Religion plays an important role in Little West Lake daily life. The *salah* sounds five times a day from the minarets of numerous mosques, and after Friday prayers men with Islamic headwear fill the streets, greeting each other with an exuberant *salam aleikum*. Several times a day the thundering noise of the Beijing-Lhasa train drowns all conversation in the neighbourhood. The raised track splits Little West Lake in two: in the south the neighbourhood ends in the street with the slaughterhouses, in the north at a busy boulevard with large department stores. In between is Little West Lake itself: a collection of disintegrating *danwei*, and self-built flatlets and flats built by former peasants, ranging from five to fifteen floors in height. On the ground floors these lift-less, concrete and tile buildings have small shops, storage vaults and poultry farms. Above that are large numbers of cramped, overcrowded rooms for migrant workers.

On the edge of Little West Lake you find the worst houses: low brick hovels lining dirt paths, without running water or sewage facilities. When teacher Wu walks through this part of the neighbourhood to visit his former pupils, the news spreads like wildfire. Children everywhere call his name or accompany him for a while. Via a narrow path past multiple landfills Wu reaches a small brick dwelling, where his former student Xin and her mother Wang are waiting for him. A motorcycle stands parked under a small roof at the side of the house. The lady of the house directs Wu into a simple home, consisting of a single room containing all facilities. The teacher sits himself down on a sofa pushed against one wall, while Wang places herself on the bed opposite. In between the two are a small table, several cupboards, a television set, washing machine, fridge, sink and gas cooker. The twelve-square-metre space leaves little room for manoeuvre.

Mrs Wang comes from the village of Dongxiang, in the countryside just outside Lanzhou. She married when she was nineteen and moved to the city with her husband. 'We had to go. There was no work in the village and not enough money. We owned a small farm. In years with lots of rain we had good crops, but it did not rain often. We still have the land, it is barren and dry, nobody wants to have it.' It is a familiar story in Little West Lake. The estimated 60,000 migrant workers mostly come from Islamic villages in Gansu province. Years of low precipitation made large parts of the province almost infertile. In his book *Along the Yellow River* journalist Bert van Dijk describes the farmers of Minqin village, who need to drill a minimum of two hundred meters before they hit water. The authorities have outlawed planting water intensive crops, and many farmers are moving away.[1] A researcher at Lanzhou University describes these migrants as 'ecological refugees', who cannot survive in the countryside.

After having been forced to live in Lanzhou, Mrs Wang and her husband now struggle with the same problems as many of their peers: because of their illiteracy and thick accents they can only get jobs that no one else is willing to do, such as gathering and sorting garbage, breeding and slaughtering chickens, filling and hauling bags of coal. 'At first I sold corn in the street, and later I sold many other things. The police pester you all the time, they forbid you to trade. I have worked in restaurants and hotels, I have to look for new jobs constantly.' Her husband earns money by driving people through the city on his motorcycle for a fee. Unfortunately Lanzhou authorities, as in many Chinese cities, officially prohibit his profession as motorcycle taxi driver. 'The police have already impounded two motorcycles.' Work is not the only unstable factor in their lives. In the thirteen years that Wang and her husband have spent in Lanzhou, they have moved five times.

The Wangs have three children: Xin has an elder sister and a younger brother. They are Hui Muslims, and because of their ethnic minority status, the official one-child policy does not apply to them. With a household income of several dozen dollars per month, they easily sink under the poverty line of one dollar per day. Mrs Wang sees only one positive side to living in Lanzhou: their children can get an education here, in contrast to the Gansu countryside where there are hardly any schools. She nods in Xin's direction. 'She is thirteen years old and in the fifth grade now, we really want her to go to high school later.' The school fee usually amounts to seventy-five dollars per semester, a significant assault on the household budget. Teacher Wu has arranged a waiver of Xin's school fees. Xin's elder sister has completed her education and found a job as secretary, her mother says enthusiastically. 'She has just started work for a little shop in the centre of Lanzhou. She taught herself to type. She picks up the phone, it is a good job.'

On the picture next to the television stands a photograph of the two sisters. The portrait would be funny if it wasn't so bitter. Wearing headscarves, they laugh into the camera. The sisters are sitting in a grand living room, with fireplace, Chesterfield sofas and a chandelier. Through the window behind them you can discern a French garden with hedges. But a closer inspection reveals it has been photoshopped.

'If I can make it there, I'll make it anywhere,' sang Frank 'The Voice' Sinatra about New York, but he could have crooned the same about Lanzhou. The Chinese model of urbanisation is based in essence on financial success. The cities only welcome those who can provide for their own subsistence, who have jobs, start companies of their own, in short, those who contribute towards the economy. An immigrant who cannot fulfil this requirement has to stay in the countryside where he can avoid dying of hunger by growing his own food. That is, at least, the theory. The tool the government tries to enforce this transparent model with is the *hukou*, which ensures that migrants have no rights to social security benefits in the city. If they lose their jobs, they have to return to the countryside, to their farmland. As unjust as it sounds, the system has many advantages. Chinese cities do not have to deal with the massive slums, *favelas* or townships found in the suburbs of Mumbai, Rio or Johannesburg. Millions of construction workers, labourers or waitresses may live in miserable conditions in containers, sheds or crowded flats, but they are largely spared the violence, the intimidation, the child beggars, the extreme poverty and organised crime of the slums. Those who cannot cope simply move to the countryside, where poverty is concentrated. In 2009 the average annual income in the countryside was around 750 dollars per year, while in the city it hovered around 2,600 dollars. The gap widens each year.[2]

This success-based urban model has functioned properly for a long time, but is now starting to show its first cracks, mainly because it ignores two groups. First of all, city dwellers such as Ma, who cannot benefit from economic growth because they have lost their jobs. They have to make do with a small handout and a worker's dwelling near their bankrupt factory. The second group consists of migrants such as Mrs Wang, who have few perspectives in the cities, but cannot return to their villages either, and cobble together a living in illegality. In a report on China's urban transition United Nations researchers note that 'the decline of state-owned enterprises has resulted in layoffs and an increase in the number of unemployed people, who, together with informal workers and rural residents, are facing serious problems in joining the new urban labour market.'[3]

In brief, the growth of cities in Central and Western China increases prosperity, but also leads to an increasing divergence in the distribution of wealth. There is a growing gap between rich and poor, between those who can manage, and those who cannot.

According to the so-called Gini index, income distribution in China at the moment is even more unequal than in the United States. It is an almost universal law that the poorest people live in the cheapest places. In the long run, this will create districts where all societal problems end up together: unemployment, illiteracy, poverty and crime; neighbourhoods such as Little West Lake.

That does not mean there are no successful people in the neighbourhood at all. Right beside the mosque movers are emptying a small lorry. They are lifting a gold mirror, a five-piece sofa, and lamps to the penthouse of a ten-floor flat, stair by stair, because there is no lift. On the top floor a bearded young man in a *djellaba* directs the removal men to the right rooms. His name is Ma. 'You're right, that is the most common family name in Lanzhou.' He has lived in Lanzhou for fifteen years and built this residential tower together with his family. Most of the other floors they let to other migrant workers. 'This is a disadvantaged area,' he says. 'You can see that the government does not pay any attention to this district. They do not invest here. We have to do that ourselves.'

'People call this place little Afghanistan.'

Professor Chen Wenjiang of Lanzhou University says that his city contains more areas like this one, with a population of laid-off fifty-somethings and poor immigrants from different ethnic backgrounds. 'In those districts lives a heterogeneous population that only has poverty in common. Many big city problems come together here. Half of all city crime takes place in neighbourhoods like these.' Chen says that the scope of the problem is still manageable, but he fears the rise of a new risk group: the children of migrant workers. 'The first generation of migrant workers are now in their fifties, their children were often raised in the countryside and only came to the cities when they were older. The second generation has some farming experience, even if it is not very much. But still, if they become unemployed, they can always return to the countryside and live as farmers.'

According to Chen, this pattern is slowly changing. Migrant workers are increasingly letting their children grow up in the city, says the professor. 'These children feel completely urban, they have never lived in the countryside. The oldest of this group are now between ten and twenty years old and live with their parents. Some have jobs in restaurants or as a compound security guard, and others go to school. They have no link at all with their parents' villages. The problem arises once they lose their jobs. They really have nowhere to go to.' Professor Chen predicts that this third generation will become 'the problem group of the future,' but he has no hard data to prove this. 'There has been hardly any research into this in China'.

'The school itself is a migrant, too.'

'*Hao hao xuexi, tian tian shang*', proclaim the characters above the blackboard. Studying hard will bring you further every day. Beside the famous Mao quote hangs a poster of the Latin alphabet: with A for Apple, B for Bed, but also Q for Queen, and X for Xmas. Thirty children of around six years old look expectantly at teacher Wu. In contrast to many other Chinese schools they do not wear uniforms, but their own clothes, which mostly appear unwashed. Wu claps his hands, 'end of the lesson,' and all hell breaks loose. Thirty six-year-olds storm past their school desks to the door, with chairs and children toppling over, and within sixty seconds the classroom is empty. Wu observes his pupils in a fatherly manner. To stay warm in the cold school building, he is wearing a long coat and a hat. Wu is a cheerful man, and deeply committed to the world around him. During the day he teaches to the poor children in Little West Lake.

'Many people can only see that these children are dirty and naughty. Secondary schools reject them because their level is too low. Eleven-year-old children raised in the countryside possess as much knowledge as a six-year-old in the city, and on top of this they usually do not speak very good Mandarin.' Gifts fully finance the school, from Lanzhou businesses and individuals and from the international relief organisation Oxfam. The school budget is limited. 'The school itself is a migrant, too,' jokes Wu. 'We have moved nine times in eight years because we could not afford the rent hikes.'

The current accommodation is on the second floor of a warehouse next to the railway track. The more than a hundred students are divided over three classes, taught by eight teachers, all pensioners or volunteers.

According to Chinese law, children must attend school from their sixth to their fifteenth birthdays, which rarely happens in Little West Lake. A careful poll the school conducted in the neighbourhood showed that more than 2,500 children do not go to school at all, and the true figure is probably higher. Everywhere in the district children younger than fifteen are hanging around or working as street vendors. Between 2002 and 2010 the school taught a total of 1,500 students. 'We get far more requests than we can handle,' says Wu.

The migrant school officially aims to prepare children in one to three years for regular education, and success varies. 'Last year we sent twenty-seven students to secondary school, after a year there was only one left,' says Wu. His old pupil, Wang Xin, is clearly an exception for the better. The teacher blames this on a blend of different causes. First, school fees are an obstacle. 'Public education is only free if you have a city *hukou*.' For migrant children the price is 150 dollars per semester for a good school, and 75 dollars for a bad one. Many parents do not have the money, or use it for something else. 'Some Muslims spend more money on the mosque than on their children's education,' says Wu. 'I am a Muslim, too, but I think I am entitled to criticise that.' Additionally, Lanzhou's public schools are not enthusiastic about accepting migrant children. 'They aren't very good at school and often older than their classmates, which causes frictions. They bring down the school average. Teachers will find any excuse to send them away.' Teachers have a personal financial interest, too, says Wu. With Chinese New Year, parents traditionally give teachers a *hongbao*, a red envelope with money. 'That is their grey income. Migrants don't have a lot to give, so their children are less desired.'

The authorities display little interest in the children. Wu believes they fear that acknowledging the problem will cause loss of face, but there is also a funding problem. China has a strongly decentralised tax system, in which local authorities are dependent on local tax income to finance schools and health care. 'If only high-income people can educate their children, then that group remains a privileged, high-income group permanently,' wrote World Bank researcher David Dollar, adding 'China is at some risk of falling into this trap.'[4]

送电话：13008789494

Wu is also teaching a group of adolescents. He is trying to prepare them for the labour market. 'I am trying to teach them survival strategies. Simple things, such as reading and writing, but especially how they can grow up to become good people.' This is often unsuccessful, he says. Some youngsters refuse to go to school. 'They drink and smoke, they feel betrayed by society. Many boys end up involved in crime.'

The Lanzhou planning authority resides in a typical Chinese government building with an enormous entrance of neo-classicist pillars. Inside, Wang Jianhe smokes a cigarette on the sofa in his office. Beside him stands a plant. Wang has been working since 2006 on one of the largest urban renewal projects in Lanzhou: tackling the 'villages in the city'. 'The goal is to change the bad areas into beautiful city districts.' He is clearly referring to contemporary high-rise compounds.

In the same way that the Chinese city excludes its second-class citizens, it also rejects second-class neighbourhoods: urban areas with poor housing and inferior sanitation, where many people live close together in unglamorous buildings. In practice, these are, firstly, old working class neighbourhoods such as 'Old Civilisation Street' in Kunming, and secondly, 'villages in the city,' where peasants develop their own mini-flats they let as shops or homes to migrants. City authorities see especially the latter as hotbeds of crime and neglect. To eliminate these 'urban tumours,' the authorities use a method as simple as it is effective: demolition. Wang Jianhe and his colleagues at the planning authority have ambitious plans: in a ten-year period they want to transform a total of sixty of the urban villages in Lanzhou into modern city districts. 'Land use, building style and living standard need to be improved. We will demolish the villages and build new neighbourhoods.'

The present homeowners, about 30,000 families, will receive replacement housing. Their tenants, hundreds of thousands of migrants, will need to find new homes themselves. Wang does not think this will pose a problem. 'We compensate the homeowners with several homes, so they can let those out again. Additionally, we stimulate them to follow education or to take up jobs, so they can provide in their own upkeep.' Enough space will be left for the migrants now inhabiting the 'villages in the city,' he says. 'They can just rent apartments in the new compounds.' This approach by the Chinese authorities is not unique. In recent decades the United States and Western Europe followed the same model of demolition and new construction in their own disadvantaged areas. Faith in the engineered society professes that removing bad buildings will also remove social problems. It is a belief that already existed in ancient Rome. Reality often proves less pliable.

The approach of the Lanzhou planning authority is part of a large national campaign

of social building. In total, Chinese cities are to build more than ten million subsidised homes per year. Forty per cent of that is intended for homeowners of demolished 'villages in the city.' Commercial property developers build the homes, as happened in Mr Sun's village in Shijiazhuang.[5] Of course, in many respects the new compounds offer a better quality of living than the villages in the city they are replacing. They are

LANZHOU (2010)

(2015)

roomier, fire safety is better, they have safe play areas for children and sanitation. In his book, *The New Asian Hemisphere* Kishore Mahbubani describes the impact of the latter. 'If I were asked to name the date when my life entered the modern world, I would date it to the arrival of the flush toilet. On that day I felt that there had been a magical transformation of my life. Suddenly, I felt that I could lead a life of greater dignity, suffering from less embarrassment when visitors came to our house.'[6]
The question remains, of course, whether it is necessary to tear down entire areas to install some simple plumbing. But to local administrators and property developers, financial profits of new construction form a strong incentive for urban renewal. In the end it will lead to a selection process: the poorest migrant workers cannot afford new apartments, and move to the next cheap district.

'They feel betrayed by society. Many boys end up involved in crime.'

The Lanzhou Blue Light Machine Factory also sports a faded slogan: 'Doing great deeds makes people happy.' Engineer Ma Ziying ostentatiously knocks on the wooden front door. 'Hardwood. They don't make them like that nowadays.' The retired technician was responsible in the 1970s for the construction of workers' homes in the factories. Like most *danwei*, they are modelled after Soviet originals: five floors high, grouped around two courtyards with trees and benches. The buildings themselves are simple. A few concrete ornaments decorate the brown brick facades near the stairwells. Ma Ziying: 'These houses have deep foundations, they are all earthquake-proof.'
The smallest homes were meant for singles. Ma, who himself has three children, received the largest flat: a three-room apartment. Blue Light was part of Lanzhou's industrial pride. 'Our mining equipment was famous all over China,' says Ma with conviction. He still cannot stomach the factory's bankruptcy in 2009. 'I don't understand it. We had the people, we had the machines, we had the customers, and we were the only factory in China who made these machines.' He suspects that Blue Light had to close

for a different reason. 'We went bust at a time when the coal industry in China started to flourish.' The price of 30 million dollars for the entire factory area that the property developer agreed to pay the management after the bankruptcy was, he says, 'far too low.' Ma does not want to say it out loud, but he leaves the impression that some sort of improper self-enrichment was involved in the sale.

Since then, the lives of the residents of the *danwei* have deteriorated. 'We all used to receive bonuses if the factory did well, so everybody used to do their best. That atmosphere has gone: no one has jobs anymore.' Ma is not so outspoken about migrants as his colleagues in the electronics factory, but he, too, mentions the change in the composition of the population in the neighbourhood. Homes that belonged to colleagues who moved or died are now let to migrants. A spacious apartment costs between sixty and seventy dollars per month. 'That is not only cheap for Lanzhou, it is cheap even for Little West Lake. This has become a slum.' In the courtyard the deterioration of the area can be witnessed. The school and nursery have been closed for several years. A resident has left his broken sofas outside of the stairwells.

On the site of the former Blue Light factory hall, a developer plans to build 'Greening Englandshire.' An enormous billboard shows a compound with red telephone booths beside a golf course where a man in tartan trousers is practising his swing, his Mini Cooper parked by the roadside. A warning in a corner of the image reads: 'This is a computer visualisation.' Ma does not believe that the new neighbourhood will have a positive influence on the *danwei*. The apartments in Greening Englandshire will cost at least 600 dollars per month. 'That is for the rich. Ordinary people will stay in this *danwei*.'

A couple of hundred meters from Blue Light, black smoke from a stove fills the room. 'Our money is nearly gone,' says the woman. 'I am thinking of selling our furniture, to have some cash for coal.' Her fifteen-year-old son stands around awkwardly, clearly embarrassed, staring down at the noses of his fake Nikes. Teacher Wu looks round the living room. The boy is a former student of his, who started at a public school last year. 'He had a headache today', his mother apologises. Wu nods. He knows enough.

9. GUIYANG

引领3G生

GUIZHOU - KENYA
With 38 million inhabitants, Guizhou province has roughly the same population as Kenya

GUIYANG

'SAVING ENERGY IS USING YOUR FINGER'

On dry days, Mr Wang trades in a small park near People's Square in Guiyang, the unofficial bicycle market on the riverbank. Around twenty men are displaying their merchandise between the flowerbeds: bicycles and motorcycles, both new and second-hand. Wang dresses in thick winter pyjamas, the characteristic dress of elderly Chinese city folk. On his feet he wears shiny black patent leather shoes. The market is quiet, too quiet as far as Wang is concerned, who can complain for hours on end about the lack of customers. 'Ten years ago everyone had a bicycle, now only students and migrant workers.' Wang works himself up, about the government, for instance, that removed all bicycle paths in the city to make room for cars, or about the police, who send him away for illegal street trading. They should be thanking him, he says. His trade is good for the environment.

But the most important reason for the demise of the bicycle are people themselves, who have lost interest in cycling. 'The only bicycle still gaining popularity is the e-bike.' Wang uses an electric bicycle himself, which is very convenient at his age when pedalling up the Guiyang hillsides. He does not understand why everyone seems to want a car nowadays. Surely, they are completely useless in the city? 'You're stuck in traffic jams half the time, and the other half you are looking for a parking space.' In his youth people did not own bicycles either, says Wang, but for an entirely different reason: at the time they were a luxury. Wang clearly remembers the first bicycle he bought, in 1978, a Phoenix. 'That cost 180 yuan, half an annual salary.' Back then, many Chinese dreamt of possessing at one time in their lives 'three circles and a sound': a bicycle, a watch, a sewing machine and a radio – the symbols of success at the time.

'Things have changed since then,' he laughs. That becomes clear a hundred metres down the road on People's Square, where a giant statue of Mao Zedong waves amicably at the two glass pyramids forming the entrance to the underground Wal-Mart superstore. On the square shoppers are swarming around a stage, plastic bags in hand. One by one, the bravest step forward to sing in the qualifying round of a karaoke contest. First prize in the competition is a car.

Guiyang's fleet of automobiles grows by three hundred cars per day, more than two thousand a week, more than a hundred thousand per year. The epidemic growth of personal mobility symbolises both economic success and its complications: enormous traffic jams and the destruction of the environment.

Guiyang is the capital of Guizhou, one of the poorest provinces in China with an average annual household income of 900 dollars per capita. It is also one of the least urbanised regions in the country. A large part of the population still lives as peasants amongst the paddy fields in the karst mountains around the city. Guiyang's urban core has more than two million inhabitants and all the physical attributes of a typical central Chinese megacity. Cars in the centre clog up all six lanes in perpetual traffic jams, covered by a grey cloud created by the humid climate and the dozens of factories in town continually belching thick clouds of smoke into the air. At night, the city centre changes into a miniature version of Las Vegas: hotels and karaoke bars outdo each other in garish neon lighting, vying like divas with makeup.

In this light, it is surprising to discover that Guiyang advertises itself as an 'eco-city,' the result of a strategic decision made in 2002. The local government feared that, as capital of underdeveloped Guizhou, the city would lose the economic tug-of-war with other cities in China's interior. City administrators chose to shift the struggle to another battlefield: sustainability. A sensible decision, in part because Guiyang possesses an excellent green costume, a beautiful landscape of richly forested mountains in and around the city. After some years of preparation the city joined the United Nations Sustainable Cities programme.

From that moment, Guiyang became an eco-city, according to the official UN definition a city 'dedicated to minimizing the required inputs (energy, water and food) and its waste output (heat, greenhouse gases, water pollution and waste)'.[1] A 2006 United Nations report indicated that green pastures are still a long way off. The last twenty-five years have shown 'close correlations between economic development, population growth, and increases in resource consumption and polluting emissions.' Between 1978 and 2002 Guiyang's economy grew by more than ten per cent annually, and energy use increased by six per cent per year. This caused a 'large-scale and in some cases irreversible damage to the local environment, including loss of biodiversity and degradation of natural resources, most notably water and soil.' The authors of the UN report conclude that a major, perhaps impossible challenge faces Guiyang and China as a whole in 'finding a new model of development that decouples expansion of the local economy from resource consumption and pollution.'[2]

If only that were as easy as it sounds.

Three decades of Chinese economic advance are based on industrialisation and urbanisation. These have pushed the country into becoming the second economy in the world, but wealth comes at a price: 48 per cent of Chinese townsmen live in areas with air quality so poor that it damages the respiratory tracts. The Chinese Academy for Environmental Planning calculates this causes 411,000 early deaths per year.[3] Almost 60 per cent of China's rivers do not measure up to international clean water standards. In comparison: for the United States that figure is eight per cent.[4] On top of this, China is rapidly increasing use of two resources for which it has inadequate supply: energy and water. Especially in the northern half of the country, depletion of groundwater threatens the cities in the long run, which would not just spell ecological, but also

CARBON EMISSIONS PER PERSON, 1950-2006

(Source: Carbon Dioxide Information Analysis Center, 2006)

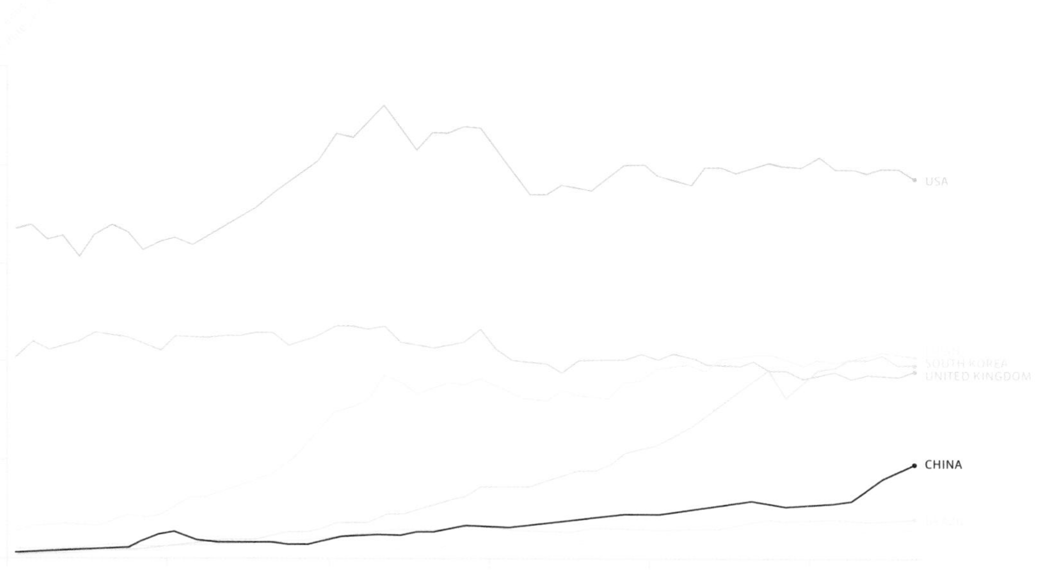

economic disaster. Chinese cities are the key to the debate on sustainability, as they are responsible for up to 85 per cent of national energy consumption. Considering continuing urbanisation, China's energy needs will double by 2025, compared to 2005.[5] Guiyang is not the only Chinese city with green ambitions. More than sixty cities nationwide have plans to build eco-cities. The most famous example is Dongtan, near Shanghai. Proposed by McKinsey and developed by the international designers and engineers of Arup and McDonough & Partners, Dongtan presented itself with great flourish as 'one of the first green cities in the world.'[6] The project ground to a halt when its political face, Shanghai municipal party secretary Chen Liangyu started serving an eighteen-year prison term for fraud involving social benefits. Other Chinese eco-cities followed a similar pattern: grand announcements in the international media, followed by zero results. Specialists worldwide are still looking forward to the first real Chinese eco-city, because this could serve as an example to the frenzied building China will continue to pursue in coming years.

Driving through Guiyang, you see signs everywhere exhorting people to 'build a sustainable city together.' Garbage bins for separate waste collection stand on every street corner, but a superficial examination shows they are not terribly effective. On the walls of Guiyang City Hall sustainability tips admonish employees, for instance next to the light switch. 'Saving energy is using your finger.' Cartoons advocating water conservation surround the forest of potted plants in the corridor.

Wen Zhongyuan, head of the Guiyang municipal department of international communication, uses the stairs instead of the elevator when he goes to lunch. 'As a civil servant I have to show the right example,' he says cheerfully. Wen is a short, slim man with a generous smile and a touch of nervousness about him. He wears a dark grey suit with a blue-striped tie, and sits behind a large table full of bowls of fruit. A large showcase in the corner of the room exhibits gifts from delegations worldwide that visited the city. The environmental awareness campaign first of all aims at convincing policy makers and administrators on the need for sustainable development, says Wen. 'Over the last year we invited several famous Chinese academics to present lectures to government and university officials on the importance of sustainability and environmental measures.'

'You're stuck in traffic jams half the time, and the other half you are looking for a parking space.'

The ecological message came as a surprise to many civil servants. 'The first time they heard it they were completely shocked,' laughs Wen. 'You have to realise that Guiyang has been developing in the traditional manner since 1978. For thirty years we unthinkingly sacrificed nature for economic growth.' The annual appraisals in City Hall reflect the change in thinking. 'Like everyone else I have to report how I contributed in my work to sustainable development in the city. Nowadays, this is what they judge you on.'

As head of international communications, Wen was closely involved with the most prestigious event that the city has organized with respect to its new status as eco-city: a large international Eco-Forum in August 2009. He starts to read from a five-page retrospective. According to the official assessment, the Eco-Forum provided 'a good basis' for the development of Guiyang, because the topic 'was good' and the level 'was high', facts acknowledged by 'national environmental specialists, important academics, Chinese pop stars, the chairman of international climate panel IPCC, high-ranking UN functionaries and, of course, Tony Blair.'

To bolster the status of the Eco-Forum, the city flew in the former British Prime Minister for a keynote speech on climate change and sustainability. The annals do not reveal what went through Blair's mind as he drove into a large Chinese city that at first glance seems the opposite from an eco-city. He flatteringly restricted his lecture to platitudes, singling out 'intelligent use of energy, intelligent building, city planning, and transport systems' as 'areas in which the government can play an important role,' and added careful praise: 'I believe that in its development as eco-city, Guiyang lies ahead compared to other Chinese cities.'

Wen puts the report aside and says that he looks back at the Eco-Forum with great satisfaction, not least because of the honour of meeting Blair and his wife. He remembers how Cherie Blair expressed her admiration for economic developments in Guiyang and the new, modern ring road. As head of the department of international communication, he believes Blair's support for Guiyang's sustainability agenda is crucial. 'He being here was invaluable, he is an influential politician whose ideas fit the concept of sustainable development.'

In July 2010 Guiyang organised the second international Eco-Forum, and again Tony Blair appeared behind the pulpit. This time he addressed the heart of the problem in his speech. 'We cannot expect counties like China and India, still with many millions living in poverty, to slow the pace of their development,' he said. 'They need to develop. We must search for ways of doing it sustainably.'[7]

Chinese cities are nothing less than emancipation machines. They absorb poor peasants and workers and transform them into city dwellers with increasing purchasing power, who can first only afford electric rice cookers, then off-the-peg clothes, then fridges and television sets, DVD players, air-conditioning, laptops, and finally even cars and holidays to France or Egypt. It is worth noting that China's East Coast cities mainly produce goods for other parts of the world, while the inland megacities are less suitably located for exports. While factories in Shanghai, Guangzhou or Shenzhen highly depend on global economic demand, factories in Chongqing, Zhengzhou or Guiyang benefit especially from growing domestic consumption.

Chinese cities are nothing less than emancipation machines.

This reality is difficult to square with one the most important goals of an eco-city, the minimisation of energy use. Mayor Zhou Yuan of Guiyang phrased the catch-22 in an interview on national radio in the spring of 2009. Developing the economy inevitably affects the environment, he pointed out, but growth achieved by 'large-scale environmental destruction' is 'not what we need'. However, Zhou argued, 'we can't give up cars or buses and go to work on foot just because the ecology and environment are affected.' That was no option either. 'We should look at this problem with a dialectic view.' Zhou explained what this meant. People would not welcome an 'ecological civilisation' divorced from economic growth. As mayor, Zhou said, he must address both unemployment and sustainable development. He could not simply 'sacrifice the environment for the growth of GDP and vice versa. I dare not say that.'[8]

The local authorities have taken dozens of measures targeting the most urgent problems: reducing pollution and improving the environment. The city council spent 30 million dollars to have all city buses run on natural gas.[9] It had the river cleaned of the worst pollutants, and established a special ecological criminal court in 2009, that so far has investigated 147 major environmental cases. During the most spectacular trial, the court condemned the property developer of Fuhai Eco Gardens to a three-year prison sentence for building villas in a nature reserve. To provide tangible form to its green ambitions, Guiyang is constructing an eye-catching project, a green buffer zone of trees

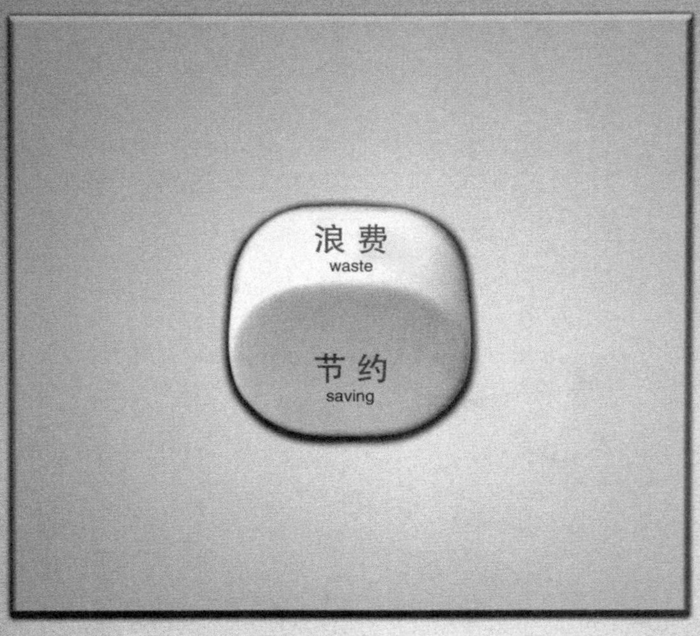

贯彻节约能源法　推进公共机构节能

节约资源　举手之劳

节约电资源，从身边做起，从我做起
共同凝聚节约的力量

中共贵阳市直属机关工作委员会　贵阳市市直机关事务管理局

surrounding the city, 88,000 hectares in size and 304 kilometres long – the equivalent of 250 New York Central Parks. Total investment: 150 million dollars.[10]

'Guiyang calls itself an eco-city,' says architect Wei Haobo. 'That is a nice political statement, but practice, unfortunately, is different.' He stands in front of a large whiteboard in Underline Office, a Guiyang architectural firm he runs with two partners. Inside, the office looks like architecture firms all over the world: young people in black glasses drawing behind computer screens, between piles of paper, scale models and design magazines scattered everywhere. Besides taking on large commercial contracts, the firm, as one of the few companies in town, also produces its own body of critical architecture, such as an open-air theatre and a community centre in a poor peasant village in Guizhou province, and a series of spacious terraced apartments that seemingly flow from the mountain into Guiyang like a river.

Wei Haobo picks up a marker and starts drawing a map on the board to support his argument. 'This is Guiyang long ago, a city with nine gates and two towers, surrounded by a river. People cultivated their own food and transported themselves on foot, that is what you could call a true eco-city.' He draws a second picture. 'Fifty years ago, Guiyang started to construct more and more factories and roads.' And a third. 'This is what the city looks like today. We are growing rapidly and are destroying all ecological elements in the process. The urban model resembles that of a Western city: roads and urban expansion emanating in all directions from a busy centre.' Wei is quiet for a moment and concludes: 'The ecological town of Guiyang has developed during the last century into a metropolis after the Western model. We are now sticking the label 'ecological' on that development, while in fact the exact opposite is happening.'

In his three drawings, Wei illustrates what is transpiring at the moment in Central China. A self-sufficient peasant society with low energy consumption and few industrial emissions has changed into an industrialised urban society with exactly the opposite characteristics. Cities in Central China are travelling the same road followed by cities in the United States and Europe in the last century. 'Look,' says the architect. 'China is building a market economy. Of course the government believes at this moment it is more important to stimulate consumer society rather than sustainable development. This used to be a city with only pedestrians. Owning a car is progress.'

Wei has only limited impact on developments, he says. 'Architects can change but a few isolated locations, not the general direction of developments. The only thing we can do is apply sustainability solutions in our own projects.' The architect proposes to meet with a good acquaintance: Liu Xiaoxing, the deputy director of a number of large sustainability projects in the city. 'She can explain to you exactly what the problem is.' An hour later, Wei parks his car in Huaxi, a neighbourhood in the south of Guiyang. 'The most ecological part of town,' he jokes. 'That just means it is underdeveloped.'
The restaurant in a large glass greenhouse has twenty tables, each with large cauldrons of the local lamb hotpot bubbling on gas cookers protruding from holes in the centre

of the table. Liu Xiaoxing is a small, powerful woman with drawn-on eyebrows. She places her purple mobile phone on the table and immediately points out the essence of the problem. 'Guiyang is a poor city.' Local government suffers from a chronic lack of funds, which forms an obstacle to necessary investments in sustainable development. This places the city in a vicious circle, she explains. 'Guiyang has an inferior basic infrastructure. That restricts economic growth, which leads to lower tax revenues, which means the city has less to spend on large infrastructural projects, and so on.'

As deputy director of the urban development company she faces the same problem, and presents an example. At the moment she is researching the possibility of separating

GUIYANG. (1995)

丢烟头处
不可回收垃圾
unrecyclable
砖瓦、果皮、剩饭、落叶等
可回收垃圾
recyclable
塑料、玻璃、金属、废纸等

GUIYANG

(2000)

the town's sewage and rain water, so that the latter can be re-used without the need for purification. The local government has hardly any money, says Liu. 'What it boils down to is that I have to look for funds myself.' That has become a little easier with Guiyang's official status of eco-city, as Beijing supports approved environmental projects with substantial sums. To complement this, Liu must raise funds from private sources. 'We first built six large water treatment plants in Guiyang. Companies and private individuals pay us a mandatory contribution for water use. In time we will sell part of our shares in those plants, and invest the proceeds in sustainable development projects.' To make Guiyang into a real eco-city a lot needs to happen, says Liu as she stirs the hotpot. 'I don't know where to start!' she exclaims. She sums up: first complete the water treatment project, and secondly, banish all factories from the city centre to downwind industrial estates. Then she would like to introduce a working recycling system for industrial waste. 'These things need to be done first. After that, we'll see.'

European and North American consumers are largely responsible for the greenhouse gasses China emits.

In international discussions about sustainability, two Chinas seem to exist. The first China is the 'factory of the world' running on 1,400 coal plants that, according to environmental organisation Greenpeace, together produce enough ash to fill an Olympic swimming pool every 2.5 seconds.[11] This China surpassed the United States as largest emitter of greenhouse gasses in 2007, and now lays claim to the title of 'largest polluter in the world.'[12] There is also a different China, the world leader in green energy investments, a country that, according to that very same Greenpeace 'builds a wind turbine every two hours,'[13] generates the most hydroelectric power in the world, is the largest producer of solar cells worldwide and is developing a promising electric car industry.[14] United Nations climate boss Yvo de Boer even predicted that this China would become 'a world leader in fighting global warming.'

Both Chinas exist. They find each other in a common goal, the development of the economy. Serious air and water pollution, a shortage of traditional energy resources and other factors that can harm economic advance must be halted. The government's intention to waste less energy must also be seen in this light, as an efficiency drive rather than a call for limits on growth.' This intention in part explains the failure of international climate negotiations in Copenhagen in 2009. Investing in alternative energy and energy efficiency? Fine! But reducing emissions? China will not commit to that for the time being. The country subtly points out that its own energy use and emissions per capita are still relatively low. It also argues that as 'factory of the world,' European and North American consumers are largely responsible for the greenhouse gasses China emits.

If Guiyang had one opportunity to live up to the label of eco-city, it was in the new neighbourhood Jinyang, an area roughly the same size as the entire existing city: 106 square kilometres. This new district has to cushion the doubling of the population expected to occur in the next twenty years. In 2008 the city administration decided to 'do anything to develop Jinyang into an ecological, digitised, new and modernised city, in order to improve sustainable development.'[15]

If you walk through the area expecting a new urban paradigm, you will be in for a disappointment. Just like most new city neighbourhoods in China, the streets are designed to accommodate enormous numbers of cars – they all have six lanes. As in new districts elsewhere, there is no busy traffic just yet; on the contrary, the area makes an empty impression, but the planners clearly have resigned themselves to the unstoppable advance of the car. Jinyang is unsuitable for pedestrians. The individual plots are too large and the streets too wide to walk from one block to the other. The reason is a financial one: according to the Chinese Land Institute, Chinese cities in 2006 earned almost 46 per cent of their income through the sale of building land.[16] Local authorities tried to increase revenue by responding to property developer's demands. These only want one thing: as large a plot of land as possible that they can develop instantly into a compound with as many towers as possible. They then construct walls around the plots, making traffic impossible for pedestrians or cyclists, ensuring that the neighbourhood focuses on motorised transport.

Jinyang has been built amidst the characteristic karst mountains, but this natural environment has largely disappeared. Developers simply levelled dozens of mountains. or split them in two to build roads and construction sites. As primary employer in the area, the Guiyang government uses several of the enormous office complexes. As most civil servants still live in the old city, while Jinyang residents work in the centre, this

leads to enormous flows of traffic twice daily. Public transport offers little respite. A monorail connecting the city with the district has yet to be built. The bus leaves every half an hour, and the journey takes almost fifty minutes. A brand new toll road shortens the trip by private car or taxi: a ride to the centre takes six minutes.

The planning museum stands in front of a roundabout with a golden statue of furiously galloping horses. Inside, Guiyang presents its ambitions. A large-scale model shows

the future district: the same endless compounds with north-south oriented housing found everywhere in China. The only green aspect is the new nature reserve with a large number of trees surrounding the city, combined with an awareness campaign. Large television screens on the outside of the museum show clips calling on passers-by to separate garbage and to conserve energy. One of the videos shows two men lighting a fire by the roadside. 'This is not civilised,' warns the pay-off line.

Dong Yun stretches himself after having napped at his desk. He stands up, switches on the light in his office, walks back to his desk and lights a cigarette, pulling an ashtray in the shape of Beijing's Olympic Bird Nest stadium toward him. Dong Yun is engineer at the Guiyang architecture and design institute, the government agency that designs almost two thirds of the buildings in the new area. He describes Jinyang as an 'enormous improvement' compared to the existing city. 'All new buildings will comply with national regulations. That means that they are 60 per cent more economical with energy than in the past. Double glazing is mandatory, as are isolating walls. Even so, 'eco-neighbourhood' Jinyang presents no radical or innovative concepts in the field of sustainable development. 'Property developers design the majority of the buildings according to their commercial plans. On the whole they do not use any new ideas, because they usually lead to higher investments. Property developers like a quick profit, that's just how it is'.

It is so cold inside the 1980s building that houses Guizhou's provincial planning institute that the officials keep their coats on while working at their desks – a common sight in the southern half of China, due to the lack of central heating. Shan Xiaogang sits down at a long oval table in the conference room. It is surrounded by a second row of chairs, at least half still wrapped in the plastic they were purchased in. As deputy director of the provincial planning department he can afford to ignore the 'no smoking' sign. He lights a cigarette, an action he will repeat many times in the next hour.

The urbanisation rate of Guizhou province is the lowest in China, Shan explains. 'Less than 30 per cent of the population live in the cities. This will change in the coming years. The city is growing. More and more people are coming in, and these people need jobs. We need to develop an industry. We can't just offer services. Manufacturing comes first.' This means Guiyang's energy needs will increase. Not only because of the development of industry, but also because of the change in lifestyle. ‘If you live in the countryside, you live like a peasant. When you move to the city, you will use more energy.’

Shan: ‘Human progress everywhere is based on industrialisation and urbanisation. No one has yet found a working alternative. We simply need industrial development. Let us stimulate that first, and we will do our best to avoid negative aspects as much as possible. There is simply no other solution.’ It is not true that China does not acknowledge the negative consequences of industrialisation, he says; on the contrary. ‘But it is a global problem. Almost all countries base their development on the American model. If China follows that lead, the world will later be using five times more energy than it is now. I fear the Earth can’t handle that.’ He extinguishes his cigarette. The ashtray is now nearly full. ‘I am happy that the Chinese government is introducing the concept of sustainability during its period of rapid growth,’ he says. ‘And not only afterward, like Europe and the United States did.’

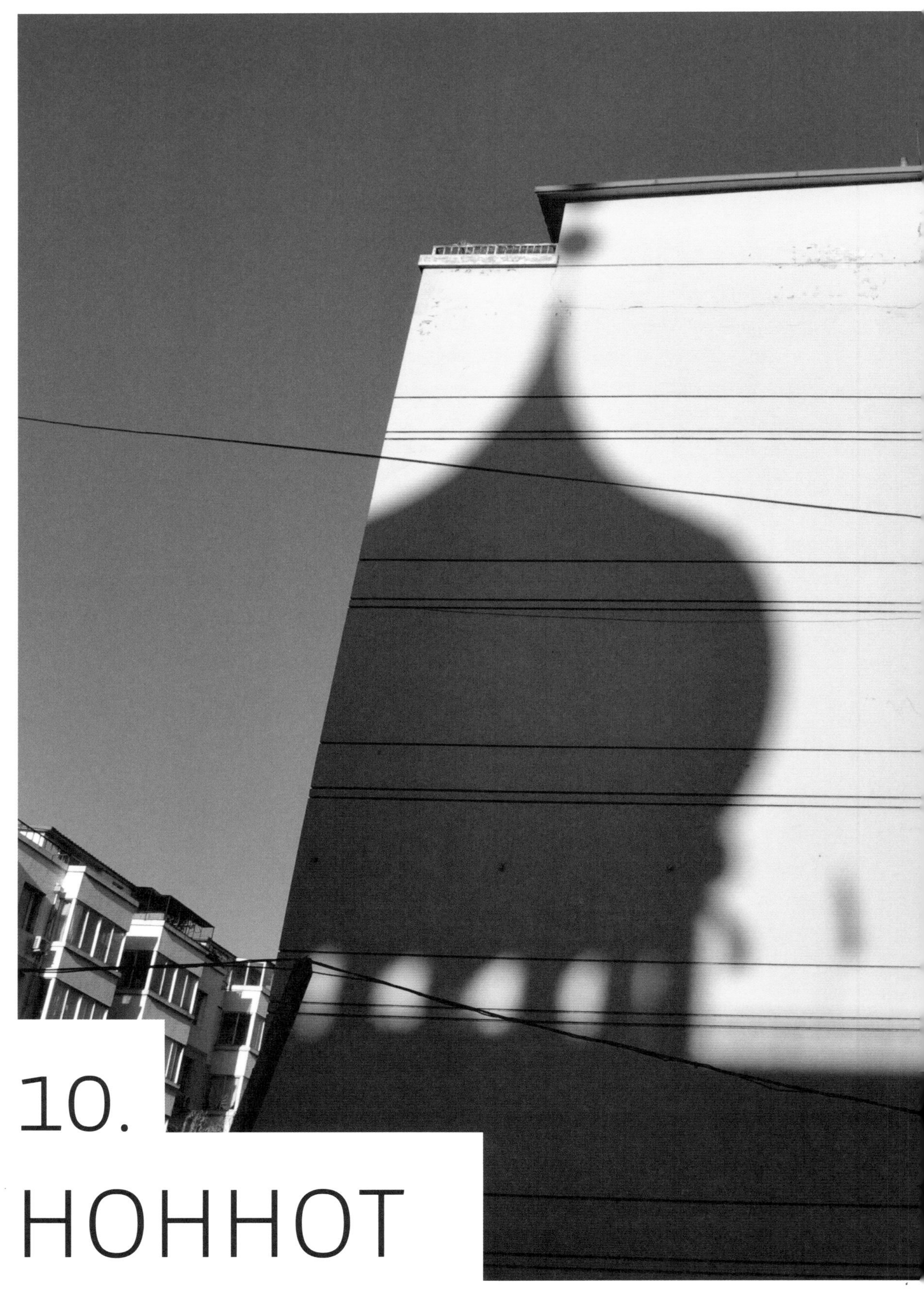

10. HOHHOT

TEN THOUSAND GALLOPING HORSES

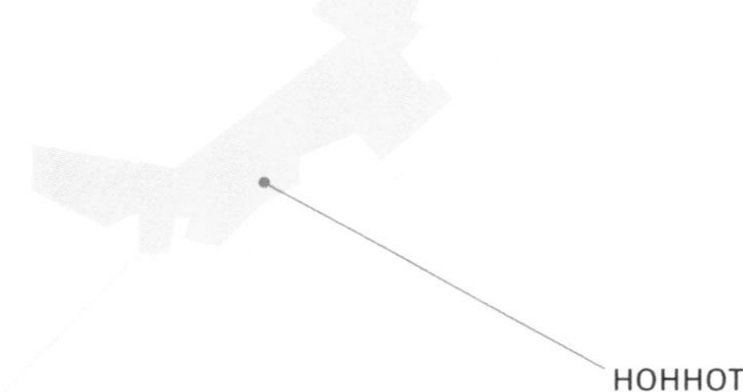

INNER MONGOLIA - NORTH KOREA
With 24 million inhabitants, the province of Inner Mongolia has roughly the same population as North Korea

A dustbin shaped like a saddle and a Mongolian nomadic tent known as a *yurt* adorn the edge of the car park. The Mongolian trident on the gate of the Park of Mongolian People's Culture is the emblem of legendary warlord Genghis Khan, onetime ruler of an empire stretching from the Pacific to the Caspian Sea. A red banner flies over the entrance to the theme park with a welcome message: 'We welcome the visitors from Beijing and Tianjin.' In an office a salesgirl hastily dons a blue dress over her jumper and jeans. She runs out and starts tearing entry tickets. Her Adidas sports shoes clash with the ethnic patterns on her dress.

On this ordinary weekday, twenty-three-year-old student Buhe is one of the few visitors to this open-air museum. He nods at the salesgirl and enters through the turnstile. According to the leaflet, the visit will teach him about the 'great history of the

Mongolian people, their legendary leader Genghis Khan, and daily life on the steppes.' The park stretches to the horizon. If there is one thing its builders have managed to achieve, it is to convey the desolation of the endless grasslands. Here, visitors witness nomadic life stripped of all its discomforts. Rather than attacking enemies from galloping Pzrewalski horses or Mongolian thoroughbreds, they shoot digital photographs from electric buggies. After viewing an exhibition on the life of the Great Khan, they can move on to a *yurt* encampment, where stone buffalo roam instead of more fearsome live specimens. The eagles they shoot at with bows and arrows are not fast-moving specks in the sky but put pictures nailed to a post. At the end of the day, the exhausted guests lay themselves down to rest in a modern *yurt* - a thirty-metre-high tent-shaped concrete building with 120 luxurious rooms, featuring bathtubs, air conditioning and flatscreen televisions.

Buhe looks around. The theme park differs tremendously from the real grasslands where he grew up. There are no grazing animals anywhere. True, there are *yurts*, but they do not resemble the traditional tents in any way. 'This gives a very basic impression,' he sighs. 'At the end of the day, it's nothing more than a funfair for tourists.'

In contrast to what its name implies, Han Chinese have formed the majority of the population of Inner Mongolia since the beginning of the twentieth century. Mongols and Han never spread evenly throughout the province. While the Han dominated the cities, Mongols roamed the steppes as nomads. Urbanisation is changing this. While increasing numbers of Chinese are starting to spend their free weekends in the fresh steppe air, more and more Mongols are exchanging the grasslands for a life in the city. The number of Mongols in the provincial capital Hohhot increased from only 14,000 in 1954 to 100,000 in 1990 and 200,000 in 2006. Their share in the urban population has also grown. In 1954 only five per cent of Hohhot's populace was Mongol. In 1990 this was ten per cent and in 2006 their proportion had grown to fourteen per cent.[1] The trek to the city is not entirely voluntary, thanks to an active policy by the Chinese authorities aimed at countering the overgrazing of the grasslands. The government has outlawed the grazing of livestock in a third of the province. As a result, more than 800,000 nomads moved to the cities after 2001.[2]

Once the shepherds and their children move to predominantly Han-Chinese Hohhot, their traditional customs and habits change irrevocably. Considering Mongolian culture is essentially agricultural, this is hardly surprising. The urban Mongol does not keep goats, sheep or camels. He does not live close to nature, has stopped sleeping in tents, and no longer uses fires of dried animal dung to heat his home. Instead of making his own traditional clothing from animal hides, he buys a pair of jeans in a shop. The new urban Mongol earns his money in factories, offices, and on construction site, or in restaurants, cafés and hotels. Streetlights, central heating and supermarkets diminish his dependence on the rhythm of seasons and the weather. Mongolian shepherds still beseech their gods for rain or sunshine. Mongolian townsmen sit bored in front of the television and zap past the daily weather forecast on CCTV-1. In the city, traditional steppe cuisine mixes with culinary traditions from other parts of China, and Mongol folk music blends with sounds from radio and television. The last thing the urban Mongol will forsake is his mother tongue, but he must renounce even that to make himself understood to his fellow townsmen. Like elsewhere in the world, emancipation of the rural population comes at the price of assimilation into urban culture. Force is not involved. The sooner the migrant adapts, the better he will do economically or socially. In order to achieve success, the former nomads willingly leave behind a substantial part of their Mongol identity on the steppes.

That same afternoon, in the middle of town, Buhe sits in a *yurt* that is nothing like the tent he grew up in, which had hinged slats covered in thick felt cloth for walls instead of reinforced concrete. This is *The Mongolian Camp*, one of the best known restaurants in Hohhot, which consists of forty concrete tents in various sizes, painted in bright pink and blue patterns. Two statues of fearsome mounted warriors guard the entrance. Outside on the car park, customers have left black Audis and Buicks beside a stretch limousine.

Buhe was born in 1986 in Alashan, a county in the sparsely populated west of Inner Mongolia. His parents, nomadic shepherds, moved their tents twice a year: once at the beginning of summer, and once at the beginning of winter. 'We lived like nomads. We followed the rain to the place with the best grass.' He remembers especially the isolation. 'I had few friends, because everyone lived far apart.' He spent most of his time with his elder brother. Several times a week, tradesmen came by selling daily necessities from baskets on their backs. 'We made all our clothes ourselves.' Buhe remembers the feeling of security and sense of community. 'We never locked our *yurt*. If we weren't at home, passersby could just pop in to get some water. Nothing was ever stolen.' He did not live on the steppes for long. His parents saw the importance of a good education. When Buhe was six years old, they sent him to live with his grandmother, a school headmaster in a small town. He was taught in Mongolian. 'I hardly spoke any Chinese until I was twelve.' He spent his holidays with his parents in the countryside. Every year in January, the family celebrated the Birthday of the Fire God, the most important Mongolian nomadic festival.

The sooner the migrant adapts, the better he will do economically or socially.

Because Buhe was a good student, he moved to Hohhot when he was eighteen to study English at the Minority University. By that time his parents, too, had abandoned most of their nomadic existence. Like many other Mongolian families, they built a house. 'Hardly anybody lives in a *yurt* nowadays,' laughs Buhe. 'Most families have sold their goats and sheep, because there is not enough grass to feed them.' His parents still keep cattle: 300 goats, thirty sheep and a few camels. These are fairly low maintenance. 'Those animals just walk to the land in the morning, they know the way. You just have to drive past a couple of times a day to make sure everything is going well.'

Buhe cannot imagine doing this himself. In the twenty-first century, shepherding is not a profession with a future. Most of all he would like to be an English-Chinese interpreter. 'I realise that will be difficult. I did not start learning English until I went to university. And Chinese is not my native language.' He is witnessing the slow decline of Mongolian culture. In Hohhot most parents prefer to send their children to schools with Chinese as the language of instruction, because 'the level of education is higher

上海
总代
批

there.' Command of the Chinese language is an absolute prerequisite for landing a good job. 'Mongol children growing up in the city often barely speak Mongolian. I notice it in myself, too. When I speak Mongolian with friends, we increasingly use Chinese expressions.' The restaurant's waitresses enter, wearing pink versions of the dress worn by the ticket seller at the theme park. They serve the food: a leg of lamb, yoghurt, bread, and bowls of vegetables. 'We hardly ever ate vegetables out on the steppe,' says Buhe. 'Perhaps once a month. Real Mongols only eat meat.'

New city dwellers such as Buhe may have removed their Mongolian costumes, but their growing presence is having an effect on the city. Even though the migrants feel they are losing their Mongol identities, the city is undergoing a partial 'Mongolisation.' The increasing presence of Mongols has changed Hohhot in numerous ways, in the first place in the increased diversity of people in the street. Judging by physique and other characteristics, most townsmen can easily distinguish Mongols from Han Chinese. The archetypical Mongol is larger, stronger and more muscular than the average Han. Mongolian men usually wear their hair long and wild, while women frequently display traditional jewellery. Mongolian names such as Bataar, Khongordzol or Chuluur are clearly distinct from Chinese ones. Most Mongols have no family names. Buhe is just Buhe, without a surname. Sometimes references can be more subtle. Having traded horses for motorcycles, city Mongols saddle their bikes with traditional cloths. The same goes for Mongolian taxi drivers, who decorate their vehicles with colourful drapes and images of Genghis Khan. More Mongolian can be heard in the street than several decades ago. 'When I arrived in Hohhot in 1978,' remembers professor Sodbilig of the Mongolian Institute, 'no one spoke Mongolian. If you did, all the children looked up in alarm, the way they do nowadays when they see a Westerner.' Today, Hohhot street signs are bilingual. Urban Mongols have their own newspapers such as *Inner Mongolia Daily*, their own television stations like Inner Mongolia TV and a Minority University of their own, where both Chinese and Mongolian are languages of instruction. In the weekends, dozens of unruly Mongolian teenagers frequent Nai Re ('friend' in Mongolian), a music venue where pounding guitar rock accompanies traditional Mongolian throat singing. There are purely Mongol neighbourhoods in the city. Ethnic riots are rare, although in May 2011 non-violent demonstrations erupted in several cities in Inner Mongolia after a Han truck driver killed a Mongolian farmer protesting against mining activities on the grasslands. According to Buhe, fights between Han Chinese and Mongols occasionally break out on the university campus, usually when excessive consumption of alcohol is involved. Mixed marriages are no exception, says Buhe. Hohhot is not the only metropolis in Central and Western China with intertwining cultures. As a rule of thumb, Chinese cities become more diverse going west. Guiyang attracts new inhabitants from Guizhou province, where a third of the population are members of minority groups such as the Miao or the Dong. Around 40 per cent of the population in the countryside around Kunming consists of Yi or Bai. The largest ethnic groups live in the far west of China, where Han Chinese are in a minority. In Xinjiang more than half the population are Uighur, Kazakh, Hui or Kirgiz, and nine out of ten inhabitants of Tibet are ethnically Tibetan.

Chi Bulag, the Fifth Incarnation of the Living Buddha of the Morui Temple, bursts out laughing. He leans back and straightens his lumberjack shirt. 'I am one of the few Mongols who still lives as a nomad. But I have swapped my horse for an airplane.' He has filled his small Hohhot studio to the brim with musical instruments and pictures of heads of state and other celebrities shaking his hand. Besides being an incarnation of the Buddha, he is one of the most famous Inner Mongolian musicians. He travels all over the world to give performances in concert halls with his Wild Horse ensemble. 'I have just returned from Helsinki.' His instrument is the *morin khuur*, a Mongolian fiddle with a neck ending in a horse's head.

Mongolian music has known less prosperous times. Chi Bulag, born in 1944, experienced the Cultural Revolution as a twenty-year-old. Mao's Red Guards not only destroyed the 'Old China,' but also targeted Mongolian popular culture, including the horse head fiddle. 'The government saw the instrument as a symbol of ethnic separatism. The Cultural Revolution claimed the lives of the most famous musicians of Inner Mongolia.' Chi Bulag walks over to one of his two pianos and picks up a picture. The black and white image depicts two men in traditional Mongolian robes. He takes a black felt tip pen from his desk and writes something under the photograph: '1906–1966' and '1924–1967'. Then he says: 'These are Balgan and Sandureng, my teachers'. After a short silence he places the photograph back on the piano. When he turns round, he says 'I have lived through a lot.'

In 1967 the bloody campaign to 'eradicate the enemy that sleeps at our side' commenced

PERCENTAGE OF NON-HAN CHINESE PER PROVINCE

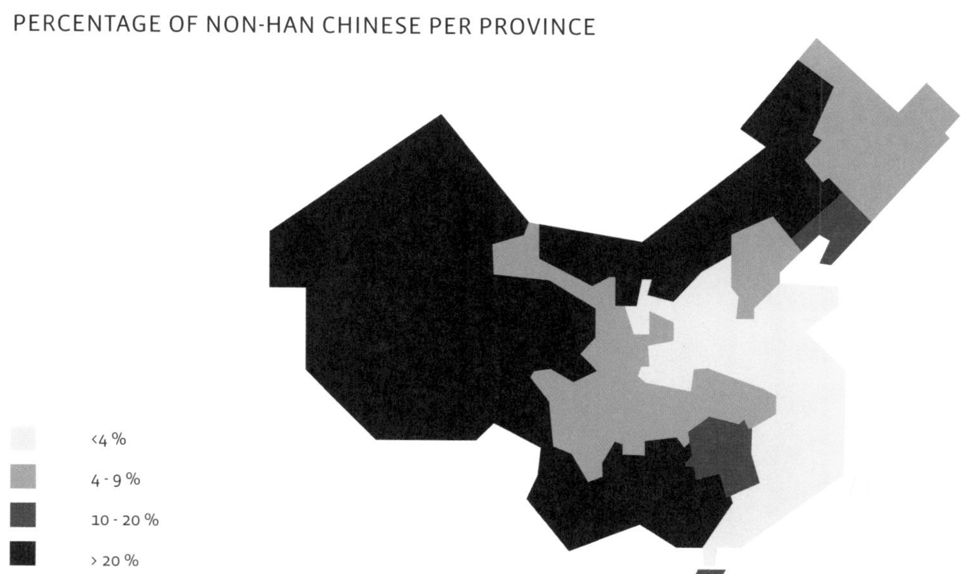

with an attack in the *People's Daily* on Ulunfu, the chairman of the provincial communist party. The paper called him 'Mongolian trash,' a separatist and a counterrevolutionary. The attacks soon spread to all Mongolian party members. Party hardliners outlawed publications in the Mongolian language, and banned pictures of Genghis Khan. In some parts of the province the authorities arrested all ethnic Mongols. In 1995 two Chinese historians presented research that described cases of branding, gouging out of eyes, and the burning alive of victims. According to official statistics, the Cultural Revolution cost 22,000 lives in Inner Mongolia, though demographic research suggests the true figure is closer to 100,000.[3]

Chi Bulag survived the Cultural Revolution. 'I played Maoist battle songs on my instrument. That saved me.' The musician saw it as his duty to keep the tradition of the *morin khuur* alive. 'You can't touch music. You have to keep on playing to pass it on to the next generation.' After Mao's death it still took several years before Hohhot musicians started to play Mongolian music in public. 'The number of musicians increased, but no one performed.' In 1986 Chi started the group 'The Wild Horse' with musician friends and students, first putting on a show in the old city museum. After that, traditional Mongolian music also gained popularity outside Inner Mongolia. Chi Bulag

started playing regularly in Japan. 'Music crosses borders,' he laughs. Inner Mongolian officials soon got the message, and used him and his Wild Horse band as a cultural accompaniment to official government delegations abroad. One of the highlights was a show in 2005 in the Golden Hall of the *Wiener Musikverein* in Austria.

In Hohhot, Mongolian music flowers as never before. The two largest universities in the city, the Shi Da and Nei Da, offer courses in the *morin khuur*. The instrument also features in modern music. The Chinese-Mongolian rock group Hanggai, for instance, travels the world playing ethno-rock on festivals. The opening ceremony of the Olympic Games marked the final step towards the acceptance of Chi Bulag in his country of birth. Hundreds of millions of spectators in and outside of China saw him leading an ensemble of eighty *morin khuur* players and forty dancers in the Bird's Nest stadium, playing his classic hit, 'Ten Thousand Galloping Horses.' The musician sees the popularity of Mongolian music as symbolic for the resurrection of an ancient culture. 'As far as I know, the *morin khuur* is the only instrument with a head. It has substance. It spreads culture.'

In the twenty-first century, shepherding is not a profession with a future.

The Hohhot tourist industry skilfully uses the Mongolian minority to satisfy the hunger for authenticity of the expanding Chinese middle class. It reduces Mongolian culture to easily digestible chunks of music, costumes, food, and excuses for excessively imbibing alcohol. Researcher Donald Sutton of the Carnegie Mellon University writes that 'minorities such as the Yi, the Miao and the Qiang are presented today to Han tourists as their younger brothers and sisters, less developed than themselves, as a nostalgic memory to the simple, picturesque country life that has disappeared in the large cities long ago.' While the real Mongolian steppe culture is slowly vanishing, it is at the same time becoming a symbol of authenticity to a growing group of Han tourists. Examples are all over the place in Hohhot: the Park of Mongolian People's Culture, the concrete *yurts* in the Mongolian Camp restaurant, and a multitude of tourist agencies offering themed trips to the 'authentic steppes.' The process is reminiscent of Kunming's revamping of Old Civilisation Street and the rejuvenation of the Xintiandi area in Shanghai, where developers constructed a bogus 'historical' reality while knocking down authentic ancient buildings. One of the driving forces behind this development is the Hohhot local authorities, who are fiercely competing for investors and desperately want to stress their city's 'unique selling points.' Other Chinese megacities do the same. Guiyang uses its green hills in its eco-city campaign, Changsha prides itself on its qualities as *Entertainment City*, Chengdu presents itself as the city of good living, and Wuhan as a business capital. When asking 'what makes our city different from all others,' Hohhot city officials apparently only could come up with one answer: Mongols. Together with local university professors, they have constructed an invented tradition of Hohhot 'steppe culture,' which ties Mongolian nomadic existence to positive urban attributes such as clean air, a green, sustainable city and the local milk industry. Hohhot uses its Mongolian background to present itself as a multi-cultural metropolis. By stressing the peaceful coexistence of different population groups, politicians hope their city will mirror famous international melting pots such as New York, London or Dubai. As an anonymous official expressed it: 'The more ethnic it is, the more cosmopolitan it is.' [4]

On the tenth floor of an office tower, four young architects are working on the details of a petrol station. The canopy consists of domes closely resembling nomadic tents. This agency belongs to ethno-architect Bayan Chagang. He designs bridges, monuments, buildings – anything as long as it has an ethnic touch. 'I want to give this city back her soul. Like everywhere else in China, foreign architecture has taken over this place in the last thirty years. That is why all cities look the same.' On first sight, China's metropolises indeed suspiciously resemble each other. This is the result of thirty years of radical communist policies of conformity, followed by three decades of aggressive state capitalism. After the 'Soviet-urbanism' of the 1950s and 1960s, further standardisation of Chinese cities followed from 1978. In the whole country, hastily constructed

Making a comeback: Genghis Khan

Chi Bulag's teachers: Balgan and Sandureng

(2000)

generic towers designed by a small group of architects replaced characteristic low-rise. Urban planners, architects and government officials looked to the same examples for inspiration: Hong Kong and Singapore, two successful metropolises with a similar cultural background.

According to Bayan, ethnic groups in China have retained a measure of authenticity lost by the Chinese in general. Indeed, 'most Chinese property developers are only interested in money. They don't care what a building looks like, providing it is finished swiftly. They steal each other's designs. But when you eat hamburgers all the time, life soon gets boring.' To be sure, he does not reject modern architecture; on the contrary.

Bayan believes China should take Japan as an example. 'After thirty years of hard work, the Japanese have developed a modern architectural language of their own. The Chinese have not accomplished this, despite having worked hard for thirty years as well.' Once the city government decided to present Hohhot as the capital of steppe culture, it supported a radical plan by Bayan. As part of the celebration of the sixtieth birthday of the province of Inner Mongolia, the government asked him to completely redesign Hohhot's Genghis Khan Boulevard. They also consulted him on a new, and more ethnic, face for Hohhot's inner-city Main Street. Bayan Chagang emphasises that his designs represent more than just Mongolian culture. 'You can see all ethnic groups

(2005)

HOHHOT

(2010)

reflected in the city: the Han, Manchu, Hui, Tibetans and Mongols.'

Han Zhiran, the provincial party secretary of Inner Mongolia, promised that the renovated Main Street would become an important, distinctive sight. 'As soon as outsiders see this street, they will immediately recognise it as Hohhot.'[5] Measured by that yardstick, he can be satisfied with the result. Along a length of one-and-a-half kilometres, all the residential buildings, shopping centres, hotels and offices bear the mark of ethnification. On the street level, new blue faux-façades with yellow decorations stand a metre from the original building exteriors. The windows now have gold-coloured frames. Traditional ornamentation covers the house fronts, ending under the roof in blue cornices. Larger and smaller concrete painted *yurts* stand on the rooftops. In the Muslim part of town, minarets and golden domes protrude above the buildings. Here, Islamic arches cover the fake facades.

'I still live as a nomad. But I have swapped my horse for an airplane.'

Hohhot's architecture of identity is strikingly unambiguous. *Yurts*, saddles and minarets, no one can misinterpret the symbols and signs. The plaster ornaments, pastel colours and domes scream at passers-by that they are walking around in a multicultural city. This form of architecture is not unique to Hohhot. Irish pubs worldwide hide concrete buildings with mock exteriors and interior panelling in an attempt to evoke the Dublin Temple Bar District in the middle of Madrid, Denver or Shanghai.

Not all Mongols are happy about the changes. Researcher Li Narangoa of the Australian National University, herself of Inner Mongolian origins, quotes local residents describing the Main Street face-lift as 'putting clothes and hats on the old concrete buildings.'[6] She typifies developments in her hometown as the 'commercialisation of a tamed ethnicity.' In a long and well-documented essay, she argues that the emphasis on minorities in Hohhot does not stem from 'any desire to promote Mongol culture and ethnicity.' She points out this 'does not necessarily mean respecting the intrinsic value of the cultural heritage,' but instead boils down to 'adapting or moulding that culture and heritage for commercial and/or nationalistic purposes.' Narangoa belies that the promotion of Mongolian culture will continue only for as long as 'leaders believe in its commercial value and see that value compatible with political and market goals.'

Urbanisation and globalisation everywhere lead to a regression of rural culture and the mixture of different ethnic groups. Like Narangoa, nationalists and anti-globalists around the world criticise the loss of the national or local identity, usually by the time it is too late and the process has largely been completed. Migrant cultures often become reduced to a manageable number of reference points: a few holidays, an ethnic cuisine, several surviving words and a single building or work of art. Usually these elements blend after a lengthy process of selection with the existing culture. Alienating about this process in Hohhot is that the government has magnified a number of elements from Mongolian popular culture and as part of a large-scale promotional campaign. It has transformed a city with a predominantly Han Chinese population into a Mongolian theme park. The huge new Provincial Museum honours the steppes with a roof of artificial grass and blue ceilings representing the skies. The new sports stadium has a Mongolian entrance. West of that begins the new Genghis Khan Boulevard, with modern 'ethnified' buildings designed by Bayan Changang. The street ends on a large symmetrical square, home to a statue of the Great Leader himself, riding into battle on horseback. In front of the statue of Genghis Khan six huge cow horns form a guard of honour. Statuettes of grazing sheep populate the freshly mowed grass surrounding the square.

Buhe sits on a stone saddle next to the memorial to his notorious ancestor. He quite likes the city's extreme makeover. 'Hohhot used to be a Chinese city like all others. Now you can see that it's Mongolian.' The boulevard with the Genghis Kahn statue makes him proud. Buhe's transformation from shepherd's son into townsman is now complete. He has recently applied for a job as English teacher at the Minority University. Sometimes he misses life on the grasslands, as do his brother and parents. But they have found a solution. 'In the autumn we went on holiday with three families,' he says. 'We took the old *yurt* out of storage and all of us spent a week on the steppe.'

11. CHENGDU

(1950)

ZAHA GOES EXTRA LARGE

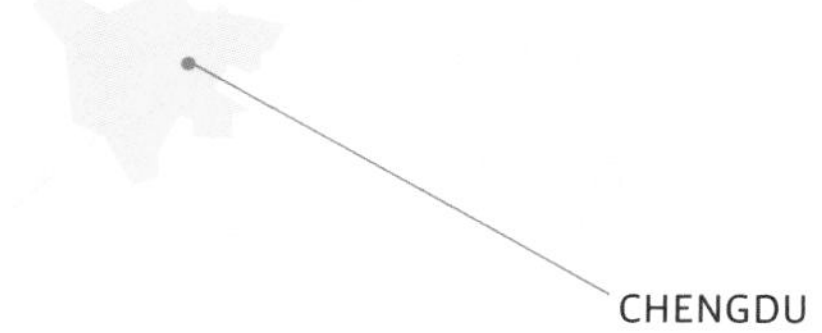

SICHUAN - GERMANY
With 82 million inhabitants, Sichuan province has roughly the same population as Germany

From his front garden Luo Fahui points a remote control at the automatic gate to let the dog in. Even though it is already four in the afternoon, the artist is still dressed in thick winter pyjamas and blue slippers. Luo is a short man with close-cropped hair, big eyes and a friendly face. He appears utterly relaxed. He walks through the large garage to his studio, a high-ceilinged space overlooked by two glazed statues of boys in underwear pierced by arrows in their chests. Dozens of monochrome paintings fill the room, displaying an abundance of faceless naked bodies.

San Sheng Xian, or freely translated, 'Three Saints Village,' is located in the countryside just outside Chengdu, the capital of Sichuan province. Every weekend hundreds of families from the city visit the famous village flower market. Tea houses and restaurants scattered among the vast bulb fields and ponds have in recent years been joined by studios and homes for artists. The most prominent artists live in The New Blue Roof, an artists' colony identifiable from the country road by a large building containing an art gallery. An arrow on a wooden notice board points at a paved path leading to The Artist Village which, contrary to its name, consists of a dozen modern villas surrounding a central lawn. A parked Mercedes and an Audi also hint at the inhabitants' prosperity.

Luo Fahui owns a Range Rover. As a Chinese artist he has reached the pinnacle of success. Art galleries from Hong Kong to Amsterdam display his paintings, and collectors pay tens of thousands of dollars for his work. Only three months ago he presented a solo exhibition in San Francisco. It was a smash hit. 'One visitor was so touched by one of my paintings that she started to cry,' says Luo. At the moment he is working on a new series of paintings. On a table in his studio lie his sources of inspiration: an American edition of *Penthouse*, the booklet *Early Erotic Pictures* by Taschen Publishers, and a photograph of a Chinese tour group. Trance music CDs are strewn all over the place. 'I like listening to Tiësto and Armin van Buuren,' he says. 'I buy most of these CDs in Hong Kong, because you can't get everything here.' The large studio windows provide a view of the fields. In the distance a farmer is building a wood fire. 'I hope they won't end up building all over that piece of land,' sighs Luo. 'The view is fantastic.'

How Luo rose from origins as an impoverished painter to international artistic stardom illustrates the growing status of modern art in China. His story also shows how, after years of neglect, Chinese cities suddenly started to deploy their artists to attain the coveted image of a creative and innovative city.

China only has a very recent history of liberty in the arts. This emancipation process runs parallel to the political and economic developments of the last thirty years. Luo was born in Chongqing in 1961 and grew up during the Cultural Revolution, in which Mao incited his subjects to destroy anything and anyone related to 'the Old China.' And successfully so: Red Guards tore down temples, closed down universities and banished intellectuals to the countryside. In justification Mao claimed that bourgeois elements had infiltrated the highest echelons of government to surreptitiously reintroduce capitalism. One of the hundreds of thousands of prisoners was later party leader Deng Xiaoping. Art served politics. According to official army guidelines the goal of art was to 'provide content to the struggle of the revolutionary people and eliminate the bourgeoisie.'[1] This was put into practice through socialist revolutionary operas such as '*The Red Lantern*' and '*The Red Women Brigade*', and thousands of posters glorifying the Great Helmsman himself. Luo learnt to draw with charcoal on walls. 'Propaganda pictures, of course, we did not dare to make anything else.'

When Chinese universities opened again in 1979, art education had to start practically from scratch. Luo enlisted as a seventeen-year-old in the preparatory training course of the Sichuan Academy for Fine Arts in Chongqing. 'It was great. I suddenly met students from all over the country. You could feel that the world was changing.' Luo remembers how his university bought an international encyclopaedia of art history, and exhibited it as a relic in a glass showcase in the library. 'Every morning a security officer would open the case and turn another page of the encyclopaedia.' Fascinated, Luo and his fellow students went there every day to sketch copies of the pictures. The arrival of the encyclopaedia marked a watershed in education. 'Until then we only studied Russian artists. Now we also got to know European artists: the French Impressionists, the German Expressionists.'

'Propaganda pictures, of course, we did not dare to make anything else.'

As the planned economy slowly gave way to a guided market economy, homogenous communist art mixed with outside influences. Western rock music found its way on to university campuses, and students traded the grey Maoist uniforms for the jeans, dresses and sunglasses in vogue in Hong Kong and Taiwan. Young intellectuals eagerly immersed themselves in Western literature, philosophy and art through books and magazines. Especially surrealism and pop art gained popularity. The new ideas spread from Hong Kong first to southern China, and then to the rest of the country.

After graduating, Luo left for Chengdu, where he rented a space barely ten square metres in size to serve both as home and studio. He remembers the 1980s as a thriving period for artists in the whole of China. 'We were poor as hell, but life was cheap. It was the best time of my life.' In Chengdu, the Sichuan Group started to make a name for itself. One of its members was painter Zhang Xiaogang, who at the moment is taking the world by storm as 'China's hottest artist.' Many of Zhang's works from those days show signs of the renewed interest in European artists such as Van Gogh, Millet or Gauguin. Luo did not belong to the Sichuan group, he says. 'I have always worked alone.' Regardless of political relaxation, artists still faced a different problem: there were no art galleries. 'We could only show our work to one another.' A friend posted his work on the notice board of the park where he worked as a janitor. 'One day everything had disappeared. Someone must have taken it.' Other Chengdu artists presented similar open-air exhibitions. They were following the example of the Beijing Stars group, who as early as 1979 had hung their work in a small park next to the National Art Museum. The Pekinese artists were ahead of times in other ways, too. In February 1989 they succeeded in exhibiting their work within the walls of the National Art Museum in the legendary *No U-Turn* exhibition, a title indicating that, as far as they were concerned, the changes in the new China were irreversible. The mega-exhibition displayed more than 300 works by 186 young artists and tested the limits of the permissible. 'A young man was throwing condoms to a group of people gathered around him; a guy in red was washing his feet in a basin plastered with images of Ronald Reagan; a long-haired man was selling fresh shrimps to a crowd of customers. Strange things were scattered around: lumps of gnarled plastic resembling human intestines; rotting surgical gloves preserved under glass; a poster announcing that a man's death sentence had been carried out was plastered on a wall of photographs.'[2] As a piece of performance art, Xiao Lu fired two bullets at her work 'Dialogue,' made out of two telephone booths and a mirror. With *No U-Turn* Chinese artists put themselve on the map of the international art world for the first time. *Time* Magazine wrote a review entitled 'Eggs, pistol shots and condoms.' A large section of the young Chinese intelligentsia was convinced that reforms would also lead to political changes. In the middle of April 1989, student protests started on the Square of Heavenly Peace and quickly spread to other Chinese cities, including Shanghai, Guangzhou and Chengdu. Artists and art students played an important role in the demonstrations, for example by building the legendary 'Goddess of Democracy' in Beijing, a white, ten-metre-high statue of a torch-bearing woman. How the protests ended is well-known. In June 1989 Deng Xiaoping deployed the army against the students to crush the rebellion in the capital. Fewer people realise that students and

RANGE ROVER
川A·61L78
EXHIBITION

security services also clashed violently in Chengdu. According to eyewitness estimates, between thirty and three hundred people were killed in the city after June 4.[3]

As for many other artists, 1989 turned Lao Fahui's artistic career upside down. Even after twenty years, he does not like to talk about the period. He drops the remark that he had to 'leave Chengdu for a bit.' He left for the southern boomtown of Shenzhen. In 1990 he moved to Beijing, where he witnessed security services still harassing students. 'They arrested them and sent them to building sites to work in construction.'

The '6/4 incident' *(liu si shijian)*, as the quelling of the of the insurrection on 4 June 1989 is known in China, forms a turning point in the rise of modern art. Artist Zhang Xiaogang speaks of a 'milestone.' 'In that year the era that Chinese artists imitated Western modern art ended (...) after 1989 Chinese art came of age.'[4] A number of artists moved to the United States or to Europe. Others forcibly withdrew from society and concentrated on developing their work, leaving the cities and settling in artist colonies in the countryside. In a period of relative isolation they produced the first paintings in a movement later known as 'cynical realism' or 'Chinese pop art' a trend that has now conquered the art world.

Two years after his forced departure, Luo returned to Chengdu. He started a job as a university lecturer and continued to paint his own work. As his art was not considered politically dangerous, he received invitations to various exhibitions. In 1996 he displayed his paintings at the first Shanghai Art Biennale. Such official exhibitions of modern art were rare in China. In 1999 art historian Francesca dal Lago wrote that 'for artists, the lack of exposure is suffocating. Neither persecuted nor openly criticized, China's avant-garde is held back – or simply ignored. And for an artist, that's far worse than public criticism.'[5]

Halfway through the Nineties a trend began that would bring change. The first diplomats and businessmen started to buy Chinese art and set up galleries. As dictated by the laws of supply and demand, prices of Chinese modern art soon started to climb steeply. The higher the amounts, the more collectors came to have a look, which again increased demand, resulting in new record prices. The March 2006 sale of Zhang Xiaogang's *Comrade No 120* for 970,000 dollars at Sotheby's first New York auction of modern Asian art caused astonishment worldwide. It was a substantial amount for a contemporary

artist. In October that year British collector Charles Saatchi spent 1.5 million dollars on a second painting by Zhang, and in November his abstract *Square of Heavenly Peace* went for a stunning 2.3 million dollars. That same month, a panorama of the Three Gorges Dam by his colleague, Liu Xiaodong, sold for 2.7 million dollars. Then, the circus seemed to be unstoppable, topping with the sale of Yue Minjun's *Execution*, in which four laughing prisoners await shooting by an equally exuberant firing squad. Hidden for years, the work appeared at a London auction in 2007, where an anonymous collector bought it for 4.2 million euros. It demonstrated that Chinese artists had joined the ranks of internationally highly paid artists. The American magazine *Portfolio* christened the craze. It contemptuously spoke of the 'Ka-Ching Dynasty.'
Famous British art critic Waldemar Januszczak expressed his disbelief in the *Sunday Times:* 'The situation is at its silliest at the contemporary end of the market, where a crop of repetitive Chinese painters trained at communist art schools to do the same thing over and over again have suddenly become the tigers of the auction rooms. In recent months, Zhang Xiaogang, churning out a seemingly endless procession of blank Chinese faces, has outsold Damien Hirst and Jeff Koons.'[6] The works of the new generation of Chinese artists certainly contain a repetitive element. But such acrid commentaries especially underline the fact that international art critics had failed to foresee the development.

International success also provoked changes within China. With their popularity now expressed in dollars and euros, local city authorities suddenly started to appreciate the potential of the artists they had ignored for years.
In 2005 Luo Fahui worked in what was then the accommodation of The Blue Roof, which was a world apart from the present villa neighbourhood. The artists' colony lay on the other side of Chengdu, under the flight path of the international airport, and consisted of a number of empty shacks and typical blue-roofed factories. Counting more than fifty artists, it had quickly become the most important art district in Central China. Local city government hardly paid it any attention. 'They weren't interested. They had never heard of us.' Curators and art traders from Europe were now foraging through China seeking interesting artists. They also ended up in Chengdu. In 2004 Luo displayed his work in the Irish Museum of Modern Art, in Dublin, which proudly

announced the exhibition *Dreaming of the Dragon's Nation* as 'the largest exhibition of Chinese art ever shown in Ireland.' In 2005 a curator from the French city of Montpellier arrived at The Blue Roof to invite Luo and four others to the Montpellier Biennale, 'the first large-scale event outside China exclusively dedicated to contemporary Chinese art.' When the artists returned from France following the exhibition, they found to their surprise an official delegation from one of the city districts expecting them. The officials invited the artists to enter the awaiting vehicles, and drove them to the countryside east of town. Upon arrival, the delegates revealed their ambitions. 'They told us this was to be the future cultural district of Chengdu,' says Luo. In a couple of years a new museum for modern art was to arise between the bulb fields, as well as numerous galleries and other cultural facilities. The officials made Luo and his colleagues an attractive proposal: because they belonged to the twelve most famous artists of Chengdu, they would each receive a piece of land in the new area, on which they were free to build a studio as they saw fit. 'It was a clever way of keeping us in the city,' laughs Luo. 'Many artists were thinking about moving to Beijing, where it was much easier to find an appropriate studio at the time.'

'Zhang Xiaogang has outsold Damien Hirst and Jeff Koons!'

The international attention for Chinese art arrived at a time when cities across the world had started to push the concept of the 'creative city.' In 2002 the American sociology professor Richard Florida published *The Rise of the Creative Class*, in which he calculated the economic value of creativity. In the book, translated into Chinese in 2003, Florida asserted that urban regions with high concentrations of Internet entrepreneurs, lesbians, guitarists and graphic designers also showed high economic growth. As far as he was concerned, young, hip, creative companies should take possession of old, abandoned industrial sites and harbour areas sooner rather than later. Previously these ideas had only proliferated in obscure squatter and artist subcultures. Florida made them mainstream at a stroke.

Chinese city governments fully took part in the international mania to present cities as innovative and creative. After years of threats with closure, Beijing authorities suddenly revitalised the famous 798 art district. The former arms factories of East German design, where dozens of artists had lived and worked for years, underwent a metamorphosis. The authorities had the factory sheds neatly plastered, the roads paved and provided with street lights, and placed Chinese and English directional signs everywhere. Soon, increasing numbers of tourists from home and abroad visited the district to look at art and consume lattes and pizza in trendy bars and restaurants. In Shanghai, a city traditionally strongly focussed on the economy, the municipal council decided in favour of the large-scale transformation of empty factories into 'centres of the creative industry,' with offices and studios for graphic designers, Internet companies, architects and marketing agencies.

The metropolises in China's interior also went to work. Chongqing changed the Huangjueping neighbourhood around the art academy where Luo Fahui had studied in the 1980s into an art district. Along a length of more than 500 metres artists have covered all the buildings in the main street in graffiti. It is a jarring sight to see graffiti, associated internationally with subculture, has been applied here at the instigation of local authorities on a scale rarely witnessed anywhere in the world. In Xi'an, the city council bought the factory sheds of the artists' district Textile Town from a former state enterprise. More than seventy artists expressed their worries in the *Global Times*. They said they hoped the area would be maintained as 'a simple place for artists to live and work' and would not become 'as commercial and successful' as 798 in Beijing. The construction of Chengdu's Art District in Three Saints Village fits the same national trend. The policy is not always successful. As the Australian academic Michael Keane put it in a lecture in Shanghai, 'the government believes it can construct a creative class in this manner, but in many places you see the artists leave as soon as the government moves in.'

Chengdu's 2007 municipal cultural policy, part of the city's Five-Year Plan, presents towering ambitions. The cultural industry is to become Chengdu's 'new economic pillar', by organising 'cultural events, conferences and exhibitions of great global influence.' Party leaders measure the success of their policies in hard economic data. The cultural industry in Chengdu must grow by sixteen per cent annually to three billion dollars in 2010, or about 4.5 per cent of the local economy.[8]

In pursuing the coveted cultural status, the officials particularly target the 'hardware.' Like other cities in China's interior, Chengdu is literally casting a formidable cultural infrastructure in concrete. Besides a new cultural district, the city will have a new City Museum measuring 70,000 square metres in size, designed by British Sutherland Architects and dedicated to 'natural history, history, popular art and Chinese shadow play.' Chengdu also has plans to build the 'largest cultural centre in Western China,' with a museum for modern art, a conference centre, three theatres, bars, restaurants and shops, designed by star architect Zaha Hadid. The website *Archinect* announced the project under the title 'Zaha goes Extra Large in Chengdu.'[9] Such stupendous cultural buildings can be seen in all Chinese cities. The problem is the programming. Lacking theatre companies, orchestras and artists with audiences to match their size, these theatres and museums stand empty most of the time.

'In China we are not afraid of "big",' says Liu Jie. 'We have known for a few years that China must change from factory of the world to a creative superpower.' Liu is owner of A Thousand Plateaus, a small art gallery in the centre of Chengdu showing work by Chinese and foreign artists. With his black-framed glasses, sports jacket and iPhone he looks like a typical representative of the cultural scene. In the pure white gallery Liu smokes one cigarette after another of the 555 brand. 'Western cities started building their cultural infrastructures more than a hundred years ago. Chengdu has only just started, but does not want to wait a century.' Liu does foresee a problem with all the new museums and theatres the city is building. 'I don't think there are too many of them, but perhaps they are too big. If you ask me, a city needs more small-scale cultural facilities, originating from private initiatives. The most interesting experimental art projects always take place without government involvement.'

The large museums, theatres and concert halls in Chinese cities almost exclusively cater to what Liu describes as 'mainstream'. To be sure, this differs from the political propaganda of the old days. It is more varied and may express careful criticism. Liu: 'By mainstream, I mean easily accessible art with a certain element of show biz.' A typical example, says Liu, is CCTV's New Year Revue, with folk dancing, comedies, acrobatics and Chinese opera. His argument is clear: if Chengdu wants to develop the creative

sector, it must do more than merely build museums and theatres. The city has to attract and stimulate creative talent.

The Chinese authorities find themselves trapped in the constraints of totalitarian rule. They need creative people, but not so creative that they will transgress political and social boundaries. On paper, art remains subservient to politics. Chengdu's cultural report still contains the mantra that cultural policy serves Marxism/Leninism, Mao Zedong's ideas, Deng Xiaoping's theory, Jiang Zemin's Three Representations and Hu Jintao's Harmonious Society. No one has forced artists to literally toe this line for years, but it does mean their art can be censored – be it literature, film, theatre, visual arts or music. An art editor at Chengdu's largest newspaper says that she cannot print the name of Ai Weiwei, one of China's most acclaimed international artists, who contributed as an architect to Beijing's celebrated Olympic Stadium, but whose political activism has made him a pariah. The studio he built at the invitation of the Shanghainese district Jiading was torn down unexpectedly in November 2010. In April 2011 security police arrested Ai and held him in an unknown location. His arrest was part of a wave of repression lasting several months in which dozens of writers, activists, artists and scientists ended up behind bars. The Beijing party leadership decided on the crackdown against dissident voices in response to the popular uprisings in the Arab world in the spring of 2011, out of fear that China would suffer a similar fate. Ai was released in June 2011, but did not dare to discuss his detention in public.

Between Ai's political art and CCTV's mainstream art, there is a large area in which artists can more or less do as they please. Ordinary Chinese themselves demonstrate an increasing interest in art. *Cosmopolitan's* Chinese edition regularly educates its readership in the purchase of art for the walls of their home. Photography is a national hobby for young people. Besides official theatres and museums, there is a lively and growing subculture in cities such as Chengdu. Not far from the villa neighbourhood where Luo lives, young artists meet each other in small bars to smoke pot and debate vigorously until early morning. Just behind the Provincial Museum, in the trendy re-C Gallery, housed in a basement under a restaurant, young curators work at the foundations of a solid art criticism. Novice singer-songwriters perform in the Machu Picchu bar to an audience of young artists, musicians and television producers. One of the two owners turns out to be a former squatter who used to organise wild parties in the Berlin squat scene. Now he looks for new challenges in Chengdu. 'The cultural field is still young here,' he says. 'My bar lies within the city's first ring road, but twenty years ago this was all countryside.'

The figures speak for themselves. In 1980 the city centre had two million inhabitants, a number that has risen in the meantime to five million. The whole urban conurbation even counts ten million people. In recent years, Chengdu has developed into the most international city in Central China. The United States, Germany, France, South Korea, Pakistan, Thailand, Singapore and Sri Lanka have all opened consulates in the city. Compared to its size and international status, Chengdu's cultural sector is still lagging behind. Part of the cause lies in China's turbulent past and in the rigid political climate that continues to pose problems for Chinese artists. Also significant is that many new city dwellers have only recently abandoned the countryside. 'Many residents come from peasant families,' says Machu Picchu's owner. 'For now, they are not interested in culture.' The former squatter is sure things will change. 'What you see now is only just the beginning.'

The present Chengdu cultural establishment also once started out as a subculture. 'I have never had a relationship with the government,' says Tang Lei. 'They know who I am, but we hardly ever have contact. They used to stare at me and say: that is Tang Lei, who likes rock music. They saw that as underground.' Posters with works by Chinese artists decorate the walls of the Little Bar. Magazines such as *Arttime, Contemporary Artists* and *Art Market* fill the bookcase. Behind the bar is a collection of CDs from just about every Chinese rock band in existence. Twenty years ago, the neighbourhood surrounding the Little Bar was countryside as well. Today it is populated by an abundance of cafés, boutiques, coffee bars and restaurants.

On 18 January 1997, when Tang Lei opened her bar in a former hair salon, she had no intention of establishing Chengdu's cultural nerve centre. 'I just did not feel like a nine-to-five job,' she says. 'I wanted to sleep in, and smoke and drink at work.' Tang is pushing fifty, but has not lost any of her youthful enthusiasm, though she has quit smoking years ago. She sips her chrysanthemum tea. Tang has followed a route full of twists and turns in becoming one of the key figures of the Chengdu art world. During the Cultural Revolution she moved to the countryside to be educated by peasants. After that she

Cultural policy in three cities: Textile City in Xi'an (top left), subsidised graffiti in Chongqing (top right), and the City Museum in Zhengzhou (bottom).

Chinese
Dragon Tiger

worked as a postal sorter and taught herself English. That knowledge provided her with the opportunity to work for a travel agency that supported foreigners visiting Chengdu. This is how she met a German professor in *Freikunst*, who invited her to study for a year in Kassel, in Germany. 'He thought I should grasp the opportunity to go abroad.' In the meantime, Tang Lei had built up a circle of artist friends. In 1988 she married the young and not-yet-famous artist Zhang Xiaogang. While her friends in the art world were contemplating their fates after 6/4, Tang moved to Germany for two years. She visited museums in Germany, England and the Netherlands, attended concerts by Sting and U2, and worked for a summer at the prestigious *Documenta* exhibition in Kassel. Back in Chengdu, Tang gave birth to a daughter. 'I started the Little Bar when she went to kindergarten.' Her first regulars were her friends, many of whom are now China's most celebrated artists: architect Liu Jiakun, artist Zhou Chunya, performance artist Yu Ji, curator Liang Kegang. The artist Luo Fahui, too, was one of the regular visitors of 'The Living Room of Sister Tang,' as they called the bar.

'I said: you can perform here, but only if you play your own songs.'

Tang Lei played a crucial role in the emergence of the alternative rock scene in Chengdu. Halfway through the Nineties young musicians played in several Chengdu cafés, where they performed covers of songs by popular bands from Hong Kong or Taiwan. 'They approached me as well, these long-haired boys with guitars. I said: you can perform here, but only if you play your own songs.' This was not always a success. 'Oh, it could be awful!' she laughs. 'A lot of times the bar emptied as soon as the band started to play!' Stimulated by house rules that banned mainstream music and permitted only original compositions, the bar quickly evolved into one of China's most famous rock venues. Tang Lei turned herself into a producer. She was determined to promote 'Chengdu rock' throughout China. In 2009 she took nine bands on tour through the country. 'I didn't make a penny, but that didn't matter. I just wanted to do it.'

In 2007 Tang Lei opened a second Little Bar, with a large stage and professional lighting and sound. At least twice a week bands perform to an audience of around three hundred young people. Artists and musicians from all over China came to Chengdu to attend the opening, 'an unprecedented event,' in the words of art critic Liang Kegang.[10] By now, the second Little Bar is a fixed address on the tours of China's most famous rock bands. Besides shows in various Shanghai, Beijing and Guangzhou rock venues, a typical 'tour of China' consists at least of performances in the Vox in Wuhan, Freedom House in Changsha, Lao Wo in Kunming, The Nuts Club in Chongqing, Guangquan in Xi'an and Little Bar in Chengdu.

Even though Tang Lei has never been involved in official Chengdu cultural policy, the Little Bar has become an institution that cannot be ignored. Since 2009 the city government co-finances the Zebra Music Festival, a large-scale, three-day open-air festival featuring pop music, hip hop and rock. With an increasing number of cities positioning themselves as trendy and creative, such festivals are spreading like wildfire over China: from five festivals in 2007 to more than seventy in 2010. In the first two years, the Zebra Music Festival attracted tens of thousands of visitors, who travelled with tents and sleeping bags to the festival area, an hour's drive outside of town. In 2010 several foreign acts played the main stage, including Taiwanese rapper MC Hotdog, whose music is formally banned in China due to his obscene lyrics. For the programming of the festival's rock stage the organisers asked the experts from Little Bar for help, who whipped together a programme of local rock bands that played for three solid days. This is how Tang Lei suddenly became involved in a mass spectacle partially organised by the government.

'The Chengdu authorities believe that rock festivals give the city prestige,' says Tang Lei. 'As in: we have music, we have culture. But they have no idea how to organise one, which is why they end up knocking on our door. We have been doing this for fourteen years.'

12.
YINCHUAN

YINCHUAN

(1950)

YINCHUAN

STACKED BARS OF GOLD

NINGXIA - DENMARK
With 6 million inhabitants, Ningxia province has roughly the same population as Denmark

Enrique Iglesias pounds through the loudspeakers. In the front of the Toyota RAV4 sit two young women in make-up, dressed to kill. On the back seat Lieutenant Zhang emits a deep sigh. After a lavish, alcohol-soaked meal with friends in one of the best restaurants in town, they visited the new A8 nightclub, and rented a private room with luxurious sofas and a karaoke machine connected to an enormous plasma screen TV. They sang the latest Taiwanese and Hong Kong pop hits, and gorged on Cuban cigars and Scotch. Like his army chums, 27-year-old Zhang comes from a wealthy family. His parents own a thriving construction company in Yinchuan. Zhang is investing the family fortune in property. He bought his first apartment five years ago. It was on the expensive side and, according to Zhang, 'not such a good investment.' A year later he bought his second apartment, a year after that numbers three and four. He lives with his wife in one of the homes, the rest he lets to tenants. 'A lot of Chinese people leave their properties empty, but I think that is a waste of money.' Zhang estimates that up till now, he has made a virtual profit of a hundred per cent. He expects a further increase in value. 'This city is developing. More and more people need homes. That drives up the prices.' Then the driver parks the Toyota diagonally on the pavement in front of tonight's final stop: night restaurant The White House.

Yinchuan is the capital of Ningxia, China's second-smallest province. The city only started to develop in the 1950s and 1960s as a result of Mao's 'Third Front' policy, which ordered the removal of essential sectors of China's industry to the interior, safe from military attack. An important military base arose in Yinchuan, a city of then barely 20,000 inhabitants. Numerous new textile, rubber and machine factories soon offered jobs to migrants arriving from the whole of China. Nowadays the city is known as 'an oasis in the desert,' the only noteworthy place within a 500-kilometre radius in an otherwise inhospitable area. After the turn of the millennium the population jumped from 600,000 in 2003 to one million in 2010. The entire Yinchuan conurbation now has about one-and-a-half million inhabitants.

Unlike many other megacities in Central and Western China, Yinchuan does not have an awe-inspiring skyline, but the city is addressing this flaw. The new district of Jinfeng, which will more or less double the existing surface area of the city, in many ways resembles urban expansion in Zhengzhou, Chengdu or Guiyang. The new Town Hall at People's Square faces a conference centre, an exhibition hall and a five-star hotel. A hundred metres down the road lies the provincial headquarters of the communist party, shaped like a French chateau. Jinfeng is a textbook example of what architect Neville Mars dubbed the 'instant-city:' a city built 'almost overnight, without history or previous context.'[1] With districts like these, cities convert China's economic growth into broad boulevards, government buildings, gleaming offices, and especially, into endless amounts of stacked new housing.

The ten-kilometre-long Baohu Street forms the main artery of the new area. Driving by car along the entire length of the road, various stages of urban development pass by on the left and right like a film. At the western end of Baohu Street the harvest lies drying in the sun amidst shabby farms built out of mud and corrugated iron. Several hundred metres to the east, villages have been razed to the ground and transformed into piles of rubble. Slightly further still, workers have placed tall billboards with adverts for future apartments, while bulldozers are levelling the land. The middle section of Baohu Street cleaves through a landscape resembling works by the world-famous artist Christo: concrete skeletons of residential towers under construction, surrounded by scaffolding wrapped in green gauze. Following this sight are the finished compounds, the absence of any activity revealing their recent completion. At the end of the road lie the apartment complexes built two or three years ago, bearing names like Phoenix Garden, Cambridge Water Town or Baohu Bay. All are very similar to Xi'an's Holiday Garden.

At ten in the evening a ghostly atmosphere pervades Jinfeng. Most roads in the new city district are brightly lit and abandoned, interspersed only by dark islands. There are no cars on the compound car parks, no shops, and no residents in the apartments. Human life focuses on the construction sites, where work continues unabated. The sound of scraping metal and churning concrete mixers carries far. A completed twelve-storey flat protected by guard dogs offers a macabre spectacle. Lights burn behind all the windows. Since the apartments all lack curtains, it is clear that, apart from the shining light bulbs, they are all vacant. Apparently the property developer is trying to attract attention with this light show. A sign in front of the gates reads 'for sale'.

In the night restaurant The White House, Lieutenant Zhang and his friends have ordered a table full of snacks: fried chicken toes, dumplings and noodles. Soon, the discussion turns to new business plans. 'We want to open a wine bar,' says Zhang. 'With European wines and Cuban cigars.' He stresses this is not to be just another café, but an exclusive private club with a membership fee of at least 15,000 dollars per year. Zhang and his friends do not expect to make a fortune out of wine and cigars, or even out of the hefty fees. They intend to use their army contacts to attract a clientele of senior government officials and property developers, and to become mediators in the largest and most lucrative transactions closed in Yinchuan: the issuance and transfer of construction land. 'That is where the real money is,' laughs Zhang exuberantly.

The scale of China's construction business is hard to fathom. Researchers predict the country will build between twenty- and fifty-thousand skyscrapers annually in the next twenty years. The construction industry employs more than 40 million workers in China, as many as the total number of inhabitants of Argentina. The country uses half of the global production of cement and steel.[2,3] Real estate is an essential pillar of the national economy. The Swiss investment bank UBS even proclaimed property development in China to be 'the single most important sector in the entire global economy.'

Real estate and government are intimately entwined. On the one hand, city governments depend on urban expansion for their income, with on average 46 per cent of their revenues deriving from the sale of building land.[4] In some cities that figure runs as high as 60 per cent.[5] On the other hand, large state-owned enterprises in the chemical, military and transportation sectors buy up this land for residential projects that often have little connection to their core business. Because of their excellent government contacts, it is easier for state companies such as Hainan Airlines, China Telecom or the China Tobacco Group to wrangle loans from state banks than for commercial parties. This pushes prices for building land to record heights. Throughout the country, commercial property developers are lagging behind. In 2003 they still managed to put their hands on 60 per cent of the building land in a city like Beijing. In 2010 this had fallen to less than 20 per cent, leaving the rest for state-owned companies.[6] Since 2005 the rise of Chinese housing prices has been unstoppable. Some researchers report that average housing prices have tripled in five years' time.[7] The price explosion in China's interior is, if possible, even more extreme than on the East Coast. The investment boom is swiftly displaying the characteristics of a hype.

Housing madness has also struck Yinchuan. Billboards advertising new projects hang from every street corner. At the airports, in restaurants and at the hairdressers slickly designed real estate glossies cover the tables. During rush hour, promotional staff throw leaflets with new housing developments through open car windows. 'Buy a house now, a guaranteed return on your investment.' Bulk text messages reach those not stuck in traffic jams. Taxi drivers and hairdressers can tell you exactly who the city's best real estate developers are; Wanda and Vanke are brands with logos as prominent as China Mobile and KFC. Home seekers start queuing at sales centres from five-thirty in the morning for the latest discounts: free washing machines, rooms or balconies with the sale of a house – while supplies last. Anyone who possibly can attempts to gain a foothold on the property ladder. The arguments sound familiar: get in now, because it may soon

be too late - before you know it, no one will be able to afford decent properties. This fear is also fanned by popular television dramas such as *Snail House*, featuring a young couple desperately seeking a home. Despite suffering hardships such as a diet of dry rice, part-time second jobs and scrimping on bus fares, they never succeed in making their dreams come true.

Apart from the shining light bulbs, the apartments are all vacant.

Sun Jianbing pours hot water on his pot of 'eight delicacy tea,' a local blend of sugar, raisins, dried lychees, wolfberries and tea leaves. Judging by his living room, he is well off. A French clock stands by the window. A large flatscreen television hangs on the wall, between two wooden Chinese cabinets. A larger corner sofa and a chandelier complete the interior.

Sun and his wife are from Zhangning, 140 kilometres from Yinchuan. He worked for years as a chef with the Chinese Red Cross, but only started to make serious money when he set up a trade in local cheese and wolfberries that he sold to restaurants all over China. Two years ago the couple decided to move to Yinchuan, because of the lack of adequate education in the countryside for their nine-year-old son. They chose for a compound called Summer Palace in the new city district of Jinfeng, next to the highly regarded 'Number Two High School'. Sun recalls that at the time he was taken aback by the high sales price of the apartments in Yinchuan. 'We hesitated for a long time whether to do it or not. In retrospect I can say it is the best decision I have ever made. Prices have only gone up further since.'

When Sun bought a home in Summer Palace two years ago, all 500 apartments in the same street were sold out in no time. Today, almost half of them still remain empty. 'Many people bought these houses as an investment,' says Sun. 'They never come here. They don't even rent them out, because they think the profits are too meagre, little more than small change.' On the ground floor of the buildings, the developers planned a 300-metre-long shopping street. Presently only a mini-supermarket, a billiards hall and a kindergarten are to be found there, all surrounded by dark and empty concrete spaces. Sun and his wife do not mind having so few people living around them. 'In large cities people don't know their neighbours anyway', they say, 'so to us there is little difference.'

The Summer Palace sales centre displays a model of the extension of the compound, which will be built in several phases over the coming years. Estate agent Ma Xiaoli sketches the price hikes of recent years: two years ago the prices were around 400 dollars per square metre, while the new apartments sell for 750 dollars per square metre. Ma cheerfully admits that speculators have discovered Summer Palace, although she maintains it concerns 'only 20 per cent' of the homes. Ma: 'Everyone in Yinchuan who possibly can buys two or three apartments. That is better than putting your money in the bank. Interest rates are below inflation, so you actually lose money when you do that, while house prices keep increasing rapidly.'

Cai Jinhai, professor at the Chinese Academy for Social Sciences, and one of China's most important economists, raised the alarm in April 2009 in the *Financial Times*. He predicted that average house prices would halve within two years. 'I expect a collapse, followed by years of stagnation.'[8] A year later he added that 'prices in secondary and tertiary cities are increasing more dramatically than in the important cities. This is very dangerous and endangers the local banks.'[9] Former Morgan Stanley analyst Andy Xie called the Chinese housing market a 'gigantic pyramid scheme.' Xie: 'Prices are based on the expected development of value. The more money and people are sucked in, the more prices increase, and expectations are met. That convinces even more people to join the party. A bubble like that ends only when there is not enough liquidity left to feed the beast.'[10]

Unsuspicious sources are also sending out warnings. Zhang Xin, director of the renowned property developer Soho, fully acknowledges the existence of a property bubble. 'This does not mean we are leaving the market. The strategy is not to giving up or leaving, the strategy is (…) to sell as fast as possible.' Significantly, Zhang warns her own customers about the dangers of speculation. 'The buildings are not fully occupied, and people should be worried about it.'[11]

In the spring of 2010 rumours circulated on the Internet that 65 million new apartments in China were not connected to the electricity network – a good indicator of vacancy. Despite flat-out denials by China's state energy corporation, bloggers and journalists throughout the country scrambled to investigate the problem, and decided to go and count for themselves. Journalist Feng Tao of the Ningxia Radio and TV Guide researched vacancy in Yinchuan through a tested method: counting darkened windows. He believed that the percentage of homes with the lights turned off between nine and eleven in the evening would give an indication of the number of vacant houses, and thus also the scope of real estate. In his research area Feng counted 872 apartments. Lights were off in 350 cases, which would point to a vacancy rate of 40 per cent. To be completely sure he returned during the day to count curtains. 'If people live there,' he thought, 'then they would at least have curtains.' He counted 170 apartments where this was not the case, around 19 per cent. The journalist concluded that the vacancy of flats in his area was probably between 19 and 40 per cent.[12] He also sought confirmation from flat janitors, who complained they had difficulties in cashing mandatory maintenance fees, 'because they cannot find many of the home owners.'

Observers of the Chinese property market are divided into two camps: those who believe a property bubble exists, and those who do not. The latter group's arguments can be summarised as follows: considering the continuing trek from the countryside to the city, the massive demand for new houses will remain strong in the coming decades. New apartments sell rapidly, which suggests a high demand. Finally, the Chinese to a large extent dip into their savings to pay for their houses. Even if prices fall, homeowners will not have any trouble in meeting their mortgage payments. In brief, argue the sceptics, the 'mother of all bubbles' is not as bad as it seems.

These arguments do not convince the critics. The American National Bureau of Economic Research conducted a study in various Chinese cities (Chengdu, Xi'an, Wuhan and Shanghai) and demonstrated that over the last decade the growth in the number of apartments was at least as large as the increase in the number of households, which means there is no shortage of supply.[13] The apartments sell swiftly because of speculation. 'People are using real estate as an investment, as a place to store cash,' says professor Patrick Chovanec of Tsinghua University in Beijing. 'They treat it like gold.'[14]

YINCHUAN

(1995)

It is true that Chinese families are only moderately exposed to mortgage debt. They have to make a down payment of 30 per cent when purchasing a first home, and have to put as much 40 or 50 per cent on the table when buying a second or third home. According to investment bank UBS the total mortgage debt is only 33 per cent of disposable income, compared to over 90 per cent in the United States. But these figures are not as hard as they appear at first glance. Analyst Mike Shedlock explains on his blog that the true Chinese burden of debt is higher because of an extensive system of private loans. 'Almost no one has the 20 to 30 per cent down to buy a place (…) Families lend, friends lend, and they all rely on each other for cash reserves. The ties of honour and reputation are all that enforce repayment. It is a great shame if you can't repay. Face is everything.'

A small TV screen in the lift of the Yinchuan Housing Department displays an advert for homes in new compounds. In twelve years a lot has changed. Until the end of the last century the department was responsible for the distribution of houses that all belonged to the state. They appointed apartments in *danwei* to all employees of local councils, government offices, state companies and universities. There simply was no commercial housing market, until 1998 when reforms by Prime Minister Zhu Rongji made it possible for employees to buy their own homes. From 1 January 1999 the distribution of new housing was also replaced by sales, and China's commercial housing market was a fact. A few months later banks introduced a new product: the mortgage.

Director Zhang of the Housing Department sits behind a heavy desk offering a view of an areal photograph of the city. Nowadays the department has the task of guarding accessibility to the housing market – no mean feat considering the speed of urbanisation. Still, Zhang is satisfied. 'We built 40,000 new homes in Yinchuan last year, 10,000 in social housing and 30,000 for the commercial market.' Housing stock increased between 2003 and 2010 from 250,000 to 400,000 units. If anything threatens accessibility to housing, it is the rapidly increasing prices. In Yinchuan the housing market started calmly in the 1990s, says Zhang. 'We saw an annual increase of between ten and twenty per cent.' By 2007 that figure had multiplied several times. The director warns against hasty conclusions. 'You have to take into account that the quality of new housing in this city is improving nearly every day. That explains a substantial part of the rising prices.' Zhang also points out that buyers from outside the city purchase over 60 per cent of

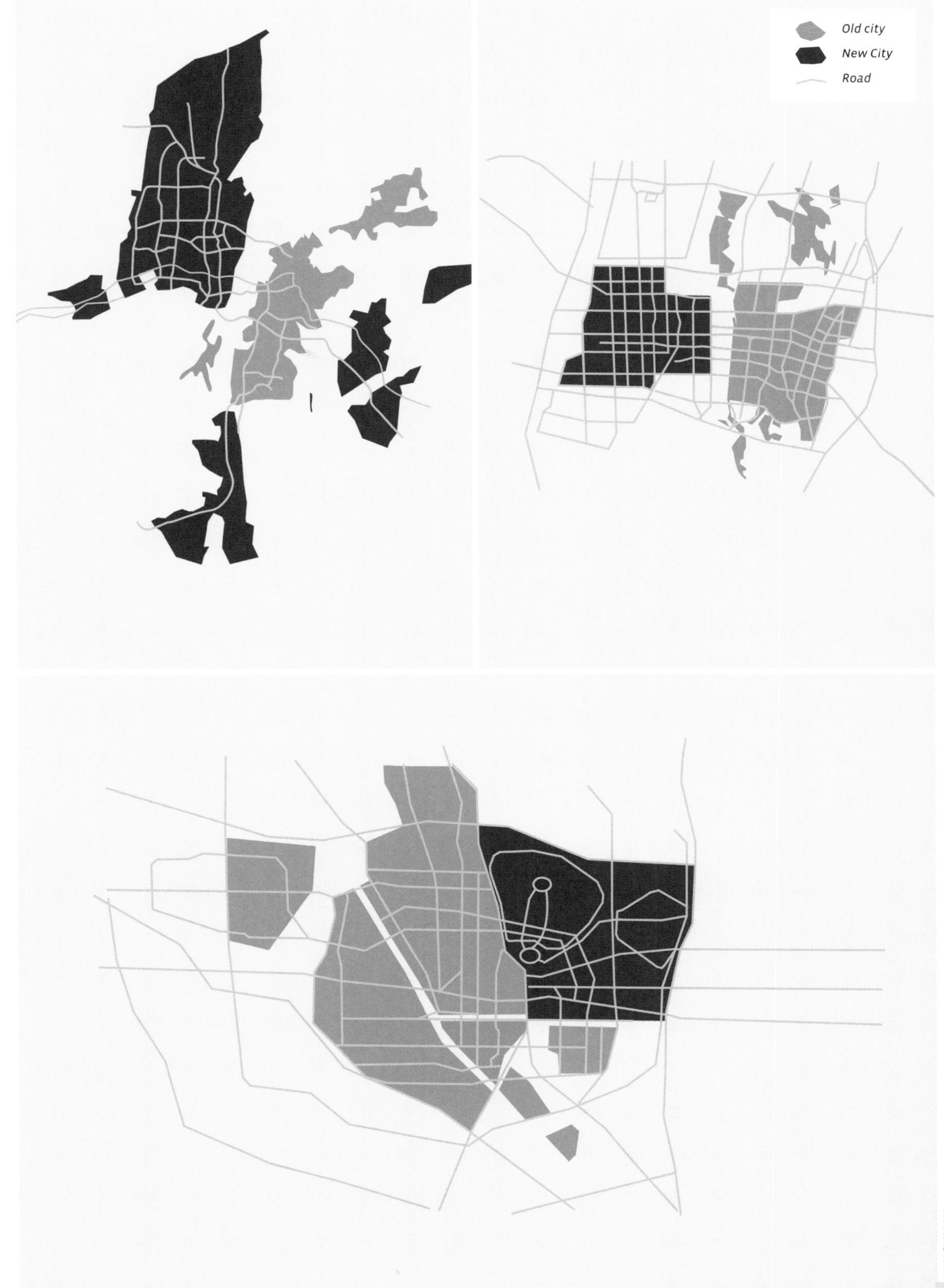

The city multiplier: Guiyang, Yinchuan, Zhengzhou and their urban expansions.

the houses in Yinchuan. 'Those are rich people who move here because we have the best schools and health care for miles around. Yinchuan is by far the most popular city in Ningxia.' He admits a tendency towards speculation exists, but dismisses the alarming reports of black window counters. 'That's just theory, people are just coming home late.' According to his agency, not more than five per cent of city dwellers own more than one apartment. Zhang sounds quite sure of himself. 'There is no bubble.'

'Everyone in Yinchuan who possibly can, buys two or three apartments. That is better than putting your money in the bank.'

'Of course there is one,' exclaims professor Deng. This professor in real estate at Ningxia University is the main authority on housing prices in the city. Deng sits in a coffee bar in the new district of Jinfeng. He wears a cotton jumper under a leather jacket and leaves a relaxed impression. The academic calmly presents proof for his assertion. At 3,000 dollars per year, the annual household income in Yinchuan is the lowest of all Chinese provincial capitals, he says. 'But housing prices are quite high, and they are growing fast.' In 2009, he says, Yinchuan was in the top three of Chinese cities showing the fastest increase in housing prices. 'After years of steady growth of about 25 per cent per year, prices in 2009 suddenly catapulted by a hundred per cent in twelve months' time.' Deng believes this makes housing prices in the city unhealthily high. He uses a personal example. Three years ago he bought a small apartment for 18,000 dollars and let it for 91 dollars per month. 'That was a healthy situation. The relationship between the value of the house and the annual rental income was one to sixteen.' In the meantime the professor's apartment has quadrupled in value, with no end in sight to the boom. 'But the rent I can get for it has hardly increased. That shows the market has overheated.'

Deng scribbles the calculations on a notepad to support his words. He sketches a market with artificially high demand and an artificially low supply, a situation that guarantees high prices. 'In most big cities outside of China, young people start their housing career by renting a house with some friends. After that they rent a home for themselves, then they buy a small house, and if they do well they might move on to a bigger house.' Chinese family relationships clash with this pattern, says Deng. Tradition demands that a young man buys a home before he asks a girl to marry him. 'If such a boy can't afford a house, the family will help out. Due to the one child policy both parents and grandparents can contribute money, keeping the fire under the housing market burning and inflating demand.'

At the same time supply remains unnecessarily low, because many of the purchased

apartments are not for sale. 'The Chinese don't have a lot of possibilities to invest their savings. They can buy stock, but prices aren't stable. They can bring their money to the bank, but interest rates are low. So they choose real estate.' Part of the housing stock is not used as a home, but as a savings account for family capital. 'These homes lose their intrinsic function as a dwelling. If that goes on for long enough, housing prices will sooner or later stop reflecting the market value of a home.' Deng estimates that in the most expensive compounds fifteen to thirty per cent of the flats serve merely as objects of speculation. 'We have done research by going door-to-door and interviewing people.' Also feeding the bubble are local governments and state companies building compounds where employees can buy flats at cost. 'Many government officials have more than one home.' The professor believes that the Chinese government is aware of the bubble, but

YINCHUAN (2010)

struggles with a dilemma. 'On the one hand prices are too high, on the other hand the real estate sector is enormously important for economic growth.'

'As soon as prices start falling, people will stop buying anything at all, and things will go from bad to worse.'

Deng is pleased that the government is taking measures, but doubts if they will be adequate. The 2010 National People's Congress forbade 78 state companies in various sectors to develop any new real estate projects. It increased the down payment for second home from 40 to 50 per cent, which immediately doubled the number of unofficial loans. Shanghai introduced the 'one family, one house policy.' The measure promptly led to 'fake divorces' in families desiring more than one home. In 2011 a number of cities experiment with a real estate tax of between 0.3 and 0.5 per cent. Deng: 'I don't really believe this will show a lot of results.' What if the Yichuan bubble bursts? Deng Yu leans backward. 'As long as prices are increasing, people will keep buying. They have never known any different. But as soon as prices start falling, they will stop buying anything at all, and things will go from bad to worse. The sales of steel, building materials, kitchens, furniture and anything else linked to construction will collapse. Then other sectors will follow.' He refers to the bursting of the real estate bubble on the Chinese island of Hainan at the beginning of the 1990s, which caused long-term economic stagnation. Ultimately the bubble could also cause a financial crisis. 'Both buyers and property developers are borrowing money. Look at the crisis in the United States. Something similar could happen to China.'

13. KASHGAR

KASHGAR

(1950)

'IN THE EAST THERE IS SHENZHEN, IN THE WEST THERE IS KASHGAR'

KASHGAR

XINJIANG - AUSTRALIA
With 22 million inhabitants, Xinjiang province has roughly the same population as Australia

The taxi driver cranks up the volume on the radio. 'From Uzbekistan,' he shouts, when we ask where the frenzied music comes from. His solid physique, moustache, bushy eyebrows and thick hair mark him as a Uighur. Outside it is ten degrees centigrade below zero, inside the heating is roaring at full blast. We drive through a dry and barren landscape, infrequently dotted by villages of earthen houses. Men in fur hats and women in headscarves are walking along the motorway. Occasionally we overtake a donkey cart laden with people, sheep, building materials or a combination of all three.

It is January 2011, and we are en route to China's westernmost city, Kashgar. This former Silk Route trading post is not only very far from the East Coast, but also difficult to reach. From Shanghai it was a five-and-a-half hour flight to Urumqi, the capital of the boundless and sparsely populated Xinjiang province. From there the flight west to Kashgar took another two hours. During the trip we enjoyed crystal clear views of the inhospitable landscape below, the snowy peaks of the Tianshan mountain range, with offshoots running into the Taklamakan desert. It is not difficult to realise why only five per cent of this province is suitable for human habitation.

Reaching the city outskirts after a twenty-minute taxi ride confirms our suspicions. Kashgar differs massively from the cities we have visited over the last two years. The usual ingredients of a new Chinese metropolis are lacking. There are no construction sites stretching for miles on end, hardly any real estate adverts, and no motorways clogged with traffic jams. Apartment blocks of at most six floors cover the largest part of the city rather than flats measuring twenty or thirty stories. We do not see any international shopping chains, and hardly any Chinese ones. Instead, Kashgar has a thriving class of small tradesmen, countless clothes shops, nut sellers, butchers and tiny restaurants. This is a pint-sized place compared to megacities like Wuhan or Chengdu. The urban core has just about half a million inhabitants. Differences in income with the Chinese East Coast are considerable. If the average monthly salary in Shanghai is 365 dollars, residents of Kashgar make no more than 140 dollars per month.[1] You could say Kashgar manifests all the main attributes of the cities we have visited in exaggerated form: of the sixteen, it is farthest from the sea, its economy the least developed, and the percentage of Han Chinese the lowest. Ninety per cent of the population is Uighur, eight per cent Han and two per cent Kazakh, Tajik, or Kirgiz.[2]

That China's development has mostly bypassed Kashgar becomes apparent on Sunday morning, when we visit the city's most important cattle market. On a dusty 500 by 500 metre field, sandwiched between the motorway and a railway track, several thousand men in black coats, beards and fur hats stand amidst their wares: tens of thousands of sheep. Over the centuries, the sales process has changed little. Buyers lift the animals, tap them all over, look them in the mouth, and buy them after a haggle. Most shepherds and tradesmen accompany their flocks on foot. The market could be a nice folkloristic tourist attraction, if not for the fact that it represents a substantial section of local business. In 2009 the agricultural sector accounted for a third of Kashgar's economy. In terms of jobs that share is much larger still.[3]

When Deng Xiaoping announced his 'getting rich first' strategy, he placed Kashgar at the bottom of his to do list. Now the East Coast has become a thriving urban zone and Central China has started developing vigorously, the government has finally found time to turn its attention to the Far West. At a meeting of the Politburo in May 2010, President Hu Jintao announced the establishment of a new Special Economic Zone, the first one in fifteen years. To the surprise of many the choice fell on Kashgar. Commentators at home and abroad saw the ambitious plan as a response to the ethnic tensions that hit the province in 2009, which claimed nearly 200 lives in the capital, Urumqi. Stimulating the local economy would pacify the Uighurs, who feel disadvantaged compared to the Han.

Kashgar is closer to the Mediterranean than to the East China Sea, and closer to Istanbul than Shanghai.

With the new Special Economic Zone China also hopes to tap a new consumer market in Central Asia. Kashgar lies close to Kyrgyzstan, Tajikistan, Afghanistan, Pakistan, Kazakhstan, and Uzbekistan. The Chinese government counts on continuing economic growth in these countries because of their huge oil and gas reserves. In due course, Kashgar is to become the nexus between Europe and Southeast Asia. The city is closer to the Mediterranean than to the East China Sea, and closer to Istanbul than Shanghai. Various plans are circulating for an 'Iron Silk Road' of railways between China and Europe. In May 2011, a rail freight service operating five days per week was launched between Chongqing and Antwerp, a twenty-day journey. Another envisaged route is to connect Kashgar to the Mediterranean via Iran and Iraq.

Should the plan for the economic zone succeed, then Kashgar will be the jewel in the crown of the Go West project. Local party secretary Zeng Cun predicts that by 2040 Kashgar will be 'a world-class international big city.' A party slogan expresses the same ambition: 'In the East there is Shenzhen, in the West there is Kashgar,' a reference to

China's most successful Special Economic Zone to date. In 1980 Shenzhen was little more than a fishing village. Seen from the Lounge Bar at the top of the Shenzhen Grand Hyatt hotel, the Shenzhen skyline now differs little from that of Hong Kong a few miles south.

Little is known of the exact implementation of the Special Economic Zone, but the plan will certainly feature tax breaks, incentives for investors and the development of heavy infrastructure. In the run up to the decision, the national government built a new terminal in Kashgar airport, and invested 7.4 billion dollars in other construction projects. It also 'strongly urged' the wealthy province of Guangdong to invest 1.4 billion dollars in Kashgar over the next five years.[4]

In Café Pakistan in Seman Street Kashif tears a piece from his *chapati*. The 28-year-old businessman from the Pakistani city of Lahore says he has lived in Kashgar for three years now. He is in the import/export business. 'I export fruit and televisions from China to Pakistan. And from Pakistan I import cosmetics to China.' On the walls of the restaurant hang posters of a motorway winding through snow-capped Central Asian mountains. The last couple of days Kashif's table companions have viewed the same spectacle from behind their lorry's windscreen. Driver Nicolai is sweating over a plate of curry. For several years now, this former Russian army soldier has driven trucks from the Tadzjik capital of Dushanbe to Western China to pick up televisions and small household appliances. Kashgar is a regular stop on his seven-day journey. When asked what he transports from Tajikistan to China, he smiles melancholically. 'Nothing,' he says. 'I drive an empty truck to China, and return with a full one.' The traders and lorry drivers in Café Pakistan are part of a growing group of foreigners in Kashgar. 'This city is only at the beginning of its development,' says young Kashif with conviction. 'The Chinese have big plans here.'

Broadly speaking, the transformation of Kashgar will transpire according to the same pattern we have witnessed earlier in other cities in Central and Western China. Not that Beijing has a blueprint all these cities need to follow; quite the contrary. The model for the modern Chinese city has grown evolutionarily. City governments in the whole country constantly copy each others' successes and learn from each others' mistakes.

The new Chinese megacity is characterised by a rejection of old ways and a strong belief

1589403960

in progress. The results can be seen in the city centre of Kashgar, which is thousands of years old. The formerly legendary trade mission on the Silk Road resembles a ghost town, abandoned by its inhabitants. Here and there something has bitten larges holes hundreds of square metres in size into 'the best preserved example of an Islamic town in Central Asia', as historians of architecture described Kashgar several years ago.[5] Old Kashgar consisted of a maze of streets, alleys and passageways with houses, shops and mosques made of brick, wood and earth built, rebuilt, adapted and enlarged over the centuries. For that reason director Mark Foster filmed *The Kite Runner* in the city in 2006, set in the 1970s in the Afghan capital Kabul.

In May 2009 the local authorities decided to tear down 85 per cent of the old town and replace it with new construction. Just like in Kunming's Old Civilisation Street, developers are now reconstructing the old homes in reinforced concrete. The remaining inhabitants observe the demolition and reconstruction with mixed emotions. They expect that some of their neighbours will be returning this summer to walk the straight new streets and to live in modernised housing with plumbing and running water. Like all other metropolises in China's interior, Kashgar will be a city without slums and without history. That is to say, almost without history. In the interest of tourism, the remaining fifteen per cent of the historical town will be redeveloped into a romanticised version of the past. Even now, visitors have to buy tickets to enter old Kashgar, where they can view the Tuerxun family's *traditional* pottery, have tea in the Ali family's *original* court, or buy cloths in the *authentic* carpet shop owned by the Mukeni family. Not completely coincidentally, the tourist enclave lies right next to another attraction, the Great Bazaar, where holiday makers buy fur hats, tea sets and silk.

In complete accordance with the established pattern, Kashgar is developing an administrative and business centre in the south typical of Chinese urban expansion. The fact that Shenzhen's planning authority is advising the city of Kashgar says a lot about the type of district that will arise. There will be wide roads, high towers and undoubtedly also a central square with an imposing new town hall, a cultural centre, a five-star hotel and a conference centre. After completion of the district, the residential towers, parks and museums will probably stand empty for a long while, as we saw in Zhengzhou, Chengdu and Yinchuan. China builds prior to use, a result of the fact that the government drives most developments. The eastern Chinese province of Shandong has already built a giant complex for cargo handling in Kashgar, awaiting the expected future flow of goods. Seeing such new heavy infrastructure in a state of disuse evokes associations with the *grands travaux inutiles* of the former Soviet Union, but the realities of Soviet communism cannot simply be equated with present day state capitalist China. Thirty years of abundant East Coast growth has shown that timely investments in airports, motorways, interchanges, railway lines, bridges and buildings often prove themselves prudent in the long run. Though some of these projects will have to be written off as useless, the authorities see that as acceptable collateral damage. While not the epitome of efficiency, it does prevent capacity problems that could slow down growth.

The all-pervasive top-down approach differs strongly from the more bottom-up transformation of Indian, South American or African cities. There is grass-roots expansion in China as well, especially on the city margins. As it expands, Kashgar swallows dozens of villages. Like Mr Sun in Shijiazhuang, the villagers respond with pragmatism, creativity and entrepreneurship. In the countryside around the city thousands of peasants are already demolishing their farms and replacing them with four- or five-storey buildings, with two goals in mind. First, they hope to let the small residential towers to migrant workers flooding Kashgar. Secondly, they hope to assure themselves of as much compensation as possible once the houses are marked for demolition. It is only a matter of time before the houses built by the self made architects will disappear. They will eventually be replaced by large-scale, linear, orderly and uniform city districts that consist mostly of guarded walled compounds, the dominant housing type in modern Chinese cities.

Not only do the new rich and middle classes live in their own closed enclaves, the same goes for migrant workers from the provinces. They work as labourers, factory workers, cleaners, hairdressers, chambermaids, garbage collectors, security guards, delivery men, packers or prostitutes, and sleep in container homes on construction sites, in dormitories on factory grounds, or in 'villages in the city'. They create an informal economy of their own with their own restaurants, semi-legal clinics, gambling halls, cinemas and massage parlours.

This way, the new Kashgar will display a typical Chinese tendency towards zoning. All compounds, 'villages in the city', villa neighbourhoods, *danwei* and construction site settlements are part of the largest zone of all, Kashgar itself. As Special Economic Zone it differs in status from other cities in the surrounding area, the province and the rest of China.

An impressive network of roads, anticipating an increasing mobility of the townspeople, will soon connect the various parts of the city. In the south of Kashgar, not far from the cattle market, we can already see the start of that development. Thousands of cars are parked in the open air on a large dirt field. In the front stand passenger cars, both new and second hand. Behind these are the taxis, and after that, busses and lorries. Thousands of men with leather jackets and fur hats walk between the vehicles. A ten-year-old Volkswagen Santana sells for 500 dollars. It will not take long before the cars sold here will be creeping along the motorway in endless traffic jams.

'I drive an empty truck to China, and return with a full one.'

On Saturday evening we smoke a water pipe in the Hantaji, a club on the third floor of a shopping centre in the centre of Kashgar. Around a central dance floor twenty- and thirty-somethings sit chatting on sofas. They are drinking beer, whisky or soft drinks, and eating dried figs, almonds and raisins. In front of an immense video screen a singer in black tie croons one Turkish, Uzbek or Uighur hit song after the other. People dance in pairs – man/man, woman/woman, man/woman. The women dance with gracefully twisting hands and swinging hips, the men by victoriously throwing their arms into the air. The number of Han Chinese in the club is a grand total of zero. They can be found four metres lower, on the second floor of the same building, in a different club. There is less dancing going on here, and more dicing. The guests are hardly talking to each other, but that is impossible anyway. Loud hip hop blasts from the loud speakers.

Uighur and Han may live in the same city, but they inhabit two different worlds. They have their own languages, alphabets, newspapers, magazines, radio and TV stations.

Their children attend different schools. They dress differently and eat different meals. Uighur pray five times daily in the direction of Mecca, while Han Chinese burn incense in temples. The chasm is so extreme that the two population groups even live in their own time zones. The Kashgar Han have set their watches to Beijing, while the Uighur live by the geographically more straightforward local time.

Modern Chinese cities are not only spatially zoned with compounds or special development areas, but also socially. The most important dividing line runs between migrant workers and townsmen, a separation often coinciding with a gap between rich and poor. In Central and Western China, segregation often also has an ethnic element. As long as the Uighur middle class have enough money to spend in nightclubs such as the Hantaji, that is not a problem. The danger lies in the forming of neighbourhoods where poverty and hopelessness coincide with a high concentration of a certain ethnic group – that is a recipe for tensions.

At the same time, the Han-dominated local communist party will not hesitate to use the local Uighur culture for the *branding* of the city. Just like Hohhot is using Mongol steppe culture to create the image of a multicultural metropolis with lots of greenery, fresh air and healthy dairy products, Kashgar will probably exploit the concept of 'Silk Route Culture': *doing international business while enjoying a cup of sweet tea.*

On both sides of Kashgar's Revolution Street dozens of posters show the still modest Kashgar skyline morphing into impressive Shenzhen high-rise. The strength of Chinese cities lies to a large degree in projecting of an image of success before anything has actually been achieved. You constantly feel yourself surrounded by the future, by virtual skylines or by completed buildings, ready for future use. Together, these form a futuristic and hope-inspiring décor.

Like all Chinese cities, Kashgar is focussing on physical growth. The strong state guarantees insane construction speeds, and the implementation of an ambitious modernising agenda without major hiccups. Cramped, dark and unhealthy homes will make place for light, spacious, and airy accommodation. The current inhabitants will collectively jump into the modern world. In ten years or so Kashgar will have taken on the appearance of a world city with an impressive skyline.

Once this physical transformation to modern metropolis is complete, the emphasis will shift from construction to the non-physical aspects of the city: breathing life into transit hubs, business districts, High Tech Development Zones, into new theatres, museums and sports stadiums. This will present the local leaders with an important and difficult choice: do they want Kashgar to become something more than merely a gigantic collection of people and buildings? The example of Little Bar in Chengdu, which blossomed from an underground rock bar into one of China's most promising live venues, shows that China's cities have enormous potential when it comes to developing their soft side. However, authorities still often hold back its expansion with restrictions on political, artistic and academic freedoms.

'In thirty years I will be controlling my international empire from here.'

After two days in Kashgar, the receptionist at our hotel notifies us that the secret police have been making inquiries about us. The following day, they start phoning us non-stop. They want to know what a foreign journalist and architect are doing in Kashgar, where we are going, who we are talking to and how long we are planning to stay.
Foreign visitors to China's emerging megacities will not immediately notice that China is not a free country. Street life is surprisingly familiar; you could be in New York, New Delhi or Rio. City dwellers enjoy many freedoms; they can decide where they live, work, shop, whom they marry or what they want to study. At the same time personal rights and political freedoms are strongly restricted. The government decides how many children you are allowed to have. Press freedom and freedom of opinion stretch only to the extent permitted by the ministry of Propaganda. Websites such as YouTube, Facebook and Twitter are blocked, and their Chinese counterparts severely censored. Writers, lawyers and artists who speak out too explicitly against the system disappear from urban society: they are either abroad, in prison cells or kept at an undisclosed location. The rulers of Kashgar follow China's national model of *harmony*, aimed at keeping *stability*, resulting in a society from which most sharp edges have been filed.

Chinese political leaders are discussing the future of the system at the highest levels. In recent years Prime Minister Wen Jiabao repeatedly avowed his 'devotion to political reform' in interviews. 'The supreme criterion for assessing the performance of officials is whether the people feel happy and satisfied, rather than skyscrapers.' Wen argues that China must 'push forward reform of the political system', increase citizen's democratic rights and place checks on state power. The fact that his own state media censors his speeches illustrates that he has not enough supporters in the Politburo for his far-reaching proposals.

At the same time, Chinese citizens are pushing the margins of the permissible, often with the connivance of the authorities. The wealthy have more than one child simply by paying a fine. Local authorities, for instance in Shanghai, subvert national policy by actively promoting couples to have a second child. City governments in Chengdu and elsewhere have discovered that avant-garde artists can provide income and prestige. Totalitarian dictatorships are not supposed to have a functioning civil society, but the Chinese state allows and stimulates environmental NGOs to operate more or less

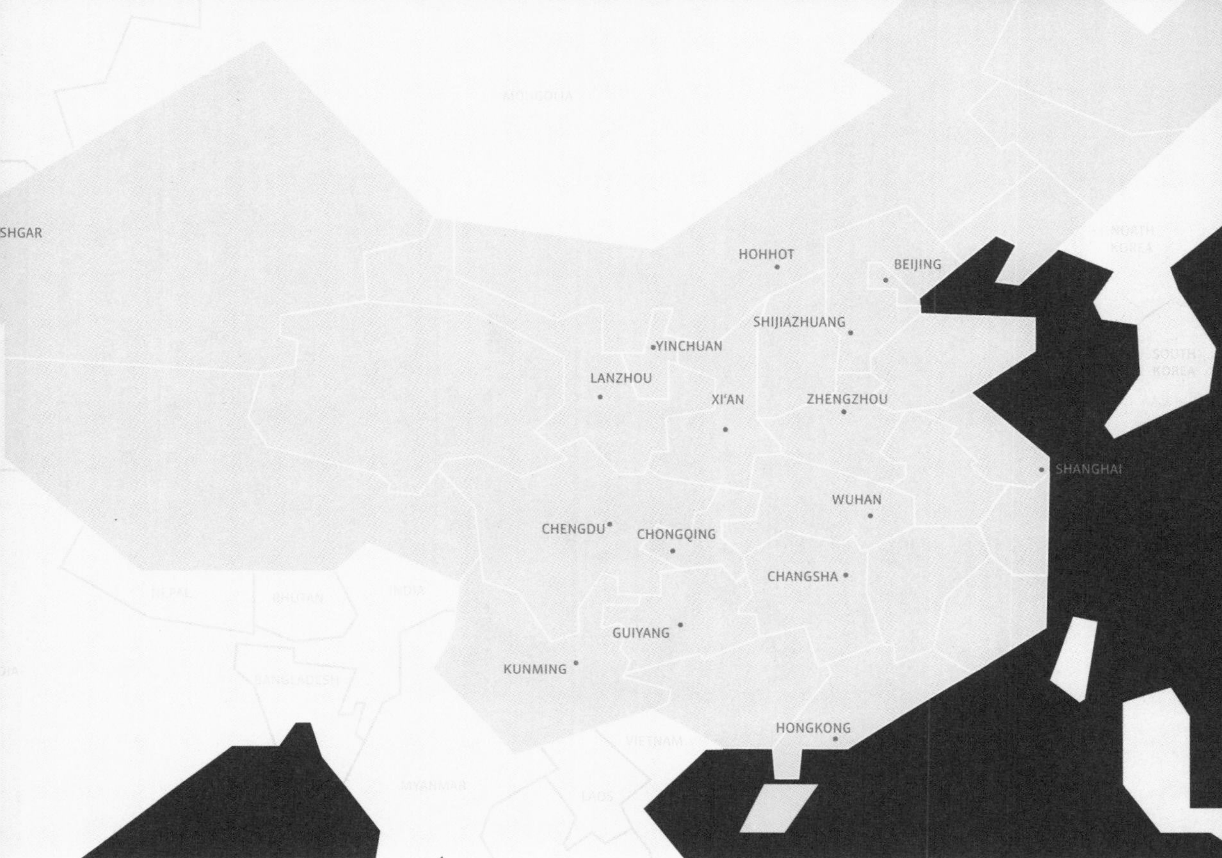

independently. In all Chinese megacities, locals like teacher Wu in Lanzhou organise themselves to defend the interests of migrant workers. In 2006 the Chinese government even invited Greenpeace to act as a consultant on the new energy law. Local investigative journalists target corruption or, like reporter Feng Tao of Ningxia Radio in Yinchuan, the dangers of real estate speculation. Authorities tolerate and even encourage them, provided their writing is not aimed against the power of the communist party. Overstep that boundary and, like internationally famous artist Ai Wei Wei, you could find yourself in a prison cell.

Successful media companies like Hunan Television are already churning out hugely popular TV shows and reality series, but attempts to set up a Chinese Al Jazeera have failed. The colossal museums built all over central China are full of endless calligraphy and abstract paintings that might have shocked China's polite society thirty years ago, but world class art remains an exception. The glitzy skyscrapers in the Central Business Districts fail to deliver what their spectacular exteriors promise. They are half empty, and often mainly house small companies like wedding planners and estate agents.

建工集团欢迎您
形象 质量第一 用户至上
大祖国 建
经 济

拆
两

Chinese megacities have already become the 'factories of the world,' a direct result of economic liberalisations introduced since the 1980s. They now face the choice of permitting greater freedoms at the risk of political dissent. Allowing greater intellectual and creative liberty could tap into the potential of a highly literate workforce of what soon will be the largest urban society on the planet.

After dinner in Café Pakistan, Kashif returns to his home office, located in a large building on the other side of the street. Inside are numerous small spaces where businessmen live and work. 'Here almost everyone is from Pakistan,' he says. 'A bit further down the road there is a similar place with Uzbek entrepreneurs.' The young Pakistani's office is on the seventh floor. Besides a bed and a desk with a computer, the cramped room is full of trade goods: soap, toothpaste, eyeshadow and shampoo. As he fills the glasses with a Chinese *baijiu* and Sprite cocktail, Kashif says he eyes the future optimistically. 'Mark my words,' he says. 'In thirty years I will be controlling my international empire from here.' A broad grin appears under his moustache.

EPILOGUE

When we were sitting in the high speed train from Shanghai to Zhengzhou two and a half years ago, we had barely a notion of what to expect. What drove us was a high degree of curiosity about this unfamiliar metropolis. We had prepared our trip as well as we could, but we had not come across more than fragmentary descriptions of the city. Our guidebook reported that Zhengzhou was 'a not unattractive mini-metropolis' and a 'pleasant place to spend the night' when visiting nearby tourist attractions such as the Shaolin temple. We took Wikitravel´s advice to heart to meet a certain Hank, a 'local inhabitant of Zhengzhou who speaks fluent English, knows all episodes of *South Park* by heart and provides access to anything remotely interesting in the city'.

A week later we flew back to Shanghai, tired but satisfied. We had looked around in amazement at this fascinating city, which was being transformed from an insignificant industrial hub into a modern Chinese megalopolis. We had visited dozens of places and talked to countless people (including 'Hank,' who turned out to be a critical, sophisticated and articulate twenty-something with a refreshing perspective on developments in his town). Why, we asked ourselves, shouldn't we write a book on the amazing phenomenon of nascent cities in modern China?

Back in Shanghai, we developed the idea into a research proposal and established the Go West Project, a multidisciplinary think tank dedicated to the study of the rising megacities of Central and Western China. In two years time we visited sixteen budding metropolises, of which thirteen ultimately ended up in this book. Some cities we visited twice, or even three times. We spoke to hundreds of people: senior civil servants, academics, architects, businessmen, property developers, journalists, migrant workers, millionaires, artists, shop assistants, taxi drivers and soldiers. We could not have written this book without their frankness and willingness to share their stories with a foreign journalist and architect.

The completion of this book is in part the achievement of a number of special people who have collaborated with the Go West Project over the last few years. First of all we must mention Song Xinlin, who we met in September 2009 in Shijiazhuang where she acted as our local guide. She astonished us almost immediately with her boundless curiosity, spontaneity, and ability to win over people. Barely a month later, she moved to Shanghai to strengthen our team as our permanent research assistant. Xinlin conducted preparatory research for the book and was our interpreter during most of our travels. She also coordinated various exhibitions of the Go West Project in Shenzhen, London and Amsterdam.

In writing the book, a three-headed shadow editorial board advised us. In Shanghai Remko Tanis, who constantly travels all parts of China as correspondent for the Dutch GPD-newspapers, read all the chapters. His remarks and suggestions substantially improved not only the consistency and structure of the text, but also made it more relevant to contemporary developments in China. The second co-reader was architect David Mulder of XML Architecture Research Urbanism in Amsterdam. He challenged our arguments, asked us to 'turn them upside down' or 'follow them to their logical conclusion' and so helped us to avoid the beaten track. Photographer Ruben Lundgren of the duo WasskinkLundgren provided us with several days of his time to advise on establishing a narrative in the pictorial story. All three have made their own mark on this book with their constructive criticism, for which we are profoundly grateful.

The Go West Project could only exist thanks to generous support by a number of sponsors. Among the first believers were Ian Bennink and Jan Jonkers of Arkelson Architectural Services. Internet company Redkiwi sponsored the Go West Project website. For the research we received a generous contribution from the Netherlands Foundation for Visual Arts, Design and Architecture (BKVB). Support from both the Netherlands Architecture Fund and the BKVB Foundation made publication of the book possible.

We cherish many good memories of all the people we have interviewed in the last few years. More than once we would only briefly 'drop by,' to end up saying goodbye as good friends many hours later. In Chongqing we debated until late at night in a coffee bar after a sumptuous meal with Zhu Ye and Wei Haoyan of the unsurpassed magazine Urban China. A year later we repeated a similar evening in Guiyang with architect Wei Haobo, Haoyan's brother who for the occasion had invited just about everybody who was anybody in local urban planning to a teahouse.

In most cities we used local research assistants to make preparations and establish contacts. We met our first assistant Kong Xiangyu in Zhenghzou. He worked as a manager in a Japanese restaurant, but spontaneously took a week off from his busy job when he heard we were looking for a local guide. Lu Xiaotian (Chongqing), He Shuopeng (Taiyuan), Guo Qiangian (Taiyuan), Ailisi (Hohhot), Chen Hui (Wuhan), Xiao Qian (Chengdu), Wang Huijing (Changsha), Yao Jiahe (Yinchuan) and Sadik (Kashgar) all showed similar dedication when preparing and carrying out research in their own cities. Christine Haas assisted us in Shanghai with a data analysis in which she compared cities in Western and Central China to ten well known global cities.

Many of the people presented in this book we spoke at someone's advice, who knew somebody, who new someone else. Such a cascade of meetings can come about surprisingly quickly in China. In Hohhot we met deputy director Wang of the Provincial Museum in the morning. He suggested we have lunch with a Mongolian acquaintance of his, who put us in touch with a musician named Qingele, who in turn took us along to see Chi Bulag, the most famous musician of Inner Mongolia, who invited us to dinner at the end of the interview. And so we found ourselves that very evening eating too much lamb and drinking too much *baijiu* with Chi Bulag, Qingele and the brother of the mayor of Hohhot.

It is a misunderstanding that Chinese officials are by definition difficult to approach. Some interviews with senior civil servants were very awkward, but they were outbalanced by various very candid conversations, with for instance Shan Xiaogang, deputy director of the provincial planning department of Guizhou and Gao Xuemei, director of the Street, Bloc and Building Protection Office in Kunming. Often a shared meal helped break the ice. At lunch in Yinchuan, Lieutenant Zhang was still looking around nervously, as he did not like being seen in uniform with foreigners. Less than four hours later we sat down to an alcohol soaked meal with a dozen of his colleagues, which would form the start of a lengthy exploration of the city's night life.

At times we asked ourselves whether it was not presumptuous for foreigners without solid knowledge of written Chinese to write a book on a topic like this. Architect Liu Jiakun from Chengdu remarked that as outsiders we had the advantage of a fresh view. 'Looking at China with blue eyes,' he called that.

Over the last couple of years, several specialists have kept us on the right track. In Shanghai we reflected regularly on the running investigation with architect Neville Mars, author of the book *The Chinese Dream*, and with Bert de Muynck and Monica Carriço of research group MovingCities. Vice dean Li Xiangning and urban planner Su Yunsheng of the Tongji University Faculty of Architecture gave their views on Chinese urban planning. Stefan Landsberger, professor of Culture of Contemporary China at the University of Amsterdam shared his ideas about the modern Chinese society. Carl Fingerhuth, professor of Urban Planning in Zürich and author of *The Kunming Project* shared his invaluable knowledge and collection of photographs for the chapter on Kunming. Annette Nijs, director Global Initiative of Business University CEIBS in Shanghai and author of *China with different eyes* provided us at crucial moments with suggestions to bring the Go West Project further. Michelle Provoost of the International New Town Institute followed the Go West Project closely from its inception, and helped with publicizing the results, for instance with an exhibition in 2011. John van de Water of Next architects and writer of the book *You can't change China, China changes you* occasionally provided input, usually by phone and remarkably often from an airport somewhere in China. Preston Scott Cohen, professor of architecture at the Harvard School of Design, helped us get in touch with a number of key figures in the city of Taiyuan.

During our excursions we regularly met foreigners from the relatively small expat communities in their cities. Almost without exception these were people with stories to tell. One example is Ryan, a young South African in his twenties. He had been sent by

his father from Port Elisabeth to Zhengzhou to expand the family sheepskin business. In Changsha we met Hans Ackermann, who has been acting for years as the unpaid advisor to the local government. He surprised us and local officials with his direct mode of questioning. 'No, no, no, we're not asking that! Just answer the question!' In Kunming architect Roelandt van Ierssel took us along urban expansions and historic new construction in Kunming. In Wuhan Maren Striker introduced us to his employer: the local city planning authority. Gijs Gruijters showed us the way in the artistic underground scene of Chengdu.
A project like this not only has peaks. Perhaps the deepest crisis occurred in the presence of singer-songwriter Daniël van Veen, who advised us to keep focussed and avoid being sidetracked. With his razor sharp analysis of our biggest obstacle, he helped keep the Go West Project on track.

We have not only travelled through China the last couple of years. In our hometown Shanghai the Go West Project also behaved as a nomad. Our first ideas for the book originated in a coffee bar in one of the city's large shopping centres. After that our office found itself on the nineteenth floor on Zhaojiabang Street looking out over ten empty skyscrapers, in a creative centre near People's Square and in an apartment on Julu Road with a view of a tennis court on the roof of a Mexican restaurant. We wrote the book in the office of architects Bittor Sanchez-Monasterio and Nicolas Salto del Giorgio of byn studio, located in a villa in the former French Concession. We made the finishing touches in the Dutch Design Workspace, housed in a disused factory in Jing'an, one of the nicest neighbourhoods in Shanghai.
This book would have never come into being without our publisher Martien de Vletter of SUN architecture, who from the very first beginnings had confidence in the project and in its success. Job Roggeveen of studio Job, Joris & Marieke provided the Go West house style and book design. Historian and writer Martin Mevius translated the original Dutch text into English. Both Job and Martin contributed valuable ideas and new concepts that very much improved this book. Dozens of people have helped in their own areas of expertise. *Volkskrant* picture editor Heike Gulker, chief curator Frits Gierstberg of the Netherlands Museum of Photography, and Corinne Noordenbos, head of photography of the Royal Academy of Art in The Hague, all granted us extensive

periods of their time and advised us on photography and image selection. Dramatist Caspar Nieuwenhuis provided us with his knowledge of story building. Both Laura Mitchelson and Christina Antoniou reviewed drafts of several chapters of the English text.

We especially thank the Dutch representation in China. One of the most prominent, active and loyal followers of our progress was consul general Eric Verwaal in Shanghai, who once even organised a dinner with the theme Go West, to get various people together and so help the project. Consul general Ton van Zeeland in Guangzhou and Machtelt Schelling, head of Culture at the Dutch Embassy in Beijing, were instrumental in making our participation in the Shenzhen/Hong Kong Architecture Biennale 2009 possible.

The support of the people closest to us over the last few years has meant a lot to us: our parents, our brothers and our friends Wendy, Vincent, Paulus, Ernst, Jaap and Natasja. We dedicate this book to those who encouraged us most of all to persist and who continue to inspire us: our beloved Rosalie and Clarisse.

Michiel Hulshof
Daan Roggeveen

Shanghai, July 2011

NOTES

1. Zhengzhou – 'This is a business town'

[1] Clarence Kwan, 'Urbanization in China – Another 280 million people by 2030', Deloitte Chinese Services Group, May 2010.

[2] Jonathan Woetzel, 'China's Cities in the Sky', *McKinsey What Matters,* 7 January 2011.

[3] McKinsey Global Institute, *Preparing for China's urban billion,* Shanghai (McKinsey & Company) 2009, p. 53.

[4] Dali L. Yang, *Beyond Beijing: Liberalization and the regions in China,* London (Routledge) 1997, p. 29.

[5] National Bureau of Statistics, *China Statistical Yearbook 2000,* Beijing (China Statistics Press) 2001.

[6] Wang Jianwei and Li Zhongzhi, 'Introduction to the China Surface Transportation Financing and Investment System', lecture at TRB Financial Committee Summer Meeting, New Orleans, 21 May 2010.

2. Shijiazhuang – How the city moved to Mr Sun

[1] Yasheng Huang, *Capitalism with Chinese Characteristics,* New York (Cambridge University Press) 2008, p. xvi.

[2] Jehangir S. Pocha, 'Shanghai Building Boom pits architects of East vs. West', *Boston Sunday Globe,* 10 September 2006, p. 2.

[3] Shijiazhuang Council, 'Suggestions by the city administration of Shijiazhuang for the speeding up op the reform process of the 'villages in the city'. 25 February 2002.

[4] Eye witness account, *tianya.cn,* 4 January 2010.

[5] *Yangzhou Wenbao,* 22 September 2009.

3. Chongqing – Building the largest city in the world

[1] Neville Mars and Adrian Hornsby, *The Chinese Dream – a society under construction,* Rotterdam (010 Publishers) 2008, p. 678.

[2] National Bureau of Statistics, 2008.

[3] 'China rumbles as millions join holiday rush for home', Xinhua, 3 January 2009.

[4] 'Migrant workers find a champion: NPC deputy fights for the rights of poor labourers

toiling in the cities', *South China Morning Post,* 16 March 2006.

[5] 'Integrating into the city, migrant workers experience three big changes', Xinhua, 17 April 2006.

[6] Chongqing Social Security and Labour Employment Analysis, Bureau of Social Security in Chongqing, first quarter 2009.

[7] *Chongqing Ribao,* February 2008.

[8] Aris Chan, *Paying the Price for Economic Development: The Children of Migrant Workers in China,* Hong Kong (China Labour Bulletin) 2009.

[9] Jamil Anderlini, 'Call to end China citizen registration system', *Financial Times,* 1 March 2010.

[10] Chongqing government website, 25 March 2010.

[11] 'City's builders deserve chance of better life', *Global Times,* 11 November 2010, p. 10.

[12] *edu.people.com.cn,* 12 January 2006.

4. Wuhan – Canary Wharf in Central China

[1] John Friedmann, *China's Urban Transition,* Minneapolis (University of Minnesota Press) 2005, p. 57.

[2] Harry Alverson Franck, *Roving through southern China,* New York (The Century co.) 1925, p. 75.

[3] Freda Utley, *China at War,* London (Faber and Faber) 1938, p. 32.

[4] Thomas J. Campanella, *The Concrete Dragon,* New York (Princeton Architectural Press) 2008, p. 33.

[5] Richard McGregor, *The Party,* New York (HarperCollins) 2010, p. 81.

[6] Li Jiangfeng and Douty Chibamba, FDI & Urban Restructuring in Wuhan, *International Business Management* 2 (5), 2008, p. 207.

5. Xi'an – 'Heaven for young leaders who enjoy life'

[1] Adrian Hornsby, 'Hey fuck! Where'd the city go?' in: Neville Mars and Adrian Hornsby, *The Chinese Dream – a society under construction*, Rotterdam (010 publishers) 2007, p. 205.

NOTES

[2] *New Book of Tang*, Volume 37: Geography, around 1060 A.D.

[3] Wang Feng and Zuo Xuejin, 'Inside China's Cities: Institutional Barriers and Opportunities for Urban Migrants', *American Economic Review,* 89, pp. 276-280.

[4] Dorothy J. Solinger, *Contesting Citizenship in Urban China: Peasant Migrants, the State, and the Logic of the Market,* Berkeley (University of California Press) 1999, p. 101.

6. Kunming – A new future for Old Civilisation Street

[1] Ian Buruma, *De toekomst van China,* Amsterdam (Olympus) 2007, pp. 187-188.

[2] Wang Runshang, About Wen Ming Street, personal document, 3 December 2004.

[3] Wang Xuehai, 'Good design is rooted in cultural exchange', in: Carl Fingerhuth and Ernst Joos (red.), *The Kunming Project: Urban Development in China – a Dialogue,* Basel (Birkhäuser) 2002, pp. 61-66.

[4] Emilie Gomart, 'Re-reading Preservation', in: Rem Koolhaas, *Content,* Köln (Taschen) 2004, p. 458.

[5] Werner Stutz, 'Old Town Preservation in Kunming', *disP 151,* November 2002, pp. 73-78.

[6] Carl Fingerhuth, 'Urban design for Kunming', in: Carl Fingerhuth and Ernst Joos (red.), *The Kunming Project: Urban Development in China – a Dialogue,* Basel (Birkhäuser) 2002, pp. 47-60.

[7] Ibid.

[8] Ibid.

[9] Ibid.

[10] Interview Michiel Hulshof / Daan Roggeveen with spokesman Zhi Jian, January 2010.

7. Changsha – Millionaires in Little Venice

[1] Hainan Clearwater Bay, 'The Richest People in China 2010', *Hurun.net.*

[2] Income gap, a woe for China and US, Xinhuanet, 12 October 2010.

[3] Jean Baudrillard, 'Simulacra and Simulations', in: ed. Mark Poster, *Jean Baudrillard, Selected Writings*, Stanford (Stanford University Press) 1988, pp.166-184.

[4] Adolf Loos, De Potemkinstad, Ver Sacrum, juli 1898, in: Hilde Heynen, André Loeckx,

Lieven De Cauter, Karina Van Herck (red.), *Dat is Architectuur,* Rotterdam (010 Publishers) 2001, p.27.

[5] Willy Lam, 'China's Brain Drain Dilemma: Elite Emigration', in: The Jamestown Foundation, *China Brief,* Volume X, issue 16, 5 August 2010, pp. 2-4.

[6] Cheng Anqi, 'Rich and elite make China emigration leader', *China Daily,* 8 June 2010.

[7] Chris Hogg, 'Wealthy Chinese flock to the West', website BBC News, 27 July 2010.

8. Lanzhou – 'If the factory prospers, I prosper'

[1] Bert van Dijk, *Langs de Gele Rivier – Watercrisis in China,* Amsterdam (Business Contact) 2011.

[2] Liu Yimeng, 'Income disparity in China: status quo and prospects', website Institute of Ideas, 16 June 2010.

[3] UN Habitat, *State of the World's Cities – Case study: China's urban transition,* 2008/2009.

[4] David Dollar, Poverty, *Inequality and social disparities during China's economic reform,* World Bank Policy Research Working Paper, April 2007, p.13.

[5] Wang Qian, 'Gvt to build 10 m homes', *China Daily,* 10 March 2011.

[6] Kishore Mahbubani, *The New Asian Hemisphere,* New York (Public Affairs) 2008, p 15.

9. Guiyang – 'Saving energy is using your finger'

[1] Hans Orville, Creating Eco-Cities – An urban contribution to climate change action and green society, 31 August 2009.

[2] Michael Kuhndt et al., *Policy Framework Study,* UNEP, 2006, p. 9.

[3] Erich W. Schienke & Neville Mars, 'The Green Edge', *www.burb.tv*, 2008.

[4] McKinsey Global Institute, *Preparing for China's urban billion,* Shanghai (McKinsey & Company) 2009.

[5] Zou Ji (red.), China National Human Development Report 2009 – 2010, UNDP China, 2010.

[6] Steve Schifferes, 'China's eco-city faces growth challenge', *news.bbc.co.uk,* 5 July 2007.

[7] Tony Blair, 'China's cities and villages are leading the world on climate change', *www.tonyblairoffice*.org, 30 July 2010.

NOTES

[8] Transcript 'Guest at China National Radio', Guiyang government website, 11 March 2009.

[9] Li Zhenshan and Pan Xiaodong, *The sustainable cities China programme* (1996-2007), UN Habitat and UNEP, 2009.

[10] Zhao Shijun, 'Guiyang maps out new growth strategy', *China Daily,* 16 May 2005, p. S5.

[11] Yang Ailun e.o., The True Cost of Coal: an investigation into coal ash in China, Greenpeace Beijing, 2010.

[12] International Energy Annual 2008, *www.chinafaqs.org.*

[13] Martin Lloyd, 'China builds a wind turbine every two seconds', *www.greenpeace.org,* 18 February 2009.

[14] International Energy Annual 2008, *www.chinafaqs.org.*

[15] 'Development Wave in Jinyang', *www.gygov.gov.cn,* 1 November 2007.

[16] Yu Meng, 'Land sales shouldn't continue', *People's Daily,* 27 December 2010, p. 17.

10. Hohhot – Ten Thousand Galloping Horses

[1] Li Narangoa, 'Nationalism and Globalization on the Inner Mongolia Frontier: The Commercialization of a Tamed Ethnicity', *Japan Focus,* 15 November 2006.

[2] Geoffrey York, 'Mongolian herdsmen no longer free to roam', *The Globe and Mail,* 6 March 2008.

[3] Kerry Brown, 'The Cultural Revolution in Inner Mongolia 1967-1969: The Purge of the "Heirs of Genghis Khan"', *Asian Affairs,* vol. XXXVIII, no. II, July 2007, pp. 173-187.

[4] Li Narangoa, 'Nationalism and Globalization on the Inner Mongolia Frontier: The Commercialization of a Tamed Ethnicity', *Japan Focus,* 15 November 2006.

[5] *Beifang Xinbao,* 21 September 2006.

[6] Li Narangoa, 'Nationalism and Globalization on the Inner Mongolia Frontier: The Commercialization of a Tamed Ethnicity', *Japan Focus,* 15 November 2006.

11. Chengdu - Zaha goes Extra Large

[1] Stefan Landsberger, *Paint it Red,* Groningen (Intermed Publishers) 1998, pp. 6-21.

[2] Francesca Dal Lago, 'The Avant-Garde Has Its Moment of Glory', *Time,* 27 September 1999.

[3] Edward H. Lawson and Mary Lou Bertucci, *Encyclopaedia of Human Rights,* Washington DC (Taylor & Francis) 1996, pp. 250-251.

[4] Michiel Hulshof, 'Zeepbel of miljoenencircus? – Hedendaagse kunst in China', *Vrij Nederland,* 19 April 2008, pp. 58-73.

[5] Francesca Dal Lago, 'The Avant-Garde Has Its Moment of Glory', *Time,* 27 September 1999.

[6] Waldemar Januszczak, 'The Real Thing', *The Sunday Times,* 29 April 2007.

[7] Wu Ziru, 'Trouble in Textile Town', *Global Times,* 19 October 2010.

[8] CPC Chengdu, Cultural Developmentplan of the 11th Fiveyearplan for Chengdu, 23 January 2007.

[9] 'Zaha goes Extra Large in Chengdu', *www.archinect.com,* 20 October 2010.

[10] Liang Kegang, 'Building an artistic bridge for two of my favourite cities', *Artzine,* 2008.

12. Yinchuan – Stacked Bars of Gold

[1] Neville Mars and Adrian Hornsby, *The Chinese Dream – A Society Under Construction* (010 Publishers) 2008, p. 680.

[2] U.S. Geological Survey, Mineral Commodity Summaries, January 2008.

[3] *www.worldsteel.org,* 20 April 2010.

[4] Yu Meng, 'Land sales shouldn't continue', *People's Daily,* 27 December 2010, p. 17.

[5] McKinsey Global Institute, *Preparing for China's urban billion,* Shanghai (McKinsey & Company) 2009, p. 87

[6] David Barboza, 'State-owned bidders fuel China's land boom', *New York Times,* 1 August 2010.

[7] Patrick Chovanec, 'China's Real Estate Riddle', *chovanec.wordpress.com,* 11 June 2009.

[8] Jamil Anderlini, 'China property prices "likely to halve"', *Financial Times,* 13 April 2009.

[9] David Pierson, 'In China real estate fever is rising', *L.A. Times,* 26 April 2010.

[10] Andy Xie, 'China counts down till the next bubble bursts', *Caijing,* 5 August 2009.

[11] Kit Gillet, 'Interview with Zhang Xin', *CIB Magazine,* 19 January 2010.

NOTES

[12] *bbs.yinchuan.soufun.com,* 20 August 2010.

[13] Jing Wu, Joseph Gyourko, and Yongheng Deng, 'Evaluating Conditions in Major Chinese Housing Markets', National Bureau of Economic Research, July 2010.

[14] David Barboza, 'Chinese city has many buildings, but few people', *New York Times,* 19 October 2010.

13. Kashgar – 'In the East there is Shenzhen, in the West there is Kashgar'

[1] *China Statistical Yearbook 2009.*

[2] *China Statistical Yearbook 2009.*

[3] Website Hong Kong Trade and Development Council, *www.hktdc.com.*

[4] Isaac Stone Fish, A New Shenzhen, *Newsweek,* 4 October 2010, pp. 24-27.

[5] John Gollings, George Michell , Marika Vicziany, Tsui Yen Hu, *Kashgar: Oasis City on China's Old Silk Road,* London (Francis Lincoln Publishers) 2008, p. 12.

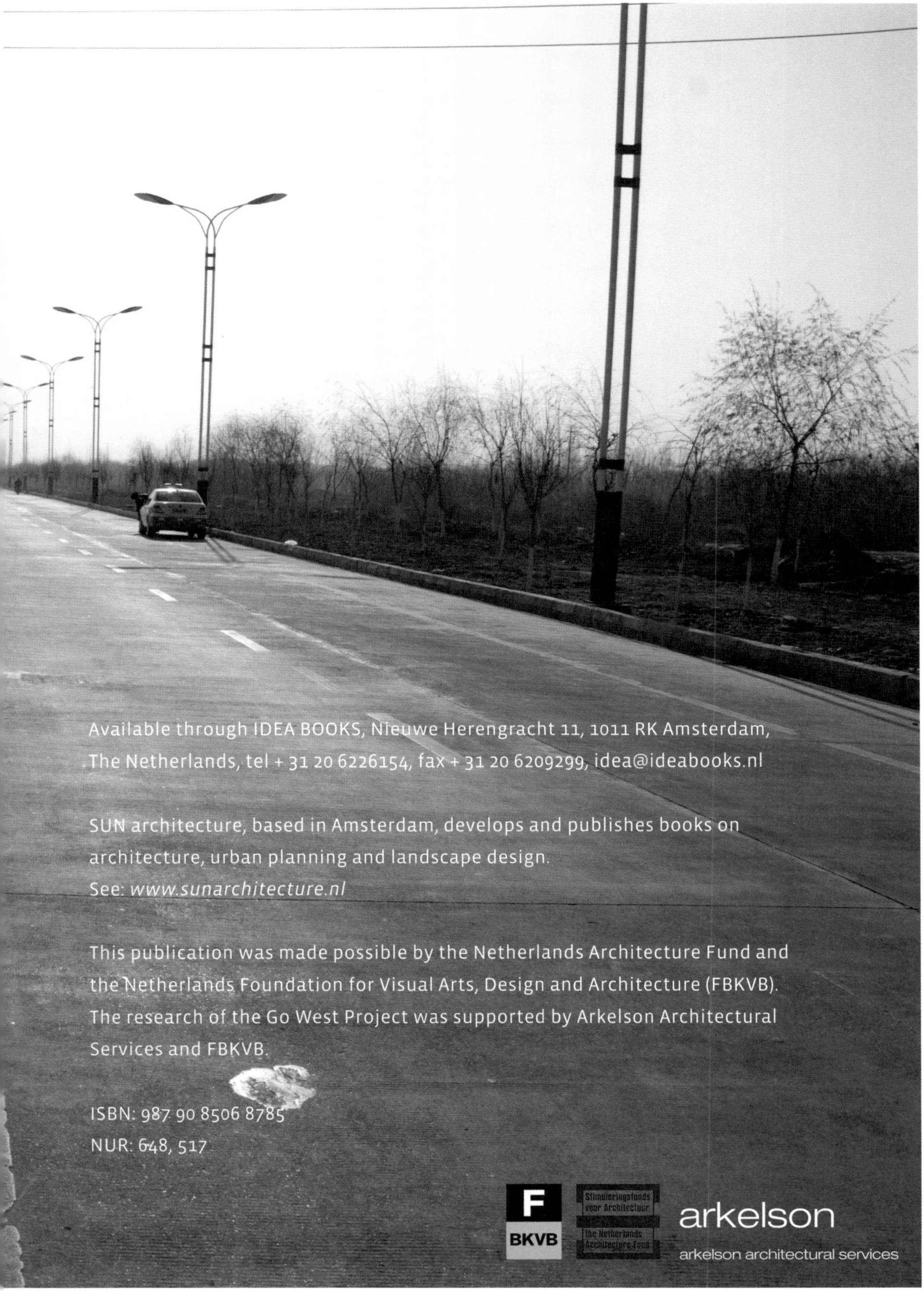

Available through IDEA BOOKS, Nieuwe Herengracht 11, 1011 RK Amsterdam, The Netherlands, tel + 31 20 6226154, fax + 31 20 6209299, idea@ideabooks.nl

SUN architecture, based in Amsterdam, develops and publishes books on architecture, urban planning and landscape design.
See: *www.sunarchitecture.nl*

This publication was made possible by the Netherlands Architecture Fund and the Netherlands Foundation for Visual Arts, Design and Architecture (FBKVB). The research of the Go West Project was supported by Arkelson Architectural Services and FBKVB.

ISBN: 987 90 8506 8785
NUR: 648, 517

arkelson
arkelson architectural services

COLOPHON

Authors:	**Michiel Hulshof, Daan Roggeveen**
Research:	Song Xinlin
Photography:	Daan Roggeveen, Michiel Hulshof
Translation:	Martin Mevius
Copy Editor:	Dutton Hauhart
Production:	Nico Buitendijk, Ton van Lierop, SUN
Lithografie	Michiel Hofmans, Image Degree Zero
Graphic Design:	Job, Joris & Marieke
Printing/binding:	Drukkerij Wilco
Publisher:	Martien de Vletter, SUN